The Life and Times
of a Railroad Engineer

Best Wishes

Bud Hoekstra

Bud Hoekstra

Printed 2012
in the United States of America
by White Birch Printing
501 W. Beaver Brook Avenue
Spooner, Wisconsin 54801

Second Edition Printed 2014

Library of Congress Cataloging in Publication
Data Hoekstra, Bud

ISBN 978-0-578-10329-7

DEDICATION

To Kathryn Anne Hoekstra, my wonderful mother.
I hope after all the disappointment that I caused you,
may this book ease the pain. You were always on my mind as I wrote.

Love,
Your son

ACKNOWLEDGEMENTS

I would like to express my gratitude to the following folks without whose help this book would not have been possible. They are: Tim Bassett, Mary Lou Clark Cardwell, John Friedell, Bernadette Friedell, John Friedell, Jr., Mary Olsen, Father Andrew Ricci, Rod Ripley, the staff at the Railroad Retirement Board in Chicago, Darin Pollei, Lester Dean at the National Railroad Historical Society and to the cast of seemingly thousands of people that I worked with. And lastly a very special thanks to my wonderful wife Jerrilyn whose dedication, perseverance and desire to implement the works found in this book through the newer technology and an acute willingness to learn.

CONTENTS
Book I
Illinois Central Days

CONTENTS
Book II
Soo Line Days

PREFACE

Shortly after I completed the first part of this book, I decided to offer it to a friend, most knowledgeable in the literary field, for his perusal and perhaps some constructive criticism. He dedicated a good amount of his time to the manuscript, for which I am most grateful. A day or two later he told me that he had finished reading a good portion of the book and complimented me on my writing style and then asked me "what is the point of the book"? Up to then, I hadn't given it much thought. He went on to say—you aren't a house hold name and so you cannot rest on your laurels, no one's going to buy a book simply because it has Bud Hoekstras name on it.

My book is intended for a person that may or may not hold trains, railroads or both, near and dear. Within the book there contains a vast array of railroad information. It isn't intended to be a biography, yet the book has to start somewhere and what better place than a young boy going to work on the railroad. If you are contemplating a career on the railroad, you will find the book more than informative.

Those 42 years encompassed much humor both sardonic and genuinly funny. As anywhere else, the railroads had more than their share of characters, both good and bad. You didn't have to have a degree to work in train service. Most of the guys were regular Joe's trying to make a living.

Many changes occurred within the industry during my tenure, AMTRAK and the Staggers Act to name a few. The book mentions each and all events in a concise manner.

I talk of locomotives and train handling which were my two favorite aspects of railroading. Terminals where I worked, and their physical characteristics are discussed with a certain introspect. I go "in depth" with train wrecks that I was familiar with.

Of course you can't have a book of this kind without a discussion of rail management vs. labor.

Finally, I speak of my own thoughts about the industry and what I feel can be done to make the railroad a going enterprise and a good place to work.

The book embraces 42 years (1959-2001) or six decades of railroading. If you are interested in trains, people and railroads in general—you'll enjoy this book.

BOOK I

Illinois Central Days

Chapter 1

Chicago

I was born on June 19th, 1943. We lived on the far south side of Chicago. I spent my formative years pretty much riding or driving east or west on 103rd street. If you went west from Halsted Street, you would encounter a railroad. You would encounter the same situation going east. I guess I had a strong penchant for trains from the onset. My mother told me in later years that, as a mere tyke, I would stare for long periods of time, at a certain cereal box that had a train skirting its perimeter.

To the west was the Rock Island, which was crossed by the Pennsylvania Panhandle Division at Vincennes Avenue. Next would be Rock Island's Beverly commuter branch, then the B & O Chicago Terminal. Lastly was a personal friend of mine, the Grand Trunk Western. There were other tracks further west, but they weren't exactly in my sphere of activity.

Going east and only a half mile away was the Chicago & Eastern Illinois. Actually the Chicago & Western Indiana owned the track, but the C & E I moved the lion's share of cars across it. 103rd Street ran under the Illinois Central and because of that, I never paid much attention to the IC. As we went east, usually on the way to my Aunt Grace's, we would go over Nickel Plate's Calumet Yard. The C & W I double track main line paralleled Calumet Yard. Once in a while if we were lucky, we would see a plume of steam at the east end of the yard when one of their Berkshires was leaving town with a manifest. During that time I watched the Erie come across Torrence Avenue with a freight train. He had to be going at least 70 MPH. I was really impressed!

We used to hop the panhandle trains as they were the slowest, hence, easiest to get on and off. One time we crawled into an empty gondola and couldn't get off. We jumped on the train at 104th Street and couldn't get off until we hit 59th Street. We weren't really knowledgeable about urban geography or the general machinations of a railroad, much less anything else. We thought we were going to end up somewhere around Milwaukee. That pretty much took care of our lust for "flipping trains".

Our friends, the Pritchard's, lived on Sacramento Avenue. The Grand Trunk paralleled that street at that point and they hauled ass. The "Trunk" was the last railroad coming into Chicago with steam locomotives pulling their passenger trains. One night we were sleeping over at the Pritchard's house. I had to get up to go to the bathroom and as I crept back to bed, in the darkness came this banshee in the night. It literally scared the hell out of me! It was a Grand Trunk night train coming into Chicago from Detroit.

Actually we spent most of our "track time" on the C & E I (or C & W I). Their tracks were close to our center of operations (Fernwood Park) and it enabled us to do our beer drinking. For some reason the cops never tried to "grab" us around the tracks. They sure as hell weren't a bit shy about chasing us around Fernwood Park, though.

Now that I think about it, I probably learned how to read from the writing on the boxcars. We would spend many happy moments watching the trains go by. Those cars came from places like "Pennsylvania", "Frisco", "Monon", "Rock Island", and on and on. Back then there were plenty of railroads. There must have been at least 85 major railroads. Each railroad had its own logo and some had two or three. Chicago & Northwestern, including its subsidiaries, had at least ten logos. Great Northern did many interesting things with Rocky, their well-traveled goat. Pennsy had a bunch and C B & Q (Burlington) was no slouch either. Then there were the cars with the mysterious names such as Nickel Plate, Katy, Monon, and Wabash to name a few.

I would always ask my dad questions. He couldn't always answer them. He would always say, "I have seen the same cars you have seen, maybe a hundred times more, but never once did I ever wonder about where a boxcar came from or where it was going. I did often wonder when I would see the caboose, though". One day I asked my dad how the railroads kept track of the cars in a train. He said, "don't worry, they know where every car is". I later found out that that wasn't entirely true, but nonetheless, the roads did a fairly good job of keeping their cars within their grasp.

I was becoming fascinated with railroading, but hadn't yet established that it could one day be a potential career.

It wouldn't be until the summer of 1959 that my first railroad experience would occur. My friend Rich Katula and I were looking for summer jobs where we could find them and this day we would be seen doing the "south side of the loop". We happened to pause at the "Illinois Central Railroad" employment office. Katula said, "Let's go in". I said, "are you crazy, they're not going to hire high school kids for anything". We bantered for about two minutes and I relented. We went in and they actually let us fill out applications. At that time I had no idea, albeit good or bad, that this day would change my life.

On November 18th, 1959 the IC called Rich and I to work. It definitely cast a new lifestyle for one Arthur L. Hoekstra. I would become: A.L. HOEKSTRA 313200, MAIL HANDLER, I.C.R.R. Not the most glamorous title, but it would be a beginning. Welcome to the world!

Chapter 2

Mail & Baggage

Along with all other passenger hauling railroads, Illinois Central had its share of mail contracts to honor. Most IC trains had RPO's (Railway Post Offices). In these cars the mail was sorted by postal employee's en route. This had to be heavy stuff because all of those guys carried pistols. Parcel post (packages) was another way to fill a mail, baggage or express car. The heaviest commodity was bulk mail. Bulk mail consisted of heavy sacks of catalogues, such as, Sears Roebuck. We called these sacks...slugs. The Chicago end of the mail operation was archaic, however, extensive. It definitely had that "paid for" look. Railroads liked to get their money's worth out of a facility.

IC traditionally hired high school kids to take up the slack during the Christmas rush. I think that this particular year was a real blockbuster for mail handled. When they hired us, there were about three or four guys ahead of us. A couple of those guys had worked the previous year. They hired about 20-25 guys after we hired. In fact, they hired three of our buddies.

Being high school kids, we were assigned to the "afternoon" shift. Afternoons were pretty much 3-11 or 4-12 on the railroad. Katula and I showed up for work using our temporary commuter train passes, which was another perk. Here we were, sixteen years old, entering a man's world for the first time. Of course we were apprehensive. This was to be an adventure hosted by someone else...this was to be an organized adventure! None of our adventures were ever in control, this one would be.

We were to report to the office of the Mail & Baggage agent, but never quite got there as we were headed off by a fellow named Tom Kee. Mr. Kee sort of reminded me of a good guy in a 1930's flick. A hero type, a guy that could do no wrong and could be in many places at one time, Tom Kee was the General

Foreman, second in command to a fellow named F.G.Neuman, whose title was "Mail & Baggage Agent". The way it worked was, Neuman ran the show days, and Kee took care of the afternoons. There were no nights.

After a brief welcome to his world, Mr. Kee stood back, looked at us, and offered some constructive criticism as to our "work attire". He said that we would also need gloves and he directed us to one of the guys that just happened to have about thirty pair. In addition to that he had snuff, chewing tobacco, condoms, and with a pause he volunteered that he was getting some more of those "eight pagers" the guys liked. I guess they made for easy reading. Now that we had our gloves, we were ready for work. I don't remember where they sent Katula, but I would be working with Leonard. Now Leonard wasn't the most affable person I ever met. I think Leonard simply wasn't happy. Mr. Kee said go down to #3 platform and report to Leonard was what I said when I found him. I also added that my name was Bud. Leonard acknowledged the introduction with a grunt. Good. We were gonna be a team! I sort of got off on the wrong foot with Leonard. It wasn't but about an hour after our partnership was established that Leonard asked me if I would plug this cable into the mail car next to ours. Now Leonard was only about 5 ft. 6 in. and weighed around 300+ which prevented him from doing a lot of normal things. Well...I didn't quite plug this cable into its proper place. I did cause the cable to arc and sparks of various electrical colors exuded from places where they shouldn't have been. It didn't look like I would be called to do that job again. Not long after that happened, maybe ten minutes, Tom Kee walked up to me and told me to go out to the shed and meet #8 (northbound Creole) on track #7. I wanted to do that, but then I probably should have appealed to Mr. Kee for clearer direction. He laughed and said he was sorry, he forgot I was new and added that he did that a lot. He carefully explained where I was to go and to report to Walter Kapp. As he watched me eagerly depart for my next assignment, he stopped me, called me back and informed me that I had just committed a cardinal sin. You cannot step on the rail. Step over it, but don't step on it. Can Do! After #8 was said and done, it was time for lunch. Rich and I went up to the depot restaurant and explored that part of our new surroundings. After that, the day flew by. It didn't take long to learn the work. Anything intricate would be referred to someone else. There wasn't a whole lot of intricacies to begin with.

Now you have to remember that we are two sixteen year old kids that have been tossed into an entirely new lifestyle. We not only had entered the adult work force, we were asked to still be high school kids. It was like when the school bell rang we would jump into a phone booth and emerge as something else, only with gloves on.

Looking back on it I have to say that it was a terrific experience. In this we were exposed to a vast array of personalities. Guys from all walks of life worked here for a very average wage. A promotion at this time called for a 13 cent a day raise to "lead man". I am sure that there had to be some resentment. If you look at a guy that has worked the same job for 20 years and a high school kid shows up and on his first day he is making the exact same money as you, wouldn't that make for a bad work relationship?

All in all those guys were good to us. It was fun to load a trailer and bullshit with the guys while we were dragging sacks. As I said before, there were all kinds of people doing this job and that made it interesting.

One old fellow that comes to mind was a pleasant chap by the name of "A.J. Beale". When you saw A.J. his rubber stamp greeting was always "fine day". A.J. lived about 220 miles downstate in the little town of Farina, Ill. During the work week he must have had a room somewhere on Wabash Avenue. I can't remember what his days off were, but you always knew when it was time for A.J. to catch #25. Farina was a flag stop for #25 and of course it always stopped for A.J. Kinmundy, was the first town north of Farina and A.J. always joked that if you couldn't do it today—you sure Kinmundy. Mr. Beale was pure country working and living in the big city.

There were many stories to be told mostly good…some bad. I will end this part of the chapter with the story of a fine gentleman by the name of Joe Oppferman. Now Joe in his day was a very strong man. When I met him he was still a very strong man. Already in his sixties, he worked the hardest job on the platform. That would be #3 platform with the slugs. He was Leonard's day counterpart. I think Joe just wanted to mind his business, work hard, and avoid any of the day to day bull shit. Now Joe has arms as big as my legs and I remember him never looking like he was in a bad way. One day I asked him, "Joe, can't you work a better job than this? I mean this is the worst job on the platform". He agreed with me, and went on to say that over the years he acquired a comfort zone and learned that accepting what the rank and file didn't want, he would be happier. I then asked him, "Aren't these slugs getting a bit heavy?" Joe simply replied, "heavy for you maybe, not so bad for me", and then he grinned. I probably weighed 140 pounds soaking wet at that time.

Christmas came and went. Rich and I expected to get laid off at any time. The new year came and we were still working. Finally the axe fell on the 6th of January. We both bought suits to wear for St. Helena's Hi-Club Christmas dance. It was nice to be making a "good piece of change" as Tom Kee used to say. Now it was time to go back to school and be kids again.

Toward the end of January the IC called us back to work. I can't remember if that was due to the economy or maybe there were a few retirements. Now it's push come-to- shove decision time. Katula had no problem with that. He stayed in school and severed his railroad ties. I thought that maybe I could get away with doing both, which turned out to be a mistake. Katula was already a junior and held a high scholastic average and went on to graduate. As for myself, I always struggled academically and didn't have the patience to be taught subjects that I didn't feel were necessary. In addition to that were other factors pro and con. I wasn't exactly a scholar, however high school was a "candy store" when it came to the opposite sex. That was a definite plus. Thinking about it over the years the underlying tie breaker was the fact that a certain "fear" element prevailed. I can see why a kid can't get a proper education when he's constantly subjected to intimidation. Our particular situation at Fenger was precarious to say the least. The prevailing gang had us outnumbered about 100 to 1 when you factor in the wannabe's and the ass kissers. In any event, learning was deterred by the ever present thought that the bad guys wanted not only to kick your ass but also to re-arrange your teeth. We were outnumbered because our guys went to other schools and then some of them didn't go to school at all. Still…I tried to do both. One day the science teacher caught me sleeping. I simply could not stay awake in his class (or anyone else's for that matter). Now we have an appointment with the principal. Mom and I and one Clarence T. Richardson. Mr. Richardson presented me with an ultimatum. He said, "You can stay in school or you can go to work, obviously you can't do both". Being the cocky kid that I was, my answer was "you're not paying me $75.00 (clear) a week, I'm gonna go to work", and that was the end of that. Right then and there I launched my career. Seventy-five bucks a week in 1959 was a lot of money for a kid. It was about at that time that Rich and I went different ways as he graduated and I held down a full time job.

Now I am a full time employee, making lots of money (for my age). Once I got my feet on the ground and learned the ropes, I began to look around. Probably the first thing that I noticed was that a fellow that hired out after me was now driving a tractor on the day shift. I wondered about the seniority system and that maybe this guy was somehow exempt from that because of some unexplained breakdown in the union agreement. I felt that I should avail myself to that effect, question the powers that be and maybe I could also be working days. I really didn't think that I would get anywhere with my request for a move to another shift. After all this un-balance of labor rights didn't take place overnight and wasn't going to go away overnight. One thing for sure…I was going to find out. I really wasn't too worried about how the union was going to persevere. However, I was concerned about Bud Hoekstra. My request was granted and I moved to the day shift. Sometimes you have to shake the tree.

As afternoon guys, we would always take 15 minutes for coffee and 30 minutes for lunch. I found out the first day that the contract called for 10 minutes. Tom Kee was being generous. The day foreman, "Murphy", was not. Coming back from my day shift coffee break, "Murph" was there to inform me that coffee breaks were taken 10 minutes at a time. Welcome to the "day shift", Bud!

"Murphy" was a euphemism for an Italian name. "Murph" was very Italian and intimidated a lot of people. He would stand there in whatever a gangster would wear if he was watching his wife plant tulips. He always had a cigarette in his hand or a stub of a butt protruding from his face. "Murph" was a piece of work.

Right from the "get-go" "Murph" and I didn't quite hit it off. As a young kid, I wasn't smart enough to be afraid. Whenever we would lock horns he would send me up to Neuman's office and then Neuman would take a crack at me. We did that twice to no avail. That must have been Murph's version of the rack. It was as close as he could get to punishment and not leave a scar. It must have been frustrating for him. Murphy gave me much food for thought over the years as he was one of a very few persons that I have come across in life that inwardly delighted in intimidation. I often get a chuckle when I think of him.

I had the habit of walking along the mail platform with my hands in my pockets. Every time Neuman saw me doing that he would icily tell me to keep my hands out of my pockets. This happened quite often and didn't dawn on me until many years later that the reason for that must have been for safety purposes. Why didn't he explain that to me in the first place? There's something else that I just thought of. Neuman always wore a top coat and his hands were always in his pockets! One day Neuman caught me leaving work about 15 minutes early and the next day that 15 minutes was deducted from my time card. Neuman was a most fastidious man.

Central Station was wholly owned by the Illinois Central R.R., however over the years it played host to New York Central subsidiaries—Michigan Central, and the "Big Four". "MC" trains were long gone when I came along, however there were two "Big Four Route" trains each way. One was called the Sycamore and the other was the James Whitcomb Riley. Both trains ran to Cincinnati however the "Riley" carried sleepers which ran over the Chesapeake & Ohio to either Norfolk or Richmond, Va. Mostly during the summer the "Riley" would at Indianapolis, Ind. pick up what we called "book cars". Most times only one, quite often two. These were express cars that were loaded to the maximum with encyclopedias. If I remember correctly, each set of books weighed 65 pounds. At that time I never gave it any thought but after being in engine service for some years, I can see the engineer on the "Riley" cringing when he found out he would have a book car or two to pick up. The interesting thing about that was that the cars would be tacked on to the hind end of the train. Imagine a bull whip with a couple of chunks of steel at the end of it. Now imagine that you are riding a train, sitting in the diner trying to enjoy a beverage when these "book cars" roll against the train. Even the best "hoggers" would have trouble with that. Not good operational procedure, however it fills the bill when you don't give a damn about passengers.

If the "Riley" was on time the book car would be spotted for unloading by around two o'clock. That would allow the day shift to unload the entire car. The summers of 1960 and 1961 were hot ones and it took a lot out of guys. It would be 90 degrees outside and in the car it seemed like 120 degrees. These cars always showed up at the end of the day. If Murphy had a favorite time it would be in the heat when a book car would show up. I wouldn't be surprised that his favorite movie scene was the one where Flash Gordon and the gang are shoveling coal into this huge furnace and guys are collapsing everywhere and being whipped where they lay. I'm sure that if "Murph" could have had that particular background music piped in, he would have. The whip would have been a nice touch also. While the conveyor belt is being shoved into place, we should take time to talk about favoritism. There surely were pets and there was no shortage of whipping boys. Murphy had his pets (I think they were actually Neuman's pets), and Murphy had his favorite guys to browbeat. When word that a book car was in the works, I automatically made plans to be there. I wasn't in the clique, nor did I want to be. I knew that the work, while unpleasant, wouldn't kill me. I worried about some of the other guys though. A couple of those guys were in their sixties and shouldn't have been in there. My guess is that the only reason they were there, was because at one time they spoke up or ruffled someone's feathers and because of that they would end up their careers working like slaves instead of retiring with dignity and respect. It was comical in some respects, I mean watching four of their most expendable lackeys trying to feed around ten or twelve brown noses on the other end of the conveyor belt. We in the car would be busting our asses while the "pets" would engage in casual conversation while carrying the occasional box to its proper place. It dawned on me that this wasn't eighth grade anymore...this was actually happening.

One day as I was pondering my dilemma, it all caught up with me. I looked at Murph with that silly cigarette stub in his face and I wondered how he ate. As I thought the thought, I began to laugh. The more I looked at this imposing humorously intimidating figure, I laughed harder and harder. I laugh better when I'm not working and I could see that Murph wasn't comfortable with that. That made it even funnier. Finally I heard the conveyor shut off and Murphy told me to "go see Neuman". I still can hear it. I told him that he had better come with me because I didn't know what I was gonna tell him. What am I gonna say, I mean I've never seen Neuman begin to smile. Was I going to get him laughing…would we become buddies? I think not. Neuman wasn't there anyhow and it was 3:30. I was somewhat smug as the car wasn't completely empty and the leftover boxes of books were on the floor and that makes them even heavier. The afternoon boys wouldn't be happy.

The next morning en route to work and planning the day's activities, I reflected that my first move would probably be to "go see Neuman". Surprisingly, nothing was said.

That day not only did I get a reprieve, I would get a promotion. My new job title was "lead mail handler" and I would be making 13 cents a day more. I was close to nineteen bucks daily. That was the good news, the bad news was that I would be taking Joe Opferman's place. You know, Joe with the tree trunk arms? I'm not sure what their thinking was. Were they trying to teach me responsibility? Was this a feeble display of humor? Or were they trying to slowly kill me. Working in Joe's place was like having your own personal "book car" that never quite gets empty.

I weighed about half of what Joe weighed and I'm sure he was at least twice as strong as me, but those slugs always weighed the same. I can't remember if I had the job for one or two weeks, but I would overcome this too. They weren't going to break me.

About the second day into my sentence I had heard that there was a car of mail that had caught fire around Memphis. That afternoon, Neuman caught me leaning against the side of the door of the car I was loading. In addition to not working, I was also smoking a cigarette. Neuman didn't have his top coat on this day as it was probably 100 degrees. Smoking in the car wasn't the way you wanted the boss to see you and Neuman told me so. He also mentioned that I would better understand why (not to smoke in the car) tomorrow. I knew exactly what he meant. Neuman may or may not have known that I knew about that car coming in from Memphis. It was a car of mail that caught fire.

Throughout my tenure on the mail platform, I came to the realization that railroading was in my blood. Every day cultivated that emotion more and more. My ultimate ambition, had I a choice, would have been to become an engineer. I would stand along one of the tracks in the shed waiting to meet one of the passenger trains. Sometimes the engineer would have to call for more power, which to me literally shook the ground. This was music to an eighteen year old kid that happened to finally realize what he wanted to do in life. I would think about this quite often, usually when I was lifting a box of books or a slug full of catalogs. I began asking questions. What are the requirements to become a locomotive engineer? It was established that you would first have to be a fire-men. Beyond that I had no idea. I wasn't particularly mechanical, I didn't even have a high school education and probably most importantly—I had no clout, nobody to put in a good word or to pull a few strings. The one factor that I was sure of was that I wasn't going to spend the rest of my life on that mail platform. You also had to be eighteen to work anywhere in the operating department. I had that by a couple of days. It was time to walk across the street to the em-ployment office and talk to someone. I introduced myself to this gentleman, told him I had worked two years on the mail platform and didn't feel that I had much of a future there. I went on to say that I was really interested in trains and would someday like to work in that service. The interviewer tried to tell me that my chances of working in train service at this time were slim and none. He explained that they would be taking the fireman's jobs off as the diesel's fired nicely all by themselves. It was just a matter of time. He wasn't very en-couraging. I then asked if I could at least fill out an application, he replied that it wouldn't help, but then again it might not hurt either. I wasn't living at home at the time and my mother called shortly after I got back from work that night. She told me that "the Illinois Central wants you to report to the Master Me-chanics office at Markham". "They want to know if you would be interested in working in engine service". Would I! I can't describe the feeling of elation I ex-perienced.

Once I got my feet back on the ground, I knew that I would have to call the clerk at the Mail & Baggage and advise him of my impending career change. I then thought about the gentleman that interviewed me at the personnel office. Was he testing me? Obviously he was trying to discourage me. He must have known that they were hiring fireman. It would always be a mystery however I would always be indebted to that man. Could Neuman pull the rug out from under me? Would Neuman want to do that? I mean I was sort of a pest and this would be a great opportunity to make me disappear. If he sanctioned the transfer, he would be doing us both a favor. Everything worked out without a hitch and I was even able to carry my vacation over.

As I look back in retrospect, the experience I had working for and with those guys didn't hurt me one bit. I left there a better person and I had a pretty good idea what work was about. Murphy was a one in a million person. If I hadn't seen it for myself, I would have argued that guys like Murphy only existed on television. If they were manufacturing pain and suffering somewhere....Murphy would be on the Board of Directors. Frank Neuman at least the Frank Neuman

I knew (or didn't know) was pretty much a man that went by the book. I'll be honest with you, Neuman probably could have fired me long before the "car that caught fire incident". There were a few mornings when I just couldn't get out of bed. We started work at seven and the phone would ring and it would be Neuman, his usual terse comment went something like this—"gonna come to work?" Sooner or later if I kept it up I would be toast or at least unemployed. Neuman went a little deeper than I felt he was capable of. He just may have had a heart after all. And now that chapter of my life would be over.

Amtrak came into existence on May 1, 1971 and with that the IC lost the mail contracts and trains came off. The mail platform was living on borrowed time. It too would become history. Most of the guys ended up working in commuter service or working at Wildwood unloading automobiles. Central Station would soon vanish from the Chicago skyline. It would be the end of an era.

Chapter Three

Engine Service

On the following morning, I reported to the Master Mechanic's office at Markham roundhouse. The guy at the roundhouse hands me a couple of books and points to the Chief Clerks office and says, go over there. Tell 'em you want to talk to Ed Wolfe. I talked to Ed Wolfe and he gives me a heads up about what happens when you work the extra board. He then introduces me to the pair of crew callers, both men were on the telephone at the time. Wolfe makes a call and then sends me over to the administration building. Report to Mr. Bob Morgridge and with that he hands me a couple of more books. I was walking, and luckily the admin building was within walking distance. I found Mr. Morgridge to be a gracious man. Morgridge handed me yet another book. This was entitled "Illinois Central Railroad Operating Rules". He went on to tell me that I should read this tiny, catechism like book and report back to him at 3:00 PM the next day. Riding home on the commuter train I nosed into this book as I didn't have a lot of time to properly digest its contents. Almost all of it was beyond comprehension. If it was going to be a test, I would be in bad shape.

The next day I saw Mr. Morgridge and we went through the rulebook. This took over an hour and there was no test involved. Morgridge did say that if I was serious about working in engine service, there would come a day when I would have to know it cover to cover. Now I had to take the student trips. There was one trip to Champaign, one trip to Clinton and three trips in the yard. The yard trips would be one in the lower yard (Congress St.), one in the coach yard and one at Markham, on a transfer job. He urged me to complete these trips as soon as possible, as if I didn't, I would get run around. I wondered what "run around" meant, but didn't ask. I would later find out. Of course I wanted to make a road trip. The caller suggested that I ride #63 to Clinton the following day. #63 is called for 1:30 PM on this particular day. I got there early and it seemed like I waited forever before someone showed up, representing our crew. Sunday afternoons can be quiet, even on a railroad. This day was no different. Finally a gentleman that I would have guessed was the engineer came into the room. I asked him if he was on #63 and he said that he was and why was it that I wanted to know? My reply was, I'm the student fireman that will ride with you. I extended my hand and stated that my name was Bud, the rest of it is on the slip. "Student firemen submitted a form to each engineer they rode with and were graded appropriately". He said that I'm the engineer and my name is Joe Overend. Then the fireman showed up along with the brakeman. We exchanged pleasantries. The regular fireman was Ernie Martin and the brakeman was Jim Collins. Just looking at them told me that these guys are rails! How cool can you get! I was excited. I couldn't wait to get out on those big road engines. Martin showed me around the engines and then we tied on to the train. The whole time I'm wondering why we're not on our way to Clinton. This is before I realize that there are certain requirements that have to be met, and brakes were an important prerequisite. We received our air test, got our "highball" (proceed) and then began to leave Markham, at which time Mr. Overend invited me to go back on the third unit and observe. By the way, don't touch anything. This bright sunny day was probably one of the best I ever had. The train was made up of auto parts destined for St. Louis and points beyond. If I remember correctly, we had something like 80 loads and 5 empties. Three GP9's would handle that tonnage in stride. Watching the train head around the wye at Gilman was the most impressive thing I'd ever seen, thus far. Leaving Markham, Mr. Overend mentioned that we had no pickups or setouts and with any luck we might get across the Gilman Line without meeting any trains. The Gilman Line is IC's Chicago-St. Louis single track railroad. The actual "line" comes off the mainline at Gilman. From Gilman to St. Louis the mileage is 214. It turned out that we had no opposing trains to meet and had a good run. Arriving in Clinton I walked down to the depot with the crew and was told to talk to the yardmaster or call the dispatcher to find out about what time the next northbound freight would arrive. It turned out that I would have about 3 hours to kill. That would give me time to eat and do a little exploring. The northbound train would be #62 and it also had three geeps, but because most of the cars were empties, it wouldn't be a bad trip barring anything unforseen. The engineer was Finbar Heintz with fireman Frank Manke and brakeman Earl Pease. Pease volunteered to ride a trailing unit and Heintz motioned the fireman to run the train. Martin and Manke were close to being examined for their engineer cards, and they probably got a lot of OJT. I sat in the brakeman's seat and Heintz sat behind me in the fireman's seat. Manke came back up to the cab and announced that the power looked good. Heintz handed him the train orders. Manke read them and handed them back to Heintz commenting that "the railroad was ours" (meaning no opposing trains on the Gilman Line). Heintz gave the orders to me and after I read them and handed them back, he asked me if I understood them. He knew that I didn't and I told him so. He then began to explain the three orders that we had. He told me that the first thing that is done is to check the order numbers against the clearance. After that, you look at your orders. The first order was our "running" order. This particular order conferred to us "right over all trains East Junction to Gilman. The other two orders were slow orders.

We were on the move and Heintz had the window slightly ajar which enabled me to hear those 567's roar as they were advanced in 80 RPM increments. The night was cool and the drone of the engines and the harmonic sway of the train lulled me into a state of slumber. This would be a problem in my career as it took me a long time to overcome the spell the pulsating diesels cast on me and others too. I awoke hearing Heintz calling over to the fireman something to the effect "this guy is sleeping already. I don't think I'll sign his card". The fireman went along with the ruse, agreeing with him. I tried to stay awake but had difficulty. I was perplexed as I was both interested and very much excited about my new venture. Sleeping was the last thing I wanted to do for more than one reason. I tried to mention this to Heintz, but couldn't find the words. He must have understood as he signed my card anyhow.

My second road trip would be to Champaign. This trip would be with Engineer George Ensminger and would be a quick one as we turned on our arrival and went right back to Markham. That was to be the only time I had ever heard of that happening in pool freight service going to Champaign.

The third venture would be on a transfer run called the "wobbly". The "wobbly" ran between Markham and the Chicago Junction R.R. (NYC) and return. The "CJ" yard was adjacent to the Chicago stock yards. The old timers called it the "wobbly" because back during the war the crews usually worked sixteen hours daily and everyone around the "CJ" was inebriated. Our engineer commented dryly that "they weren't the only ones that were drunk" Of the five crew members on this job, the average seniority was 38 years. The first four guys had over 40 years, but the fireman with only 16 years pulled the average down. Interesting point was that Engineer Carl Moore was also Wayne Johnston's brother-in-law. Johnston happened to be the president of the IC.

I had two trips to go, one to the coach yard, the other to the lower yard (Congress St.). That came and went. Both jobs were day jobs and both engineers had over 40 years. One of them mentioned that he was laid off from 1920 to 1937. The other guy didn't say anything. Bob Morgridge stressed that I get these trips in as quickly as I could because I didn't want someone else to jump ahead of me. Now it was time to bring my signed card and other papers to Morgridge for approval and also an informal "book of rules" test plus a seminar on safety. Luckily he was there and was receptive to my meeting him at the administration building at Markham. This took about two hours and I was approved for work. Bob said you had better call the caller and mark up. I marked up and the caller said I was many times out on the fireman's yard extra board. The fireman's extra board served all yard and transfer jobs on the Chicago Terminal with one job at the Chicago Produce Terminal (CPT). If the fireman's extra road list was exhausted they would borrow from the yard list, same with passenger service, but they never seemed to be short of fireman in passenger service. The extra road list also protected the Kankakee switch engines, Gibson City switcher and the locals and work trains beyond the terminal. It mattered not what time of day or night.

Before I go any further I should explain that I protected all of the work that I was called for. However I did all of this without the use of an automobile. There isn't sufficient time or space to explain why I didn't have a car. If it hadn't been for the IC electrics (suburban service) I would not have been able to work the extra board. The through trains enabled me to protect Kankakee assignments and there was always the occasional freight to ride when called for an outlying point beyond Kankakee. Gibson City (Bean Job) comes to mind. And of course I could not have gotten to the IC electric nor the CPT without the benefit of the Chicago bus system. Yes, the good old CTA (Chicago Transit Authority). Accolades to them all!

The Chicago enginemen's seniority district encompassed the electrified suburban service for which there were 40 jobs for engineers only. The fireman came off the commuter runs in 1926-28 when the IC went from steam to electric. All yard jobs went to the Chicago board except Hawthorne which went to the Freeport board. We had one job there however. The produce terminal had one fireman's job. All transfer work went to the Chicago board. Road work would be encompassed between Chicago, Champaign and Clinton, Ill. This would include all through passenger and all road freight runs and all jobs at Kankakee. All of the locals of which there were six also went to the Chicago board. New York Central ran two trains each way into and out of Illinois Central Station. These were the James Whitcomb Riley and the Sycamore which ran over NYC's "Big Four Route" to Kankakee where it entered the IC for the final fifty-five miles of the trip. IC engine crews brought these trains into Chicago on the final lap of their journey.

My first pay trip was on the 4:00 PM North Pulldown with Engineer Charlie Alspach. We both caught the job off of our respective extra boards on a beautiful Sunday afternoon. We did North Pulldown type stuff all day and night. I'm sitting on the fireman's side wondering when these guys are gonna go to lunch when at about 10 o'clock the engine goes into the oil track at Harvey. The engineer gets off and heads for the yard office. Five or ten minutes later he comes back up on the engine and looks at me and says "don't you want to go home"? I came back with "but it's only 10 o'clock"! We're tying up-go home was the final word. I didn't want to be presumptuous and ask was I getting paid for eight hours, but I sure was hoping. I later found out that our early tie-up time was called an "early quit". I later reflected that I was trading eight hours of hard labor for six hours of "looking out the window" for $3.50 a day more. I was on a roll! Charlie Alspach was a good guy, but it was hard for me to believe that he had seventeen years. He told me that, like a lot of guys, he started firing steam engines when he was sixteen. Charlie, like so many of the rails, had a nickname, I had found out. His was "Preacher". One day he was firing passenger for an engineer that also had a nickname-Bill "Blueyes" Egan. It seems that when the train pulled into Kankakee, Egan handed Charlie a five dollar bill and told him to run over to one of the taverns and get a half pint of Kentucky's finest. Charlie anguished over what to do or rather what not to do and so he compromised by purchasing a quart of milk, and so Egan tagged him with the "Preacher".

Most of the jobs that I worked were downtown or Congress St. Some guys called it the "lower yard". Basically it sat in a recession along the electric line. It split Grant Park from 11th Pl. to Jackson St. From Jackson St., it pretty much fanned out and became a hodgepodge of tracks all the way down to the Chicago River. You had the IC freight house, the Chesepeake & Ohio freight house and the Nickel Plate freight house. There was the banana house, slip "A", the pier, and a piggyback ramp. These little yards were the "lower yard" and were governed by a separate yardmaster at Jackson St. The main mission of Congress St. was to make up the "west end trains". These trains for the most part were "hot". SE-1 (southeastern merchandise) also originated here and consisted mainly of cars pulled from the freight house. Once it left Congress St., it didn't stop anywhere, other than to change crews.

Congress St. had a lot of "tight" places. You definitely had to know what you were doing. Some of the clearances weren't wide enough to accommodate a man. It was a dangerous place, especially when you looked at the speed factor. On afternoons there were five jobs that started between 2:30 and 4:00 PM. Most of the switchmen worked another job. Now enter the "early quit" factor.

19

You have five crews all running to catch the 7:25 or 8:25 PM commuter train (no later). These guys were good. They were virtual technicians when it came to switching boxcars. Watching them work with their lamps was amazing. They could literally "talk" with their lamps. When a new man came on one of those jobs, they would tell him to get up on the engine and stay there, otherwise he would only be in the way and not only could be a danger to himself, but to others, too.

There were about 15 jobs around the clock. The one job I usually landed on was the 11:00 PM "Trimmer Pier" with Art Kanya. Art worked the job on a regular basis and was a good guy. I ran my first switch engine under his watchful eye. One fellow rail likened Congress St. to "instead of building a ship in a bottle, we're switching in one".

The 26th St. job was based out of Congress St. and used to take cars to R.R. Donnelly, the big printing mogul. Like a lot of places, you pulled the cars that were ready and re-spotted the cars you brought with you. The job was always good when the usual routine prevailed, however when business was good they always wanted another pull. As the 26th St. job was around the clock a re-spot could sometimes wait as circumstances dictated. On this day the regular fireman wasn't available and so I was called for the job. Crews that always work together frown on a new guy because they don't know him, hence they don't trust him. The engineer kind of counseled me as to what my additional duties might be. He said, "You won't find this in your Fireman's Handbook." Before I could ask him to elaborate, the conductor (switch foreman) comes up on the engine, gives me the onceover and then hands me a twenty dollar bill and tells me to "go over and get a pint of this and a half case of that". I had a hard time telling him that I was only 18 and that they wouldn't sell it to me because the law in Illinois was 21. I'm sure that it had been years since this gentleman had had to deal with that particular problem. I really felt "out of place" but what could I do? I didn't see any of them the rest of the night as they usually worked on the engineer's side. The 26th St. always shoved back to Congress St. I later asked the engineer if they got their booze. He simply muttered, "Don't worry".....

And then there was Carl Tetzloff, the Freeport engineer that worked the night "produce terminal" job. The guys on the fireman's extra board had the uncanny ability of knowing what job they stood for before they answered the phone. Some jobs they avoided like the plague. This was one of them. Some of those guys would pester the callers to no end. I would not do that and would take any lumps when it was my turn. It seemed like my turn was coming up more than it should have. I would have to mention that to the crew caller. The job wasn't exactly a plum especially when you consider that it took me an hour and a half, on three different buses to get there. It's only 20 minutes in an automobile from where I lived. Of course the job had to be a night job. Getting off the bus, I would then have to walk what seemed like a mile. I remember one night it was pitch black and then a clinging fog rolled in. All of that and then the frosting on the cake was Tetzloff. Tetzloff was one of those guys that looked like he always had a headache. I don't think Carl ever got any awards for congeniality. As an additional "perk" the job always worked 8 hours. At the end of the night, I usually would get a ride to the bus (it wasn't Carl). One interesting aspect of the job though, it usually always had a Fairbanks-Morse engine furnished by the Santa Fe which along with the IC had joint ownership of the Chicago Produce Terminal.

Another "plum" that I was called for was the Gibson City switcher called the "bean job", it worked sixteen hours. I was told that I would be there for two days and could "deadhead" on #65 which left Markham around 4:00 AM and with any luck might get to Gibson City near the 8:00 AM starting time. Engineers don't like to slow down a big freight train for any reason, much less for a "deadhead". The question was always "how fast can you get off"? There was never a cheerful answer to my request. We got there a little after eight I was able to get off. The engineer was just getting on the engine when I waved to him telling him I was there. The engineer, a Mr. Art DuBois was a nice guy. He had lots of seniority and told me that when the "Bean Job" opened up, he sold his house in the Chicago area and moved his family lock stock and barrel to Gibson City. Art was able to work that job for one year before he could be bumped out of there, and it happened. "Heinie" Hendricks bumped him and ultimately retired from there. In later years after Art and his wife had moved back to the Chicago area, my wife and I used to go over to their place and we would play cards. Gibson City was about 100 miles from where I lived and the lack of personal transportation placed an acute hardship on myself and those affected by it.

And then winter came and I found myself on the bottom of the board. One day the phone rang and I was directed to the 5:30 PM switch engine at Kankakee. I was being "forced" as I was the youngest fireman. Well okay, I guess. I was less than enthused but had no choice. Next I would have to make travel arrangements. The James Whitcomb Riley would leave the city at 3:55 PM and arrive in Kankakee at 4:45 or so. That would give me time to eat and then walk down to the yard office. The yard office had an upstairs bunk room that was on par with a jail cell. It was winter and every time I touched one of thse metal beds, I would get a shock. I hated it, and tried to go home when I got the chance. Number 2 the northbound City of New Orleans would get into Kankakee around 10:40 PM when it was on time, which was never. This would work out for me. On more than one occasion I was able to go home because of this. Because it was usually late, it created a dilemma for the crew. The last electric train out of Randolph St. was the 2:25 AM and if you missed that, it was a two hour wait until the 4:25 came along. No one wanted to spend two hours at 27th St. (roundhouse) if they didn't have to. One night Johnny Graham was the engineer on 2. Graham was a 1910 man and was also number two on the seniority list. That night #2 was late, but I don't think it was because of bad power. Authorized track speed for passenger service was 79 MPH. Graham had it up to 101 and that was going uphill. Making up time on the City of New Orleans had an ambiguous effect, you tried to maintain the "on time" tradition and coincidentally catch the 2:25 out of the city. Cab rides were fun.

I worked that 5:30 Kankakee job for about a month give or take a few days. The board was cut again and that was my swan song. I would spend the rest of the winter laid off and at least life would be a whole lot easier. No more rawhiding going back and forth to work.

I wasn't off but a couple of months, if that, and I was called back. One beautiful spring day I was called to fire 1/63[1] with Charlie Beebe. Charlie had 40 years under his belt and was a nice old guy. We were coming off of the mainline onto the Gilman Line when Charlie stands up and says that he needs a break and that I should get over on the hogger's side. I couldn't believe it. Wow! The first time I would handle a big freight train. Thinking about that event years later, I realize that there wasn't much trouble to get into as it was uphill for about ten miles and the only thing I touched was the whistle cord. Charlie then took over. It was a unique experience for me. The return trip was awful. We were listed for around 8:00 AM on 64 with three GP9's and about 85 empty auto parts cars. We were cruising along at about 50 when we get a bell. I go back to troubleshoot the trailing units and discover that the second unit is dead. No fuel in the sight glass means the engine is starving for fuel. I couldn't do anything with it. I finally went back up to the lead unit to tell Charlie and get out my GP9 manual. Charlie said that he threw off a message at Farmer City to advise the Dispatcher that we were down to two units. By that time the third unit goes down. Nearing Gibson City we get an approach which probably means that the Dispatcher is heading us into the siding for a meet with another train. That will be good, I thought as that will give Charlie a chance to look at these two engines. That was pretty much what Charlie did, too, look at them. He may have known more about those units than I did, but not much. We are now resigned to the fact that our projected short day will now be a long one. We would need a shove over Guthrie as our single geep wasn't enough. Once we got over Guthrie we would be okay until Kankakee. We would need a helper from Kankakee to Steunkel Road, 25 miles. Surprisingly we would not exceed any tonnage ratings. We got over the road but not without egg on our faces. That night I received a phone call from Mr. Bob Morgridge. He asked me what happened and all I could tell him was that we lost the rear two units because they weren't getting fuel. Once I finished my explanation, Morgridge proceeded to tell me what happened. Each unit has a plunger adjacent to its fuel tank. If the plunger is pulled out the engine will die for lack of fuel. He never said anything about how those plungers got pulled out, though. In retrospect my feelings are that we were sabotaged at Clinton.

Summer was coming to an end and about that time it was determined that a temporary career change was in order. This decision would make everyone happy including me. And so off I went, U. S. Army here I come!

I would like to close this chapter with a brief word about steam for those of you that might be interested. When I went firing (9-11-61), there was one steam locomotive sitting at the Markham roundhouse. I don't remember its number but it was a 3600 class engine. Wheel arrangement was 0-8-2. IC was one of the very few roads that employed these beasts. It definitely had that "paid for" look about it. IC serviced a stone quarry owned by Material Service Corporation. On rare occasions because of heavy rain, a diesel could not get down into the quarry because a portion of the track was washed out. The rule was "diesel locomotives are prohibited from operating over rail that has water in excess of three inches over the ball of the rail". Hence the "bow down" or "hand bomber" was retained for emergency flood service. The guys that fired those engines during the war always less than affectionately referred to the 3600's as "bow downs" (sans stoker). They were used as "hump" engines and the fireman would work 16 hours keeping one of these engines hot. I am told that it was back breaking work. The 2613 was said to have made the last revenue trip on the Cairo turn between Carbondale and Cairo, Illinois on the 27th of January 1959. I later discovered that this engine worked out of Paducah in April of 1960 in company service. Later that same year it worked in excursion service on the Louisville & Nashville. The Illinois Central was quite proud of the 2600 class. Twenty were built as new during the war and they pulled everything and anything. What I just related to you about steam is pretty much as close as I would come to it.

---

[1]Some days there would be as many as three 63's, 1/63, 2/63, etc., etc.

Chapter Four

The Army

When I wasn't working, I was getting into trouble. My dad and I didn't get along worth a darn. We had a houseful of kids and my mother was beginning to worry about them. There was no doubt about it, our arguments were becoming more and more disruptive. Factor in a couple of minor scrapes with the law and you have a recipe for the military. I was living with my aunt and uncle at the time. He held the rank of buck sergeant (E-5) in the Army National Guard and he talked me into going into the army. We had to run around and get letters of endorsement, etc., etc. We finally got it all put together. However there was the little matter of "military occupational specialty" (MOS). You have a little bit of leverage when you join and if your particular specialty is available, that is what should be the general proviso. Papers were flying everywhere, but yet we never discussed that impending MOS. The U.S. Army had its Transportation School at Ft. Eustis, Virginia and also had a railroad battalion stationed there and that is what I wanted. I mentioned it to the recruiter and he retorted "that's right, you wanted to be an engineer" as he must have wrote the numbers 113.0. I just had unknowingly become a pioneer or to be more blunt, a combat engineer. The combat engineers were like the infantry in fact if there was a shortage of infantry, they would move a company or two of the engineers into the line. When you think about it, the infantry had it better, they could at least duck or shoot back. Try building a bridge while the enemy is shooting at you. I didn't get a chance to railroad in the U.S. Army, but I did get railroaded! On the following night I would get to ride Pennsylvania's "Kentuckian" from Chicago Union Station to Louisville, Kentucky. That meant Ft. Knox. Would that be the only train ride I would get from the U.S. Army?

Aside from being the nation's "gold depository" the army likes to call it US-

ATCA. (U.S. Army Center Armor). I would of course have nothing to do with "tanks" as my sole purpose of being there was for basic training, eight weeks of it. Here we have a couple of hundred kids, some of them away from home for the first time. There also were a few draftees among our ranks. These guys haled from mostly Illinois, Indiana, Ohio, Pennsylvania, and West Virginia. Being from that part of the country was about the only thing we had in common. There were a couple of draftees that shouldn't have been there as they didn't read or write very well. They were totally out of their element (weren't we all). Our platoon sergeant wasn't playing with a full deck either. He was an E-6 or E-7. It was difficult to tell because the army sometime after Korea changed its NCO (non-commissioned officer) structure and walked away from that with a touch of confusion. Situation normal. Let's call him Sgt. Hill. There were four platoons of trainees in the company. The powers that be always promoted competition among the platoons. We were the third platoon, but should have been the fourth platoon as we always were last in company activities. I think this drove Hill crazier than he already was. Anyone making a mistake while performing "close order drill" was not only screamed at, but physically berated. He had three or four guys that he singled out for that purpose. It was easy to make a mistake if you didn't know your left from your right, to begin with. Hill definitely had an irascible side.

Racism is and probably always will be a social disease, beyond cure. I was beginning to discover that the particular brand of racism we were subjected to, would be in reverse. The black guys, while a minority, were more than caustic when away from the eyes of our superiors. One day I was on KP and my job was to dole out two bacon strips per man. Now we're down to four strips of bacon and with one guy left besides myself to feed. I put two strips on his tray and he reached in to grab a third strip. If he gets away with it, I only get one strip of bacon. I rapped his hand with the tongs at which time he commenced to call me everything but a white man. I could have used an interpreter as I couldn't discern some of his invectives. This guy was a black man from Gary, Indiana. Some of the stuff he mentioned was understandable, like when he screamed that "when I get you in the barracks, you're gonna wish you were dead"! I now have a decision to make ....should I hang around the mess hall and avoid this guy or should I avail myself to this guy's punishment and get it over with? I opted for the latter. I tell the mess NCO that I have to use the washroom and am sitting on my foot locker at the end of the barracks. He walks in. sees me down at the end and comes charging. He was more than irate. I'm thinking "if I get up and move away from the punch he is about to throw, he's fair game for a punch of my own". I won the first round. Stay tuned. As it turned out, this guy and I were first and second in platoon "PT" (physical training). I recall he won some kind of endurance race and gave me the evil eye as he walked by. My only thought was "you may have won the race, but I'm still ahead of you". Years later I was waiting for a train and would see this guy again. I was sitting next to a switchman friend and next to him was Mr. Jones. I don't know if he recognized me, but I sure did him. They both got on the Gary train. The next time I saw my buddy I asked him if he knew the guy. He said "sure, that's Jones". Small world.

I was really glad to leave Ft. Knox. The military crap was bad enough but when you factor in the racism and throw in a Sgt. Hill or two, it changes the overall complexion (no pun intended). We were in our seventh week. Every morning each one of us had a brief look into the mirror to see how our hair was progressing. Hill made the entire platoon get baldy sours again. Ours was the only platoon that had to do that. Our hatred for him was not unwarranted. Forget Hill, we were off to Ft. Leonard Wood, Missouri!

The prospective engineers filled a bus and away we went for Ft. Leonard Wood, located near Waynesville, Mo. I thoroughly enjoyed the ride. It was a brief respite from the rigors of the "life of a trainee". Fort Leonard Wood had a reputation for being the "armpit" of army posts. I didn't mind it at all. We had NCO's that definitely would put you in your place, but nothing like that monster at Ft. Knox. Here the guys got along better. Because Christmas wasn't too far away the army elected to ship us to our next stations and we could take leave then. From there I rode the Frisco to St. Louis and then after a very long wait, took the IC's "Green Diamond" which got into Chicago about eight o'clock that night. I enjoyed my vacation, anything was better than what I was subjected to over the last few months. The vacation was not without blemish, however. While home I acquired a "black eye" with which I got to wear at a homecoming dance. I was still wearing it when I showed up at Leonard Wood. Our platoon sergeant had fun with it.

The foothills of the Ozarks can get outright cold in the winter. Our barracks were WWII vintage and were heated by coal furnaces. Of course they needed firemen and I volunteered. After all - I was a fireman! It would be the only coal I ever shoveled. Although we were all private E-1's, the army would select someone from each respective barracks to be the "platoon guide". Ours was from the Chicago area and we hit it off pretty well. This guy was big and I didn't know it at the time, but he had an even bigger temper. One frosty morning, he stuck his head out of his doorway (he had his own room) and yelled to me something like "what's the matter, can't you keep that fire hot"? My reply was without tact as I retorted "if you don't like it, do it yourself:! I'm glad that he was wearing a towel, because I hadn't heard screaming like that since I left Fort Knox. There were no repercussions. Our orders came down for re-assignment. Some guys were going to Germany because they wanted to and some were simply going because when little Caroline Kennedy threw the dart with their name on it, where it landed was where you ended up. My dart landed in Korea. We first flew from Leonard Wood to the Bay area, spending four days at a huge replacement center. That was great because they left us alone and we got to tour San Francisco. They were grabbing guys for KP but for some un-explainable reason, they missed me. After a generous respite, it was time to go. A feeling of awe came over me when I hit the deck of that ship. Suddenly the realization of how great in size the world was humbling to me. About 1,000 of us went on this 19 day cruise. It wasn't bad as the weather was good and the food was great. The ship was named the "General Mitchell" and was operated by the U.S. Navy. Of course they couldn't simply allow 1,000 guys to loll about on deck and so every now and then they had us pull guard duty. Every nook and cranny had a guard. Some guys were painters. We stopped briefly in Honolulu and Yokohama. Next stop would be Inchon Harbor where our ship could not go. We sat and waited for this huge LST (landing ship tank) to take us off the boat and into the harbor. We would then ride a train up to Camp Casey, home of the 7th United States Infantry Division. We were herded in buses over to the local "Repl Depl" (replacement center). If I remember correctly, there were about forty of us trained as combat engineers. Those guys got on another bus and headed north. Thirteen of us were held out to be interviewed. We wondered out loud-maybe they were gonna make us generals. Seventh Administration Co. (an organic part of the 7th Inf. Div.) was short of clerks. They needed finance clerks, personnel clerks, etc., etc. I was interviewed by a first lieutenant. He was more than ponderous as he perused my file. We chatted and he concluded that the finance section wasn't for me. He did ask me if I would rather be in the engineers. By that time I was psyched up to be "one of those office fellers". The lieutenant was sure that there was a place for me in 7th Admin. I ended up working in the personnel section. I didn't quite know what the engineers had to offer, but learning how to operate a typewriter would be better. I would at least be out of the elements that Korea was famous for. Being in the U.S. Army in Korea meant no K.P., however if you happened to be in a unit north of Ouijongbu, there was a plethora of guard duty. South Korean civilians were adept at ripping off anything that wasn't guarded. One night I asked the sergeant of the guard "why are we guarding an empty swimming pool in the middle of winter". They would steal the pumps came the answer. Guard duty was about every other day. It would now be time for me to stand my first guard mount. The guards are inspected by the officer of the day. The guard that could answer the O.D.'s questions without hesitation and who looked the sharpest would get picked to be "supernumerary". I decided I would shoot for supernumerary. Lt. Lacerte was the O.D. this day. That would be a plus for me as he was the guy from finance that interviewed me. We obviously had a good rapport as he selected me. That was the good news. The bad news was that the guy that usually made supernumerary wasn't a happy camper and not making it caused him to be ill. I walked guard anyway as the supernumerary was the extra man, to be employed for that purpose. At least it was a pat on the back, an accomplishment if you will.

The guy's in admin. company were a good bunch, a little brighter than the average bulb on the tree. Most of those guys were from the east coast. Of course they would have to take us into the village and show us around. The village of Tongduchon was located about 30 miles north of Seoul. It was not unlike most towns that were adjacent to a U.S. military base, its whole existence depended on the G.I. dollar. The army frowned on "off post" recreation, however it was good for the Korean economy. The girls for the most part were clean, but you had to be careful, the threat of gonorrhea was ever near. The guys took us to a club and there we were introduced to a few nice looking ladies, dressed with an oriental flair. Their sole reason for being was to make us happy and for only $2.00! A cute Korean lady sat down next to me and asked me if I wanted to go for a walk. Well....we walked to her hooch and she asked me if I would come inside. The conclusions are yours. My only claim to fame in the "vill" was one night I bumped into "Suzie Wong". Now Suzie was known to be the richest woman in Tongduchon. She was beautiful and her rates were slightly higher. She also was the only hooker in town with a television set! I didn't have enough money to consummate the deal. Suzie said that that was okay, I could pay later. She did much for my self-esteem that night. The guys didn't believe it.

What I told you in the previous paragraph in no way is an attempt to promote myself or any other G.I. as superior to the good citizens of Korea. If you took the time to look at these people more closely, you would come to the realization that they may well be the toughest people in the world. I have seen these people walk about in spring jackets when the wind chill factor was -50 degrees. I once was solicited by a woman in the middle of a very cold winter night. I was wearing about every piece of clothing that was issued to me, she was wearing little in contrast to what I had on. Here she was out in the bitter cold darkness, on this lonely guard post, keeping warm by heating these large rocks in a fire and trying to sell herself for fifty cents. I'll never forget the poverty and will always use it as a reminder of how lucky I am to be born in the U.S.A. Land of the big

PX[1]. This isn't intended to be a social studies or geography book and so I must move on.

There were plenty of activities on main post and a bus service to get you there. The EM (enlisted man) Club was always popular to most of us. There you could drink for a reasonable price and listen to the latest tunes on the jukebox. A popular song was Tony Bennett's "San Francisco". We spent many a night crying in our beer while Roy Orbison crooned away.

Admin Co. had its good points which far outweighed the bad points. The main problem with being a 201 file clerk in an office was that the workload was overwhelming. The average day was ten hours or more and I usually spent a part of the weekend at my desk. This was done when we weren't scheduled for guard duty which occurred about every other day. I had some good friends there and we had a blast. Six months went by and I was becoming more and more disenchanted with each day. I concluded that I needed a change, get out in the open and see what that's like. After nine months I finally got my transfer back to the engineers. It was to the "bridge company" no less.

Welcome to Co. D (Bridge) 13th Engineer Bn. (combat). My new home wouldn't be far from admin co and I still hung out with my buddies from there. I think I was there about a week when it became time for us to build a floating bridge. Well, being the bridge company, why not? Trouble was, we didn't have a floating bridge. ROK[2] Army did. We gave it to them after the war. Now we were borrowing it. We drove over to the ROK Army compound to get it with 5 five ton trucks. Floating bridges have lots of components, the most prolific being 16 foot lengths of aluminum weighing about 120 pounds each. These were called "balk", lots and lots of balk. We loaded it all up on the trucks and away we went back to Camp Casey where our ever vigilant superiors made us unload it so that our trucks would be combat ready for any situation. As soon as we unloaded the trucks, the ROK's called back and wanted their bridge. We had to load it back on the trucks and deliver it to them, which meant unloading it again at their compound. The next morning they said we could come and get it. We loaded it up again and brought it to our camp. It was like they were watching us, getting a sadistic glow from it all. Of course, our most astute superiors were also tired of this game, so this time we left the bridge on the trucks, actually took the bridge out and built it, loaded it back up and unloaded it at the ROK compound. Did we give it to them or did they give it to us? Who said Orientals don't have a sense of humor?

It wasn't long after we had lifted that last piece of balk off the truck that I realized that I had done more physical labor in the last three days than I had in the nine months before that. Maybe a typewriter wasn't so heavy after all. A few weeks later I was able to get my driver's license. That was a good thing. Another door opened. About the time I arrived at Delta Bridge the company was also assigned two second lieutenants, both recent graduates of West Point. One early morning I got a call from the sergeant of the guard. He told me that President Kennedy was killed. He didn't know the details. With that I must have nodded off, later I was awakened by the officer of the day shortly before six. I was in deep shit as sleeping on guard duty was a court martial offense. I quickly blurted our "Sir, did you know that President Kennedy was killed yesterday?" Hearing that, he forgot all about me and went scampering down the hill towards the company CP. I don't know if the incident was forgotten, but nothing was said. We shared an NCO club with the neighboring S & T (Support & Transportation) battalion. The difference was that the club was on our compound, and some of our guys would forget that we're all in the same army. We had some guys in Delta Bridge that didn't necessarily get tougher when they drank, however they did get meaner. The more they drank, the meaner they would get. I never saw one of those S & T guys in the club, but I heard that every time they would come in , a fight would ensue. I felt sorry for those guys. We had some bad people in our company. They were perfect for what we did, however.

One night after a particularly long Sunday afternoon at the club I was awakened by two of these guys arguing about something. I yelled to them "shut the #*#* up!" I must have hurt their feelings, because one of them challenged me to actually get out of bed and shut him up. Now we are outside of the Quonset hut rolling down the hill. I can't remember if I was winning or not but the other guy pulled my thumb back to get me off of him. One of the guards came down out of his tower and broke it up. The company commander got wind of it. This guy wasn't the "boys will be boys" type of CO he wanted to take it further. That following week we had a battalion inspection. Lt. Col. Rosen would inspect each one of us black eye and all. If you saw Col. Rosen and had to describe him in one word-it might be "tough". As the colonel stood in front of me, he turned to our captain and simply stated "this guy likes to fight". I was to find out shortly after the inspection that there was to be a court martial and I was named as a witness. It seems as though our fight would be co-incidental to the army's investigation into alleged black marketeering. The next time I saw those guys they were in handcuffs, they must have been found guilty.

Many years later as I was reading a book about the Korean War, I came upon Col. Rosen's name in the footnotes of a chapter concerning the exodus from the Chosin Reservoir. Most people interpret the Chosin battle as a Marine show. Col. Rosen's unit was comprised of 81 Americans and ninety ROK's. They were surrounded and the ROK's broke. The engineers held and suffered 50%

casualties. That morning they counted 400 Chinese Communists lying dead before their positions. An army engineer unit sent to build a CP for the corps commander was thrown into the fray. Rosen bitterly remembered that it took months before they got the recognition they deserved from the Marine Corps. For that, Rosen was later decorated with the Silver Star.

Mike Coller and I were both trained as combat engineers and became good friends while in Korea. We were getting "short". Finally the time came. Coller came up to Delta Bridge with our orders for re-assignment. He also had our travel orders. I can't remember where Coller was going but my orders said 11th Air Assault Division, Ft. Benning, Georgia. I do remember Coller's travel orders-he was going to fly. Mine said General Patrick, which was a ship. Coller chided me about transferring. "If you'd stayed in admin, you'd be flying with me". The guys in admin company had clout. That day that Mike brought our orders up, I had guard duty. For only the second time I ever conspired to make "supernumerary", I once again found success. And once again someone got sick and I had to pull guard anyway. It would be pretty close to the last time I would ever stand guard in Korea and beginning the following day, Monday morning I would begin "clearing post". Clearing post in Korea or anywhere to a G.I. was a little bit like the Mardi Gras festival in New Orleans. You had about fifteen agencies you needed to visit for a final briefing or de-briefing as it were. These little departments ranged from the division Chaplain's office to the NCO club. Nobody bothered you, as "clearing" was considered sacred ground. Of all the various agencies we "cleared" it seems the NCO club was given meticulous attention, more so than the others. That night after I wished Mike bon voyage as I was strapping on my guard duty shit I thought of a cliché someone once said- "A man seldom measures his successes as quickly as he does his mistakes". As I walked my post that night my thoughts wandered from "almost there to" "are they gonna make me jump out of a plane"?

And now comes the big day, spent the night at the "repl depl" then got on the train and rode it to Inchon and then catch an LST out to the big boat called The Patrick. The Patrick sat out in the harbor patiently awaiting the arrival of this mass assembly of ocean going G.I.'s. It probably wasn't the most efficient or cost effective mode of transport. There were around 1,000 guys on the ship. It would take 22 days to make the crossing. Multiply 22 x 1000 and you get an awful lot of wasted time. It was your tax dollar, but it was their party.

There were five of us on the boat from Delta Bridge. One of these guys just happened to be our 1st Sergeant. We all liked Sgt. Dodge and figured that we would have it made. We wouldn't have to perform any extracurricular duty with him being the "troop commander". Wrong again! He didn't cut us any slack at all!

The one aspect of the ship that I was looking forward to however, was the food. The navy put out some good food coming over, why would this be any different? About the third day of "rice and stew" I began to look around and ask a question or two. This would be different. I found out that although the Patrick was a U.S. Navy ship, its crew was made up of Phillipino Merchant Marine and they like rice and stew. It didn't kill us. After a brief stop in Yokohama to pick up a few marines, we headed for the big ocean. About ten days out, we are all cordially invited to see the "pecker checker" for an impromptu "short arm inspection". You stood in front of this medic and he would tell you to "milk it". If pus or mucous came out, you had the clap (gonnorrea). Everyone passed, and got to go ashore in Honolulu. We spent all day hanging around Waikiki beach and Hotel St. We didn't have any money, but Honolulu was a great diversion from the day to day monotony of the boat.

Leaving Honolulu it would only be five days and we would be going under the Golden Gate Bridge. That was a picture that waited a long time to be taken. Toward the end of our voyage on a star lit night I watched the lights of a ship that was way off to the east of our ship and probably 50 miles away. Eight hours later that same ship was conversely way off to our west. It was another reminder of how miniscule we are in this great big world of ours. The following day we began to see the Golden Gate Bridge. Luckily it was a bright beautiful day, befitting for this major event of ours. We all had our Korea bought cameras. And now it was time to take the picture. I couldn't move the film advancer hence the shutter release button wouldn't work the clicker. No picture. Talk about a bad omen!

It wasn't long and we were on our way to the Greyhound Bus Depot with our already paid for bus tickets tightly clasped in our sweaty hands. There were probably eight or ten guys from the boat riding the bus. Four of us were from Delta Bridge. Three of the guys were heading for points in Ohio. I was all set for a nice scenic ride across the good ole U.S.A. That worked pretty well until after we left Sacramento. The darkness would take us to brightly lit places such as Reno, Sparks, Winnemucca and Elko, Nevada. With every one of these stops the guys would pile off for a visit with one of the enterprising liquor merchants located conveniently to facilitate each and every liquor purchase. I think I know how the cocktail - "greyhound" came about. Now I'm not above having a drink, however my stomach would not allow it. I couldn't sleep, I couldn't drink. All that was available for perusal was the beautiful state of Nebraska as it was again daylight. I was told that Nebraska gets better as summer nears. I would find solace in the fact that all that was left was Iowa, a small part of Illinois and lastly- Chicago. We would get into Chicago about 3 AM. It definitely would be time to get off that bus, my rear end would not be able to stand much more. Getting off the bus in Chicago brings me to the realization that I would be trading one problem for another. My butt would get its well-deserved rest, however the bus was heated. It is February in Chicago. The walk from the bus depot to the subway would be more than brisk. We would persevere remember we spent over a year in the "frozen Chosen". One guy whom I met on the bus was also going to the far south side. He spent his time in the infantry. This fella was a career soldier, much older than I. As we were the only ones riding the CTA bus (final leg of our venture), we sat up front on the side seat and b.s.'ed with the bus driver. My infantry buddy was telling the bus driver that he was close to having his twenty years in at which time the bus driver casually looks over his shoulder at Mr. Denny's shoulder. Denny had no indication of rank, as he flippantly retorted that he partied pretty heavy. He was what the army referred to as a "professional private". These guys weren't good peacetime soldiers, but when the shit hit the fan - they were the guys you wanted fighting along side of you. The bus pulls up to 103rd St., I say goodbye to Denny and wished him much luck. He would be staying with his sister.

I have about one city block to walk and I would be home. I guess I earned the right to have this emotion money can't buy. I would be hugging my wonderful mother for the first time in well over a year. I would see my little brother and sisters and how could I forget about Dad? I rang the doorbell (it's 4 AM), I rang it again, the door then opened. You know the rest.

I had a great visit with the folks. It was really good to be home, but now it was time to head for Ft. Benning. Ft. Benning was located outside of Columbus, Georgia. It was and is the second largest army post. From Chicago, Ft. Benning is 841 miles by rail. Fortunately for me, the Illinois Central ran two trains a day to Florida. One to Jacksonville (with connections to Miami) the other, the City of Miami ran through to that city. Employees were not allowed to ride the "Miami" on a pass. The "Miami" also ran on an every other day basis. The "Seminole" was my train, good old number nine. I would be riding it on an employee pass, at least to Birmingham. Let me explain the arrangement the IC had on its venture to the southeast. For the first 606 miles the trackage was pure "IC". Once the train left Haleyville, Alabama, it would be on the Southern R.R. for 41 miles. At Jasper the trackage becomes St. Louis-San Francisco, the Frisco for another 41 miles ending in Birmingham. The total 82 miles were "trackage rights agreements". Leaving Birmingham, "IC" gives way to the Central of Georgia Railway which will oversee our trains to Albany, Ga., for the next 252 miles. At Albany, the Atlantic Coast Line would take over for the run into Jacksonville, Florida for 187 miles. At Jacksonville the Seminole for the most part would terminate but it did have cars for Miami. The City of Miami would operate over the Florida East Coast Railway for the final 366 miles into Miami.

My pass wasn't good on the C of G, however once in a while the C of G conductor would ignore my attempt to pay. One night in an attempt to better utilize my leave time, I would try to ride the "Miami" out of Columbus. No problem. I had my own Pullman all the way to Chicago. I should mention the power arrangement the IC had with the C of G. The only two E8's the C of G owned were painted in IC's Panama livery. They were numbered 811 and 812. Instead of Illinois Central across the "Green Diamond" on the nose, would be "Central of Georgia". The IC tried to keep these units on trains 9 or 10. It didn't always work that way and quite often these engines were seen on other parts of the IC system.

The train picked its way across the Chattahoochee River and I knew that it was time to seriously start thinking about being in the army again. I caught a bus that said "Main Post". That should be Ft. Benning I reasoned. Sure enough, it was. I get dropped off in front of the Main Post bus station. Luckily there happened to be an MP driving by and I flagged him down. He told me that the 11th Air Assault was up on "Harmony Church". He mentioned that he had an errand to run and then he would run me up there as Harmony Church is about nine miles away. He dropped me off right in front of the 11th AAD personnel office and wished me luck. Sixteen months to go!

Ft. Benning is to the Infantry what Ft. Knox is to Armor. The Infantry School was there along with Officers Candidate School, Airborne Training Center and home to the 2nd Infantry Div., the 11th Air Assault Div. and 197th Infantry Brigade. There were also a raft of aviation units. The lay of the land encompassed about 35 x 30 miles diced into six areas. They were Main Post, Lawson Field, Kelly Hill, Harmony Church, Sand Hill and a vast measure of boondocks. There were 22 ponds all fishable and all in the "DUD"[4] areas. Of course, VERBOTEN!

Ever since we set sail in Inchon Harbor I had been toying with the idea that maybe it wouldn't be so bad to be a clerk after all. The thought of jumping out of an airplane or rappeling out of a helicopter with a shovel instead of a rifle did not sit well with me. Perhaps I might be able to point out to the personnel guys that I knew my way around a typewriter. It couldn't hurt. That little dilemma was quickly surmounted when a personnel sergeant came up to me waving my DD20 (a record) in front of me. He then exclaimed, "I'm gonna keep you from rappeling, boy"! If it meant what I thought it did, I was all for it. Take your shit next door and report to a Sgt. Huisman. Huisman was a kindly gentleman that was happy to see me. Now I would have to learn how it would be to be a "pay clerk". Right now, while you get settled in, you can be our messenger boy and run paperwork between here and finance. I would do that two to three times daily. I rationalized that carrying shit no heavier than a few records was truly what I was cut out for and I would do it well.

Right after I moved into my 11th Admin barracks, it seemed like the army waited until I got settled in and then announced that we would be moving to another place. The barracks we were living in were in good shape, our new old barracks were awful. I never did figure out what they wanted our former barracks for.

I had a bond coming out of my pay monthly. That put a sizeable dent in my spending money and so I stayed out of Columbus and Phenix City. About once a month we would get a ride or hitch hike to a BBQ place called Culpepper's. BBQ to die for! About once a week we would walk down to the EM club and have chicken washed down with much beer. If the end of the month was near we would get a "chit book" as we were always close to being broke. One night we were walking back to the barracks, all drinking 16 oz. cans of beer. That was a no-no and the MP's would tell you to step back into the bushes and drink it. This night an MP stopped us and insisted that we pour the beer out. If he had known who he was talking to, he might not have done that. One of the guys with us handled the pay records for the MP's. Everyone has a name tag and that is how we got his. We shipped his pay records to Alaska. Payday was not a happy event for this guy. He pretty much figured out what happened via innuendo. We helped to make an MP even smarter than he already was!

Shortly after I got myself organized and settled in, I was fortunate to have a fellow in my barracks who happened to be a rail fan. He was Phil Hanna from Arvada, Colo. One day I was reading a bulletin board somewhere and there was a note asking if anyone was interested in trains and railroading in general. He was Charlie Kalhorn from New York City. It was a stroke of luck to have found these guys. We got to know the Central of Georgia pretty well and they were good guys. Someday I will try to look them up.

All the while I was at Ft. Benning, there was quite a brouhaha going on in Washington over the "fireman off" issue. It was coming to a head. Not too long thereafter I received a letter from the Illinois Central wanting to know if I would take $10,000 to take a walk. I declined

Good news! I get promoted to E-4. I am now a Specialist. The powers that be are going to send me to school. If I was to be an E-4 I would have to justify it by attending pay school at FCUSA. Where the hell is FCUSA you ask? I didn't know either. FCUSA stands for Finance Center, U. S. Army. It is located at Fort Benjamin Harrison, Indiana. That would be Indianapolis. I would be the ranking NCO among a bunch of recruits, the class leader sort of a mother hen. It was an adventure in command. Keep in mind that here are 40-45 individuals whom are away from home (many for the first time) and aren't necessarily happy. I pointed out to them that at least they didn't have duty to pull and weekends were their own. Shortly after I made the above speech, the good old U.S. Army decided that we were gonna play musical barracks again. We were going to spend the ensuing weekend moving lockers and bunks etc., etc.. Talk about campers that aren't happy. I sized up the situation, and it looked like we could get it done in a couple of hours. I went to the 1st sergeant and told him that we could get it done, and if we did, could we have our weekend passes? Okay was the answer with the stipulation - if you can get it done. We finished the job in less than two hours, and the guys got their weekend passes. I was now a hero. I didn't tell them that I had a date in Chicago. Chicago was 185 miles from Ben Harrison, and I wanted very much to be there.

I wasn't really proud of my academic prowess. I was never good at school nor was I good at numbers. As the class leader I was between a rock and a hard place. I had to pass and did. I wasn't exactly the class valedictorian, however.

Now it was time to get back to Ft. Benning and be a pay clerk. It was determined that I should work in the officers pay section. That was alright with me, except the NCO in charge was an asshole. More on that later.

I received my TDY[5] pay and shortly thereafter admin company would be convoying to Ft. Gordon for a field exercise. Ft. Gordon was located near the town of Augusta, Georgia. Augusta and the word "golf" are sometimes mentioned in the same sentence. Gordon's claim to fame was that it had a signal school and was the MP training center. It also had boondocks. Ft. Gordon came and went.

One late afternoon, I was hitch hiking to Main Post for the purpose of working out at the gym. I see a four door sedan come around the corner. Not your everyday four door sedan, this one had two stars hanging on its front bumper. Hitch hiking is against the rules. As the vehicle slowed, I thought that this wouldn't be an everyday ass chewing either, with a major general doing the honors-it would be a royal ass chewing. The window rolled down and the general announced that he was going to Main Post and motioned me to get in. The two stars belonged to Maj. Gen. H.W.O. Kinnard, Commanding General of the newly designated 1st Cavalry Division formerly the 11th Air Assault Div. Gen. Kinnard wasn't your typical run of the mill major general. During the Battle of the Bulge (1944-45) he was Lt. Colonel Kinnard the G-3 of the 101st Airborne Div. Kinnard was in the room when Gen. McAuliffe was issued the ultimatum by the German commander to "surrender Bastogne or get annihi-

37

lated". McAuliffe sent back a note with the simple word "nuts" scrawled on it. To this day I wish that I had had the presence of mind to ask Kinnard if that really was what was said. It eluded me. Talking with the general briefly, he was to be a pleasant man, with not much time for enforcing "post regulations". He was also glad to see that I was staying in shape.

"Officers Pay" wasn't working out. The NCOIC[6] and I didn't hit it off. I was getting ready to talk to one of the higher-ups, when I found out that he beat me to it. I have a discussion with the warrant officer that ran the show. We determined that it wouldn't be good to stay in officers pay. My new assignment would be with SP5 Gerry Henry in his section. That worked out fine. Henry

IC's Venerable GP9s leaving May's Yard, New Orleans.

was good to his guys and we did a lot of things together.

I was starting to get short[3] when they announced that the 1st Cavalry Div. would deploy to Vietnam. I had about four months left and my thoughts began to entertain visions of an early release. They weren't gonna ship me off to Nam at least not in a boat (laugh). I thought as did everyone else, that I was in an enviable position. Never fear the U.S. Army's here! They found us a nice place up on Sand Hill to while away our final two months. We had a paper designation. There were about two hundred of us and we were now the 29th Infantry, or part of it. Now after almost three years in the army, a lot of us weren't going to spit shine our boots or make our beds in text book fashion. Every morning about nine o'clock our company commander (they didn't know what to do with him either), who was of Japanese descent, would see my fishing rod displayed in a non-military manner, leaning against my locker. He didn't speak English very well. He would be walking into our barracks about the time my buddy that cooked and worked nights would be crawling into bed. The CO would see the fishing rod and mutter out loud something like, "Some day I catch fisherman". One day he did "catch the fisherman", only he didn't know it. He stopped me because I was wearing my baseball cap "rootie kazootie" style. He pointed out in his broken English that the way I wore the hat wasn't very military. In addition to that, I wasn't going to tell him I was the "fisherman". What a catch that would have been. We hung out up on Sand Hill maintaining records, doing clerk work, etc. The army doesn't easily identify with idleness. They wouldn't release us, let us go home early. Instead, lets inconvenience a bunch of folks. I did all I could and all I got was a flat "DA[7] says, no". Multiply 200 times whatever it took to keep a troop supplied on a daily basis and you have got a tremendous chunk of money. Sorry taxpayers.

And now it's time to clear post, that magical time in a G.I.'s career, especially for the last time. Clearing on Ft. Benning was very time consuming as Benning was a big place and they wouldn't furnish us with transportation. Clearing post will always have a place near and dear to every G.I.'s heart. I know it will mine. As I eagerly moved around Benning with my "clearance papers" carefully clutched in my hand, I would see some of the "Cav guys" getting ready to ship out. I wished those kids luck and I'm sure some of them didn't come back. I was proud to be a part of putting that division together.

And now the day comes. Where is the band, I wondered. I would be debriefed, handed a wad of money, and sent on my way. "REFRAD"[8] was upon us.

Number ten, the northbound Seminole would leave Columbus at 1:55 PM if it was on time. One way or another I would be on it. I thought that a pint of Jim Beam would make an excellent travel companion, especially for this most joyous of events. I am ecstatic! It's over!

---

[1]PX is like an on base department store. [2]Republic of Korea Army. [3]Short meant close to rotating home. [4]Unexploded artillery shells. [5]Temporary duty. [6]Non-commissioned officer in charge. [7]Department of the Army. [8]Released from active duty.

Chapter 5

Changes

Once I got out of the army, my life became a rapid succession of changes. One change I would not have to make: I had a job waiting for me. It would eventually lead me to my chosen profession in life.

Priority one would be to take that bond money that I had deducted from my pay and buy a new car. Yes! A new one! It was to be a fire engine red Chevrolet Impala, and yes, there would be payments. I was afraid to drive it and would leave it at home on whiskey nights. I didn't have it very long. Joe Zeibert and I drove it up to Spooner, Wisconsin and rolled it many times. It must have been a good lesson because it hasn't happened since. Luckily, the insurance bought me a new one however the "old" car had less than 500 miles on it when it happened. The insurance guy uttered the words "it hasn't been a pleasure" when we shook hands before I drove away in the new "new" car.

It would take almost a month to get back to work. We would be celebrating getting out of the service, celebrate going back to work, celebrate not going back to work, etc. It was a carnival atmosphere for sure.

During my hiatus as a guest of the U.S. Army, American railroading had finally gotten out from under the "diesel helper" issue. Arbitration award 282 was handed down by the powers that be in Washington. This mandate would cover a lot of ground. The Brotherhood of Locomotive Fireman would absorb the brunt of negotiations while the other operating unions would sit back and suck up whatever would come their way. These other unions would be the Brotherhood of Locomotive Engineers (BLE), Brotherhood of Railroad Trainmen (BRT), Order of Railway Conductors and Brakemen (ORC & B), and the Switchmen's Union of North America (SUNA). The firemen's union (BLF & E) had a large portion of engineers within its membership. Of course the focal point was to compromise the locomotive firemen and once that issue was resolved, the railroads would ultimately go after the rest of the crew. Next would be the flagmen. Later the conductor would be moved up to the engine, thus eliminating the head brakeman. Also coming off would be the caboose. The caboose would be substituted with an "end of train" (EOT) device. The engineer would have communication with the hind end through what is called a "FRED" (Federal Railroad End Device). The more sophisticated equipment would tell the hogger how many feet of train he had, and how much air pressure was back there. It was a high tech proposition. Radios would also have an effect on yard crews.

Of course the railroads told the world that once the firemen issue was finalized, that would pretty much be the end of their problems. They also said that when the diesel locomotive first came into the picture. When two bodies go into arbitration, something is usually given and something is usually taken. I didn't read the fine print but I can relate to you what came about on the Illinois Central after the smoke cleared.

With the exception of "through passenger" trains, there would be no need of a diesel helper or locomotive fireman. However, the company would retain "firemen" on 10% of the "A" jobs. Because I had a certain amount of seniority as a fireman, I was "guaranteed" a job, and if the "A" jobs were filled and I couldn't hold one, I could work a "B" job. The company did do us a favor, both young and old when they offered severance pay to the first 40 engineers that wanted it. That meant that I would be examined and become an engineer much sooner than planned. Instead of firing for 13-15 (the average) years before examination, I would now be looking at it in another year or so. Road crews would be afforded lodging and a meal allowance. Yard crews would now get holiday pay plus time and one half on holidays. The IC would usually circumvent that by annulling most jobs on that respective day. Without having a fireman, an engineer would be paid an additional $2.00 initially. This created an interesting scenario amongst the ranks. Some engineers outwardly protested the fact that they had a fireman. They were blatant to the extent of hostility. Some engineers were nice guys before this agreement came down, but their true colors would show once it was put into effect. Most of these guys were road men that were out there for the money to begin with. They didn't want to let a fireman run the engine, thus letting him get much needed experience, because they resented him. They couldn't let the brakeman run because you were there. That made them even madder, it was ugly. There were some good guys out there too. I think the railroads knew that an agreement such as that would create dissension and pit the men against one another. It wouldn't be the first time nor the last.

Eliminating the fireman wasn't the total answer, there were drawbacks. A fireman would be getting "on the job training". Running a train isn't like driving a cab, it takes experience and most railroads were wise to retain around 10% as did the IC. The Illinois Central had high standards for their enginemen. One requirement I am reminded of was the number of road trips a fireman had to have before he was examined. You needed 180 trips in either through freight or passenger or both, before you were eligible for examination. Shortly after award 282 was handed down, most railroads began to set up training programs commensurate with manpower needs. On 9-17-91 Engineer Certification was mandated. Every three years we would have to endure one week of classroom training and learn to run an engine vicariously through a simulator. "Certification" was the brainchild of the Federal Government due to a catastrophic accident in which 16 people were killed, including the daughter of a congressman, and caused a following passenger train to collide with the rear end of the already stopped light power. When they drug tested the crew, they found enough drugs and alcohol to get an army high. They weren't exactly focused on what they were doing. They must have really sang a tune to save their asses, or at least made a deal. I guess they told their interrogators that the use of drugs and alcohol were rampant in the railroad industry. The engineer got off with a pat on the wrist. I think he should have been tried for murder. At least he should still be in prison. This man along with his cohort can be accredited to bringing a lot of anguish and misery into the lives that were both directly and indirectly connected to that incident. The guy that was given the chore of setting up the engineers training program or advanced engineers training (A.E.T.) on the U.S. portion of the Canadian Pacific, went a little overboard with it. Some of the guys that had to run that damn simulator had been running an engine for over thirty years. It was a good program for new engineers, but a little bit much for us older heads. It didn't register with management that if any of us were any good at sitting in a classroom, we wouldn't be working for the railroad to begin with. It was a colossal waste of time and resources. The new director created a real nice playpen for himself at the expense of a lot of men and their families! It was another form of mismanagement.

Of course radios were new and not all of the bugs were quite out of them. An end to an era was fast becoming evident. The time when guys would literally talk to one another with their lamps was coming to a close. It would be a lost art. Years back before the army I watched a switch crew from the top of the Prudential building. Watching the switchmen conveying signs to the engineer with their lamps was quite a show, as we looked down into the darkness of the lower yard. Another lost part of Americana. Once the guys got used to using the radios it didn't take long for them to forget how they got by all those years without them. There was one old timer whose radio wasn't sending, and he couldn't get the engineer to move. For a minute I thought he was gonna go home.

The change most noteworthy, the one tantamount to my lifestyle, would be of course meeting my future wife during that time. I knew her from the neighborhood and we had talked on occasion. She was a pretty redheaded Irish girl with a wonderful smile and a great personality. We hit it off and after a period of romance, were married. I'll never forget the first time I met her mother, she gave me some words of wisdom; "watch your step, buster, she's got seven brothers"! It didn't take me long to realize that two kids that we were, weren't ready to mix marriage and railroading together, at least not for a positive effect. Not at this time.

It wasn't very long after the wedding that I would be unofficially informed that it wouldn't be long and we would be getting examined. The examination was a three part oral inquisition. They would be all day affairs and the tests would be taken over a span of about eighteen months. Now I'm under the gun and the pressure is mounting. You would be afforded three chances to take each examination. If you missed on the third try, you were done, finished, kaput not to mention the humility you would be subjected to. The IC had a special car dedicated to the purpose of explaining the nuts and bolts of how a 567C engine worked. It was also used for testing. Along with the machinery car, there was another rebuilt baggage car done up in air brake regalia. Both machinery and air brake examinations would pretty much revolve around the ubiquitous General Motors or EMD product called the GP9. IC had over 400 of them and we were uncertain as to which locomotive we would be queried on. Virtually as we opened our letters of examination, the IC was taking delivery of 40 GP40's which had a larger engine (645), was turbo-charged and had a different air brake system, 26L as opposed to the already in place 6BL system. It was to be the GP9.

Of the dates of these examinations, I am uncertain as my records from so long ago aren't always available, hence I will try to guesstimate the approximate dates that these events occurred.

I receive my letter and the day comes for the examination. The "machinery car" was spotted in its usual place at the Markham roundhouse. It was sometime in the month of October 1966. There were six of us taking the test which lasted about ten hours. Mr. K. G. Carriere, a southern gentleman from Louisiana would be conducting the test. The machinery car was his appointed domain. One guy flunked for the third time. I felt sorry for the guy. One down, two to go.

During this time in our lives, it couldn't have been any harder on my wife, what with two babies in diapers and me. The pressure of the tests lurking in the near future created a dolorous person in me. I was firing the 8:00 AM Fordham and we worked out a system. We lived directly across from the IC tracks and when we would be coming from 94th St. to yard our train at Markham, I would blow the whistle (two longs, I think) and she would start getting dinner ready. After a while everybody started doing it and it became a fiasco.

Christmas came and went. January brought one helleva snowstorm. I remember getting called to work my day off for time and one half. Driving was out of the question and the trains may or may not have been running. I walked, as it was only two miles or so to the Harvey yard office. A couple of weeks later I get a call from the crew caller telling me that I would have to take two days off because I exceeded the mileage limit. Fireman in the yard are only allowed 2600 miles. One day on a switch engine constituted 100 miles. Time and a half would be 150 miles and one hour of overtime would be 18 3/4 miles, etc., etc. This 2600 mile rule was a union mandate and the company would have to enforce it. Mileage was also a way the company could measure manpower needs. I explained to our local chairman that I was doing the caller a favor, told him that I even had to walk. It was to no avail. I didn't gain a damn thing that night other than to get some good exercise. The mileage factor didn't endear me to the BLF & E. It was a ploy to gain potential membership.

About that time came the letter telling us to get ready for the air brake exam. Reading the letter, I felt that I had already encountered a snag. There were only three of us on the list. That would mean that three guys would have to answer every question normally given to a group of from five to eight. These were oral tests, by the way. It would be even worse than that, I would later find out. The air was probably the toughest of the three tests, at least for me. I would drive over to the Harvey library and study there. We would be expected to trace the piping on a 6 BL brake system explaining as we went along. It looked like spaghetti to me. During this time my wife did a remarkable job. She not only had the kids to look after, she was babysitting me as well. Tense moments!

Now comes the day. I think I woke up with sweaty palms. The air car was in place at Markham and Mr. Enzenauer was also "in place". There was no getting out of it. Thank goodness the first guy pretty much was able to answer every question that was thrown at him. I sat there and smiled a lot and nodded my head with an occasional "yeah that's right". It was a struggle for me, but not as bad as it would be for the third guy. When we went to lunch, Enzenauer suggested that he "have a big bowl of 6BL soup for lunch". We went to this guy's house and I tried to help him with it. He didn't study and he didn't pass. I did. It would be a festive night.

And now we are down to the two third mark. I can't remember what else took place during that period, but it surely was all consuming. I wasn't a happy camper and the pressure was showing. I would tell my wife that once we got through these examinations, life would be good. It truly challenged our marriage.

Our invitation to attend the "book of rules" class would be held in November. This time there were ten guys on the list. This event is always held in the Trainmaster's office at Kankakee and is renowned to last about 12 hours. My wife would be at her sister's house in Bourbonais while this session was being held. A Mr. Harper the age old rules examiner was present as was Mr. Charlie Selsor our traveling engineer and of course Norm Tutwiler, the trainmaster at Kankakee. Lunchtime came and all went well, though I had no appetite. Later in the day as we were getting toward the end of the book, I noticed Selsor began filling out cards. I counted eight cards, which meant two guys weren't going to make it. The end finally came and Selsor handed out the cards. I got one. The two guys that failed were on the third try which meant that they were through. I contained my jubilation because I felt badly for these guys. It wouldn't be long

Suggesting change, new GP40s at Memphis.

and I would overcome their anguish. I felt like I weighed fifty pounds walking out of there. That was the ultimate test. I would never have to take another test as long as I was a locomotive engineer on the Illinois Central Railroad. At age twenty-two, I just may have been the youngest engineer ever on the IC at that time. How do you spell "uforia"!

While I was in the service my friend engineer Art Kanya passed away. Art played hockey and was a super nice guy. He never once ever talked about having a terminal disease, which is what claimed him. Another old friend that was gone when I came home was the 3600 class 0-8-2 steamer. Later on in years we were to take a vacation down south. I wanted to show my wife Ft. Benning. It had changed beyond my recollection. Harmony Church was no longer there (maybe the church was). Lastly, Culpeppers Barbecue was gone. There were changes, some good, some bad, but changes nonetheless.

There was talk that the hours of service rule would be repealed from 16 hours to eventually 12 hours, this would be a gradual change, allowing the carriers time to adjust.

Change can be good and change can be bad depending on whose side of the fence you happen to be. Some of these changes are made in a haphazard manner, enough time isn't always given to assess a situation and then allow it to adequately develop. Some changes are made simply to keep up with the Joneses.

The one question I always had was when all of the technical and manpower issues are sorted out and the carriers are satisfied, when they have "hit the technological wall", will that be enough? There is also the old adage-"if it works, fix it"! Most often in management, someone will be promoted and of course he will justify his being there by making an unwanted or unneeded adjustment to facilitate change and quite often it will defeat its purpose.

I personally have always resisted change. Whatever it is that is in place, works for me. This condition comes about as I am loathe to learn. I don't learn well and when I finally do, I get good at it. It takes time that I simply don't want to give, hence resistance. Why interfere with complacency? Change was never my decision to make.

After 42 years of railroading on six different railroads[2], when you consider mergers, takeovers and all other transactions that it took to shape my career, I am very happy to relate to you the one change I had no trouble acclimating myself to and that change brings about my retirement. I can watch the game from the sidelines, I don't even have to wear my safety vest, and I now have the time to write this book!

[1]The training program lasted five days and was held in St. Paul, hence traveling was required.
[2] Illinois Central, Indiana Harbor Belt, Gulf Mobile & Ohio, Soo Line, Milwaukee Road, and Canadian Pacific

Chapter 6

An Engineer

When we received the card that said we were engineers, it was felt that besides the occasional call to "pinch hit", we would be firing passenger for the next five years or thereabouts. It didn't work out that way, much to our chagrin. The passenger jobs were sweet. For instance, you would go from Chicago to Champaign on duty at 4:15 PM, leave the depot at five and if all goes as it should you're off the engine at 7:00 PM. Less than three hours on duty rolling across the countryside at 80 MPH (actually 79 MPH.). You now have a two hour and 40 minute layover waiting to come back to Chicago on number 2. While number 2 was never on time at Champaign, you almost always made the 2:25 AM suburban train out of the city. One night, incidentally, I was firing for a fellow that was intent on making that train. We were going straight through the interlocking at Peotone. I got up to see how fast we were going and the speed recorder read 108 MPH. He should have been a pilot. We made the suburban train. Other jobs would be overnight layovers. All of these jobs were referred to as combinations. The run that I described above was called 5 and 2. The better jobs all had the following day off. If you worked 5 and 2, your total time consumed usually wasn't more than eight hours and with only a total of five hours on the engine both ways. For that you would be paid two and one half days and only have to do that every other day. No two combinations were identical, however you get the drift. Passenger train speed was 79 MPH on the north end (Chicago-Champaign), and from Champaign to Centralia, 100 MPH, provided your train was made up exclusively with roller bearing equipped cars.

When I went firing the guys that were getting ready for examination had around 14 years on the railroad. The youngest engineers were either running on the yard extra list or firing passenger. They all had around 17 years of service.

These guys were kids and fired steam engines during WWII. In 1961 there were firemen on every job even though the IC was fully dieselized. This would change drastically while I was on my military sojourn. Arbitration award 282 came down and I came back to a totally different workplace. As I previously mentioned, the company offered a severance package to the first 40 engineers that wanted it. Conversely, they also offered severance to the firemen on the other end of the seniority list. When I came home, there weren't many of us left. Out of a total of approximately 90 jobs (all jobs both road & yard service subject to our seniority district), there were only 25 or so designated firemen's jobs left. This would fluctuate according to business demands which were adjusted on a quarterly basis.

And now that the "diesel helper" issue had been resolved, another dilemma is beginning to come to the surface. Where are our engineers going to come from? It was becoming evident that the passenger train wasn't always going to be around. That provided a resource of 14 firemen that were almost always examined and available to run an engine. The regular engineers on those jobs weren't exactly spring chickens either. Both ends would be working against the middle. Back in the "status quo' days a recently examined engineer could expect to fire passenger for five years or so. That could and would be effected through ever changing economic patterns. With a surplus of qualified engineers, set back and firing either freight or the passenger jobs, the IC always had a vast reserve plus these guys were getting some topnotch experience at the throttle. Once the effects of award 282 were felt, "the era of the Sears and Roebuck engineer was about to dawn" to quote Charlie Selsor, Illinois Division Traveling Engineer.

When I began making my student trips the regular fireman on those jobs all had about 14 years and were just now starting to take their engineers exams. I would be afforded less than four years (not to include army time) to take the exams and learn to run an engine and handle a train. That's quite a contrast. I would be a Sears & Roebuck engineer, one of the first. It was a dubious honor.

While I was learning about locomotives and trains, I would work as a fireman in both through freight, passenger, and yard service. The year was 1967, a year of (for lack of a better term) "self-education". Most of my work was spent in the yard, working jobs that started out of Harvey (Markham). Probably the best job was the 7:00 AM North Pulldown with John Rassbach. John sort of reminded me of Joe Opferman, from the mail platform. Both were big men in their day and both shared a similar personality. I would always ask John about his steam days. He spoke of hand firing a test train over the Gilman line at over 100 MPH. At the end of the day we would deliver and pick up the South Shores (CSS & SB) at Kensington and then shove back to Harvey and tie up.

Before my army days I fired switch engines with Harold Falkenthal and Joe Buckley. They had gone up in status, from the extra list to a "freight turn" (another list). Falkenthal told me that he once held a freight turn before the diesel came into the picture. Once the diesel arrived all of the older heads would eschew the yard for the dieselized road jobs. "Happy Hal" knew that I was getting ready for examination and would always tell me not to try to learn anything from him because he was admittedly, the world's worst engineer, had a technique that nobody should copy and "wouldn't be out here (the road) if it weren't for paying the bills". Don LeGere also had a style of his own. Unlike Falkenthal he would urge guys to try it. Instead of starting in the eighth notch (throttle 8) he would gradually shut the throttle down to the third or fourth notch. "You don't have to drag a train to a stop" he would say. With the price of fuel being what it is today, management would love to have a bunch of LeGere's. Don originally came from Nova Scotia and was a personable guy. Joe Buckley used to say that while a lot of guys his age (16-17) were firing "bow downs" (hand fired steam engines) for sixteen hours a day, he was on Iwo Jima getting shot at all day long. Well, after the fireman issue was concluded, I remember Buckley and some young fireman engaging in fisticuffs over the $2 or 3 (whatever it was at that time) amount that the engineer would be paid if he didn't have a fireman. This came about during a cocktail party that we were attending in the bar at the hotel we stayed at in Champaign. We all knew that Joe would rather have the money than the fireman. Boys will be boys.

When you fired freight you almost always would get a different engineer because the engineers union was instrumental in keeping the "turns" at one less than the fireman had. Doing it that way would enable the engineers to work more and diminish the chances of catching a fireman. Although there were only three fireman in the pool it still was regulated as if each turn was filled with a "diesel helper".

You ran a train by the seat of your pants was the good advice extended to the aspiring young engineer to be, and to always observe the engineer that you are working with, and adopt that part of his train handling technique that you are comfortable with. Take a little of this from one guy and a little of that from another, incorporate some style of your own and you just might have the makings of a locomotive engineer. No two trains are alike, each one is different. Subsequently no two engineers are alike, either.

The Clearing jobs were considered "out of line" jobs because they started outside of the bracket. A job was "in line" if it started between the hours of 6:30 to 8:00 AM, 2:30 to 4:00 PM or 10:30 to midnight. The entire Chicago Terminal was allowed three "out of line" jobs per union agreement. Usually two of the three and at times-three (depending on business), would be jobs that went to Clearing. (Belt Railroad of Chicago) The BRC was owned jointly by thirteen railroads that fed it cars via Clearing. If a railroad had cars for another railroad and had no direct interchange with that road, they went to Clearing. At this time there were only two Clearings, one at 5 AM and another at 5 PM. Depending on the crew, these jobs could be either quit[1] or overtime jobs. I would work the day job with Willie Green. Willie liked his early quit and he would say "Why would I want to work overtime when I get to do this 7 days a week".[2] Willie was a character. Back in the days of steam, probably during the war, the company decided to crack down on drinking. Back then, the crews worked sixteen hours a day, seven days a week. When they were at home-they were sleeping, when they were at work-they were drinking. One day the traveling engineer showed up on the engine looking for the evidence. Usually if there was a jug involved, it got pitched into the firebox. The traveler knew they were drinking, but needed proof. Now Willie was small in stature and would wear these baggy bib overalls which could conceal a fifth simply by drooping the open pant leg over the jug. That would work provided Willie didn't have to move. The traveler walked away once again beguiled by the most adroit Willie Green. No wonder Willie lasted well over forty years!

Earlier, I spoke of train handling and the fact that no two trains are alike and now I would like to elaborate on this. Probably the focal point in the measure of a train, are the number of cars it has. Next would be the ratio of loads verses empties and where they are placed in the train. Once you have established the train makeup, you should make a mental note-anticipate where you may have to stop that train. At what speed are you going? How much power have you got? Do you have a "tight" trainline? Do you have a "pressure maintaining" brake valve? What is the weather like? Is it cold? Every now and then you may have a "glitch" to cope with. Perhaps a touchy triple valve back in the train that may or may not cause the train to go into "emergency" when you make a trainline reduction in the "brake pipe". This is commonly known as a "dynamiter". This condition will play a determinate role in your decision process. Another example would be to have an engine in your consist that is hunting or dropping its load. You may want to isolate that unit especially in hill and dale (undulating) territory. Once you weigh all of these factors, your mind becomes a computer of sorts. As a consequence of the prevailing terrain, along with operational needs, you now have to determine what train handling technique you will use commensurate with the anticipated conditions you will encounter. Basically there are only two methods. You can use one or the other, but never go from one to the other in midstream. The essence to good train handling is the gradual control of the slack. The two primary methods I will talk about are "stretch braking" (draft forces) and "bunch braking" (buffer forces). Stretch braking is a method of train braking where the power from the locomotives is used while a drag is established on the train by the engineer making a light brake application. As the "hogger" determines how his train is reacting he will either make a power adjustment or make a further application of the trainline (train brake). Accurate manipulation of these controls will induce your train to stop where you want it. Bunch braking is usually done in downhill territory. The throttle is gradually shut off and the independent brake (engine brake) is used to lightly gather the slack. Once your train is totally against the power, a brake application is made on the train. Additional air can be taken off the trainline to effect the desired stop. Dynamic braking is the "cat's meow" for this type of control, should you be lucky enough to have them on long descending grades. Dynamic braking to be brief, is the reversal of the current going to the traction motors which creates a retarding force. The basic tool used to facilitate good slack control is quite simply-the throttle. Gradual use of the throttle is the ticket, whether you are opening it up or shutting it down. I once had an empty coal hopper train of about 140 cars. All day long we were battling a strong south wind. I made a beautiful stop at the "crew change" point by simply shutting down the throttle. The empty cars caught the wind like sails.

As the equipment got more sophisticated, i.e., locomotives, cars and the trains themselves, so did the terminology. Since "certification" was introduced, the vernacular has changed. Today's trains are now measured in feet. As you enter a "restricted" area causing a reduction in speed you can punch the train length key on your "train information braking system" module (TIBS). Once the rear of the train clears the restricted area, the TIBS will communicate that information to you. When a crew comes to work, along with their train orders, and other pertinent information, they are given a computerized track profile indicating train length with a graph showing the location of loads and empties, tonnage verses horsepower ratio, and tons per operative brake. We now have buffer forces and draft forces. It's a whole new ball game.

One of the engineers that made a lasting impression on me was Frank Horen. I only had occasion to make a couple of trips with him. He was the regular engineer on one side of 3 & 6. #3 was the southbound Louisiane and #6 was the northbound Panama Limited. When, he was on the engine, I found Mr. Horen to be a perfectionist, concise, and to the point, meticulous in appearance, a man proud of his profession. He was an engineer's engineer. On the suburban train going home, Frank was a completely different person. He had dropped his business-like manner to be a more amiable and relaxed person. Frank had 45 years of service at that time.

1967 is now winding down. November comes and with it-good news! As I mentioned in the previous chapter, I passed the "rules" and was now a full-fledged engineer. That night my wife and I had a special time and I can't thank her enough for being understanding and helping us get through the dilemma we were both facing. We hadn't yet had a chance to truly enjoy our married life together and now it was time to get back to renewing our relationship.

[1]A quit job is where a crew is encouraged to get the work done and go home early for the full eight hours pay.
[2]Most jobs on the Chicago Terminal were 7 day jobs for the engineer.

Chapter 7

1968

After getting my engineers card the past November, I was champing at the bit to make my first trip as an engineer. It would be four months before it would happen. On a cold, windy, rainy Saturday night, March 2, 1968 to be exact, I was called to be the engineer on the 11:00 PM Yard Various at Congress St. It would be my first solo experience.

I was firing the 6:45 AM City job (called the "Wobbly") when I decided to "break in" to suburban service. For learning the electrics we were paid three basic suburban days. My plan was to lay off the "wobbly" on Friday and spend the weekend (my days off) breaking in. On Saturday I made a round trip to Richton Park and then a trip to South Chicago while being coached by the regular suburban engineer. On Sunday I made arrangements with Claude Simpson, the traveling engineer in suburban service, to ride with me on a round trip to Blue Island. On the 29th of April I was okay'd for suburban service. It was also a good way to pick up a couple of days pay. One of the points Mr. Simpson made regarding his suburban service was that you either loved it or you hated it. Simpson also mentioned that I was the first one in my class to qualify. Upon hearing this, I began to worry. Did they know something I didn't? To begin with, I wasn't exactly enthralled with the prospect of ever having to work "in there"! If you take the extra days pay and factored in a bit of curiosity, I was guilty. Had I ever been given an ultimatum-I would have been one of the guys that "hated it". Getting called for one of the many weekday combinations off the extra yard list was incongruous to say the least.

It wouldn't be very long and I would find out why I was the first and only one to break-in. For example: a road job[3] and a suburban job would be open. I would stand for the road job and the guy behind me would stand for the suburban job. It wasn't fair, but I was qualified for suburban and he wasn't. Putting in a time claim was out of the question because of a loophole. It also worked against me when I would be firing through passenger (not to be confused with suburban service) and would get pulled off of it to work some suburban combination. Everyone's favorite job to avoid was combination #49 or better known as the South Chicago loop. The job started at Randolph St. at around 8:15 PM and tied up in So. Chicago at about 3:00 AM. You would have to drive your car to So. Chicago and "deadhead"[4] to Randolph St. to start the job. Eventually you would spend the night "looping" between So. Chicago and 67th St. (mainline). This job was open quite often especially on Friday nights because the regular guy worked another job (against the rules) and had a drinking problem to boot. When you got pulled off your regular fireman's job, you would lose the round trip, hence, at least a day's pay. Another job to stay away from was the "race train" that went out to Washington Park for an evening of gambling. The IC ran catenary from Harvey over to the race track and then on to Homewood. The word was that the wire always had juice flowing through it, horses or no horses because they were afraid of some industrious thief walking away with it.

One way to take the sting out of getting called off of your scheduled job was to put in a "waiver". A waiver would at least guarantee recompense for the difference between what you made and what you could have made.

I should mention here that everyone in engine service was called to work, every day all of the time. Not answering the phone would mean that you would not work anywhere. They had you coming and going.

The IC began to receive delivery of the venerable electric coaches in 1926. Granted they were ugly, but over the years the IC would prove that beauty is only skin deep. These cars would serve the IC well and would indeed pay for themselves. They were welcomed by the public as they were quiet and smokeless. The steam engines would come off as the electrics had overhead power. The electrics would not require a fireman. One old timer lamented-we lost 100 jobs when they electrified. Another went on to say that we also got hit with the depression-I didn't work for 17 years. It wasn't a good time if you were close to the bottom of the Chicago Division Enginemen's seniority roster. To my knowledge they never coined a nickname for those cars. They were always referred to as the "1926 cars". In early 1971 IC began receiving the new modern double decker cars. The general public was tired of looking at the old cars. They were painted "army green" and looked like they were going to war, although they had already been through three of them. The seats on the elderly cars were made up of straw thatch, and many a lady would snag her nylons on them. May 17,

1971 signaled the beginning of the end for the old cars as the company ran a "Directors Special" with the new cars of course.

Sometime thereafter I would qualify to run the new cars. Besides the usual getting "used to" stuff, the main new feature was the brake system. Along with the usual "air brake valve" came a "blended in" hydraulic brake and lastly, a dynamic brake that faded out at 10 MPH. You didn't want to come against a bumper post thinking that the dynamic was going to play a major role in stopping. Conversely, you would lose the dynamic ander 10 MPH. The old cars broke better. You could take a four or six car train coming into Ivanhoe at 60 MPH, put the train in "emergency" at the end of the platform (going south) and be stopped at the other end with the brakes fully released. I was later asked not to do that as it wasn't an accepted practice. These old cars didn't last 45 years for nothing.

I was seriously considering giving up my suburban rights after all, other guys had done it. Simpson was right when he laconically commented that "it wasn't for everybody". If I was to use one word to describe suburban, it would be-awkward. When it wasn't awkward, it was boring. I often likened it to driving a bus. Wasn't I an engineer? I wasn't much for electricity either. I remember having brake problems right in the middle of the afternoon "rush hour". We were sitting at the platform at Hazel Crest with a lot of smoke coming off of one wheel. Now the first rule when you have to go beneath the train to trouble shoot is to "lower the pans" (pantagraphs). I was kind of in a bind and the whole world was watching me. My particular train was carrying a good percentage of IC officials. Also, the two trains sitting behind me probably had their share too! After I lowered the pans, I visually checked to be sure they were all down and said something to the effect "I'd better make sure these pans are down,-they don't pay me enough to get lit up (electrocuted)". This comment was overheard by some senior vice president, who offered an icy stare. Luckily the engineer on the train behind me had walked up and quickly rectified the situation. Once again they were all happy campers, albeit on their way to a late dinner.

On the brighter side of it, the girl watching was superb and if you could work in there on a regular basis, you could use your free time to work another job! If you liked to gossip, you had unlimited material to work with and you would be hob knobbing with the best in the business when it came to bullshit.

I would not have to relinquish my suburban rights after all because I transferred to Joliet and Joliet would forever spare me. Amen.

On the 31st of August I would make my first road trip as an engineer on #65 to Clinton. #65 was made up of "hot" auto parts interchanged at Markham from the Chesepeake & Ohio. IC would take them to St. Louis for a connection with the Cotton Belt for the southwest. We laid over in Clinton for almost 16 hours and got called for #62. #62 had four units and only sixty or so cars. We would follow #22 the Green Diamond. #22 left Clinton on time and then developed engine trouble. We had a 60 MPH train, but alas, we would follow him to Gilman at 30-35 MPH for the next 67 miles. Once we reached Gilman and the CTC (centralized traffic control), we were able to get around him. It didn't seem right, a freight train passing a "streamliner" but the dispatcher gave us the track and we left him in the dust. Making that trip gave me a tremendous rush. It made me proud to be an engineer. I felt that that was what I was born to do.

My wife would share in the alacrity that would come when the crew caller had good news. Conversely, she would also be a victim of the antipathy that that same telephone could bring. She held it together, no easy task.

In 1968 the majority of my time was spent firing either in the yard, or when I could-the road. I worked through passenger almost as much as I did the yard. I also worked in "pool freight" service for a couple of months. During that time I caught a trip with engineer Bill Bates. I had recently made my trip on #65 and was still coming down from good thoughts resonated from that experience. Bates was kind of a "hot dog", but was considered one of the better engineers in the freight pool. However, he would rattle your chain if he could. I never ran the engine for him but one day for some reason he had me over on the right side. We were nearing Kankakee with a northbound manifest and had to get down to 25 MPH for the K&S crossing (NYC). Bates told me that he would tell me when to "get the air". We were going 45 MPH when I looked over at him, waiting for the word. He didn't look at me. We're getting closer and I yell "now"? "Not yet", came the reply. By now we're at the point where it's now or never and I once again yell out the word "now". Bates kind of gave me a disgusted look and retorted "for gosh sakes it's too late now"! We went over that diamond at 40 MPH and Bates never looked back. The brakemen used to tell a joke about an engineer driving his wife and conductor. They were both in the back seat engaged in a romantic interlude. The wife was nervous because after all, her husband was driving. The conductor, in an effort to ease her mind whispered to her gently....It's okay-he never looks back....

October came and the Clinton-Gilman local was open. This must have been common knowledge to everyone but me. The engineers extra road list was exhausted and likewise the extra yard list. I was firing and was called to "pinch-hit". I never really minded working the outlying jobs, it would be a respite from the rigors of the Chicago Terminal and I would be out in the country for a few days and at least I would have a car. The extra road list protected all of the outlying jobs. These included the seven locals (way freights) the bean job at Gibson

City, the switch engines at Kankakee, and of course the through freights when anyone laid off of their "freight turn". Sometimes those guys would forget how that worked and somehow were only available when a freight turn was open. October is a nice month to be anywhere and I enjoyed the three days I was out there. I didn't especially relish doing someone else's dirty work, however.

Please allow me to touch upon the extra yard list and its workings. Most railroads refer to it as the extra board depending on the situation. On the Grand Trunk they call it the spare board. I personally had a lot of names for it. Extra work on the IC Chicago Terminal was broke down as follows, each service had its own little list. There was the extra suburban list, the extra road list that we talked about and the extra yard list. Any through passenger jobs that came open would go to anyone desiring that work in seniority order regardless of what his regular job was. When the road and suburban lists were exhausted, then an engineer would be called off of the extra yard list. We of scant seniority did it all. This was one extra board that you couldn't work without a car. The availability of the suburban service was a godsend, however. I should mention that every employee was issued a train pass.

In 1969 there were approximately 140 jobs connected to the Chicago Terminal located at 19 different starting points. There were six starting points in suburban, three at Markham, you had a bunch of jobs starting at Congress St., the coach yard had nine jobs. 27th St. had 14 jobs, or I should say had 14 jobs for 14 engineers. On a daily basis there were nine trains, hence, nine engineers would begin their day at 27th St. in the service of passenger. We on the extra list would see those jobs only on extremely rare occasions. Switch engines for Congress St. were serviced at 27th St. and so the engine would come out of the roundhouse every fourth trick. Thanks to the use of "spring switches" and the employment of "switch tenders", only the engineer was required to bring the engine "downtown", throw in the outlying points which were Kankakee with six jobs. Champaign, Clinton, and Bloomington each had a local that the Chicago board protected. Markham was one of the largest classification yards in the world and had around 30 jobs around the clock.

Some years were busier than others, and the extra list was always well stocked with between 10 and 15 hoggers. If the list was regulated properly, you would work every day until you made your miles, which was 3200 (remember, 100 miles constitutes a day). If there was a serious shortage of "hogs" say due to both the economy and vacations, the company would conspire with the unions and conveniently lift the miles so that an individual could work as much as he wanted to. You would meet yourself coming and going.

As a fledgling engineer, I had yet to experience a full year working strictly on the extra board. In fact, in 1968, I had yet to get "set up". That year I pinch hit twenty-two times. That was a lot better than getting thrown into the fire "all at once". My wife and I were to have some challenging times ahead of us.

Toward the end of 1968, the wye connecting the west end to go south on the mainline to Markham was finished and ready for operation. This would signal the beginning of the end for Congress Street yard.

[1]Working suburban. [2]Extra yard list protected all services when their respective lists were exhausted. [3]Road jobs were considered more desirable. [4]An employee riding on a pass.

Chapter 8

~

1969

The dispatchers voice is heard over the speaker at Kankakee Junction - KX are you there? "Go ahead dispatcher", comes the reply. "NC6 is just by Ashkum and he's gonna set out somewhere, can I bring him up three track to the junction"? "It's all yours", comes again the retort. KX then calls NC6 for a location and tells him to set[1] his cars out on track two at the hospital. Except for the fog, it was just another normal night at Kankakee Jct.

It is just after midnight and very foggy. Just before NC6 (officially Extra 9192 North) departs Kankakee, the engineer prompts the KX operator to get him the lineup at Indian Oaks vicariously through the dispatcher. Three track comes to an end at Indian Oaks where it diverges into two track. Indian Oaks sits at the top of a long hill and it was always advantageous to have a favorable signal indication and not have to stop. With 84 cars in tow, stopping would be a bit of a challenge as most of the train would be on the side of that hill. This night visibility is limited to 1,000 feet. The operator relays the message to the dispatcher. The dispatcher acknowledges the operator with a simple "okay". It was an ambiguous answer and misconstrued by the operator to mean, yes, "you have the lineup" and thusly informs NC6.

In reality the dispatcher could not extend to NC6 the track lineup at Indian Oaks as he had #25 the southbound Southern Express coming by Manteno on two track. It would be a matter of seconds and #25 would be by Indian Oaks.

Someone working around Kankakee on a locomotive hears the engineer on NC6 complain about the dispatching and further stating that they haven't yet received the signal. At this time #25 has not rounded the curve just south of Manteno and wasn't yet visible. A very short pause and another radio comment "thanks KX, now you've done it, we ran the board"!

And now, ever so suddenly, the 70 MPH passenger train[2] is confronted by a

61

headlight. Less than second's later three men would be dead and two others would miraculously live to tell about it.

The dispatchers board lights up telling him that something is very wrong. There is no communication with the head end of either train. The dispatcher begins emergency procedures.

The engineer and fireman on #25 died immediately from the collision as did the engineer of Extra 9192 North (NC6). The head brakeman on NC6 was said to have grabbed the fireman by the shirt collar, pulled him through the door and out across the front of the engine into the weeds and to safety. The engineer stayed where he was futilely blowing the whistle.

Train #25 was completely derailed. Its three locomotives and the first five cars were destroyed. The sixth and seventh cars were heavily damaged while the remaining six cars suffered only slight damage. The train was carrying 48 passengers of which five were seriously injured and 29 others were slightly injured. Members of the train crew and eight railway post office employees suffered only minor scrapes.

The Extra 9192 North would have both of its locomotives destroyed. The first seven cars would be derailed of which four of those cars and their contents were destroyed. The engineer was killed.

When road crews reported for work, the name of the game was and is to get the train over the road as quickly as possible. Crews are paid by the mile and so it behooves them to use any method at their disposal to expedite the movement of their train. It works for the company, too! Time is locomotives, cars, and crews. The faster a boxcar moves from point A to point B, the quicker a dollar is made. Use of the radio was probably the single most positive tool in the struggle to get over the road. Used properly, it couldn't be beat. I was first introduced to the radio when I came out of the army. An "old timer" spoke of it and mentioned that "if the radio is abused, it'll get you killed".

The fog played no favorites and was the overall insidious precursor in the orchestration of this accident. It would set the stage for an anathema of events. The presence of the fog could not be prevented. In this case common sense and obedience to the rules went hand in hand. When a crew asks for and accepts by word of mouth that a signal four miles away is favorable and that the remote controlled switch is lined for their movement, they throw both the rulebook and common sense to the wind. The crew of NC6 knew that a train was occupying track one at the junction, they also must have thought about #25 and the fact that it hadn't gone yet. Two track would be the logical place for it to be. It all pointed to the signal at Indian Oaks being red until #25 got by.

The engineer had 26 years of experience. The brakeman had a solid thirteen years working the road. He knew the score.

When crews are trying to get over the road, they avariciously overlook the fact that theirs isn't the only train in the picture. A dispatcher once explained it to me like this: two trains, one track, someone has to sit. The engineer of NC6 in the "heat of battle" ignored the fact that his wasn't the only train. He went up that hill with the idea of getting a "good run" and gaining momentum with it, all the while assuming the signal would be favorable to the movement of his train, due to a thoughtless radio transmission relayed by an inexperienced operator that misunderstood the dispatcher in the first place.

When NC6 came to within approximately 1000 feet of the signal, they saw that it was "all red" and by then they knew it was too late. It wouldn't be but a few seconds and they would find out why the signal was displaying a "stop" indication. It happened January 17th, 1969.

The above story would be the harbinger of sad events. The IC would be plagued with a series of devastating accidents within the next year or so.

The first half of 1969 I spent firing a variety of jobs but always tried to work the road either in through passenger or pool freight service. I was "set up"[3] for the first time on June 22nd. I would be on the engineers extra list until November. As it turned out I was set up 50% of the time that year.

Early 1969 would see the delivery of ten dynamic brake GP40's. These were the first dynamic brake units the IC would buy. The IC would embark on a "run through"[4] agreement with the Union Pacific. One of the stipulations of the pact was among other things-dynamic brakes. Actually, now that I think about it, nobody ever "saw" those units, at least not on the Illinois Central. The UP grabbed them and held them hostage out west somewhere. In return they would reciprocate with units they didn't want. UP had no GP40's commensurate with the program. The UP had the benefit of brand new power compliments of the IC and sent us their unwanted scrap.

The UP fiasco would not signal the end of foreign motive power. Due to an upturn in the economy, the IC was forced to test the rental market. Some guys sardonically referred to it as the "rent-a-wreck" program. Summer would find units from the Rio Grande, Bessemer & Lake Erie and the Katy to name a few. "Covered wagons" had come to the IC. It would be the first and last time an IC freight engineer would run "F" units. Interestingly the IC still had a whole bunch of covered wagons on the property when they sent the entire roster of six ALCO C636's to the Canadian Pacific. The C636's were the most powerful locomotive the IC had. Somebody dryly commented that "that'll give our Canadian friends something to do".

At the end of 1968, IC along with Cargill began the operation of the "rent-a-train". This was an innovative market strategy that offered optimum usage of equipment. Cargill would furnish 100 or so cars and Illinois Central would do the rest. The train would make a weekly round trip between Cargill's facility at Gibson City, Illinois and Baton Rouge, Louisiana for export. IC would realize a considerable line haul of 833 miles and would extend to Cargill, a lower rate. It was a "win, win" situation for everyone involved. This train would run about once a week in both directions. No sooner were the empties spotted at Gibson City and they would soon be loaded and ready to be moved. It wouldn't take long and the "rent-a-train" would be reduced to the "RAT". The "RAT" was a big payer for the engineer. 166 miles to be exact plus the weight on the drivers that the standard three SD40's would command would greatly enhance the pay rate.

The hoppers that this train consisted of were the largest hoppers Cargill could find. They were also the latest, most modern cars available at the time. Of course modern always meant "soybean"[5] brake shoes when it came to the freight car industry. About all we knew about these "shoes" is that they must have been cheaper to make. "Cheaper" would be the only advantage because they weren't very effective when it came to braking a train. You would have to make a minimum reduction off the train line earlier than you normally would as it was felt that the shoes needed to be heated up. Friction against the wheel of a freight car would facilitate that. When you were dragging trains around in order to heat the shoes up so that you can safely stop, the price of fuel goes up as you are using more than you should have to as you need the horsepower to literally drag the train. Loaded, this train is computed to be over 13,000 tons. A solid 13,000 tons, I might add. The first time I would catch that train off of the extra list, I had traveling engineer Charlie Selsor ride with me. Ordinarily I was never happy to see Selsor but now that I look back, I was glad he was there that day.

Leaving Gibson City this train would have to negotiate 25 miles of single track on its way to the wye at Gilman. Going north the first three miles are straight uphill to Guthrie. Once you get the train over Guthrie, it gets a good roll on it as you are now going downhill. The train is seemingly moving by itself, now. Selsor is running the engine. I feel it "pull back" here and there and Selsor shows me his track profile. He announces that we are now in "hill and dale" territory as he makes a minimum reduction on the brake valve. We were now rolling at 60 per and Charlie was controlling the speed. Looking at the profile I could see another three mile hill going into Melvin. Charlie releases the air and begins to throttle down. He then states "as you can see on the track profile, we've got three or four miles of gradual up and down, nothing too hairy until we drop off of Roberts". I ask him "how can I get one of these track profile books"? (Everyone should have one) He shakes his head and says that "they didn't want to give me one"! We laugh. We are now coming into Roberts and Selsor mentions setting the air (minimum reduction) and modulating the throttle at the top of the hill in order to keep it at sixty. Coming through Ridgeville we are now on a very gentle downhill tangent all the way to Gilman (five miles). Charlie says: "set the air at milepost 86 and hold on to it. Always figure that Gilman is going to stop you and know that the speed on the wye is 15 MPH anyway. Whether or not we've got the pot signal for the mainline, I want you to stop because I'm getting off. You can take this train to Champaign yourself"! When Charlie showed up I was sort of relieved, but I felt good about him leaving, too! Charlie was the only traveler I ever saw that showed up in coveralls. The rest of the travelers always wore suits. Bob Morgridge could get down in the grease and oil and walk away like his suit just came back from the cleaners. He never would get a drop on him!

Probably the highlight of the year for me came when one early August morning, August 14th to be exact, I was called to be the engineer on a "Republican Special" that was going to Springfield for a day of political merriment. Actually two of those trains were called and I would get the second one. When I arrived at 27th St. I was confronted with three big "E" units (passenger locomotives). I have to confess that up until that morning I had never sat on the right side nor had my foot ever graced the "deadman"[6] of a passenger engine. The regular engineers in through passenger service always ran their own engines and didn't need much relief as they were only on duty about three hours. Now there wasn't much thought given by anyone about the remote possibility of a very young engineer catching a seventeen car special over the Gilman line to Clinton. When conductor J.H. (Jim) Williams first saw me sitting on the engineers side, was when the thought processes would begin. We were no longer in the "what if" stage, we had graduated to the "what is" stage. It took me a while to convince "Jughead"[7] that I was the engineer. Once we performed the engineer-conductor ritual of comparing watches, "Jughead" would walk toward the "glass house"[8] shaking his head in disbelief. Apparently "Jughead" approached the stationmaster with reservations about the engineer that would pull a trainload of Chicago area political "bigwigs". I don't think Mr. Williams wanted to be captain of this particular ship. The wheels were in motion, phones were ringing everywhere. The big question was "where was Charlie Selsor"[9]? I was wondering the same thing. About ten minutes before leaving time Jughead would apprise me of our station stops. The stops were, 63rd St., Homewood, and Kankakee. He said nothing about a "rider". We left Central Station at the appointed time, now my foot is vibrating on the deadman and is becoming an integral part of this crescendo of vibrations. 63rd St. comes and goes without fanfare and Homewood would be next. At Homewood we have a fellow by the name of Jim Zagorski enter the cab. Apparently Zagorski was taking Selsors place while he was on vacation, but hadn't yet unpacked his suitcase when the phone rang. Zagorski was young for a traveler whose seniority ran between Carbondale, Illinois and St. Louis. He had no experience on the "northend" whatsoever. They had passenger trains down there, too, however they rarely were more than six or seven cars. We were all "pretty new" as the fireman was making his first trip. I had never even run a passenger engine, much less three of them with seventeen cars behind them. Now we have a traveler that doesn't know the railroad. The blind leading the blind, I mused. As we rounded the wye at Gilman, our running orders were in the hoop. The Gilman line is a single tracked railroad which is signaled in both directions. Both timetable and train orders are to confer right, class and direction by which all trains may proceed. Zagorski was the first to see the orders. He briefly scanned them and handed them to me as he noted "the railroads ours". They looked good to me also. Nevertheless I wasn't gonna argue with him.

We arrived in Clinton and I can honestly say that we had a good trip. Zagorski bid us goodbye as he would ride the train into Springfield. We would lay over in Clinton just over seven hours before our train would return from Springfield. Zagorski would ride the first "special" and I would be alone on the second train. I felt that Zagorski must have thought I was competent enough to do the job. Jim Williams rode the train to Springfield and return, working as its conductor. The trainmen had different work rules than the enginemen. I wouldn't see him until we stopped at Central Station. He went out of his way to compliment me on my performance. I was beaming - I was having a truly good day.

When I got home I told my wife all about the trip. The trip had a positive effect on both of us. When I was happy, she usually was, too!

In October of the same year another wreck of colossal proportions occurred at Riverdale, Illinois on the Chicago Terminal.

The crew of Extra 5055 North was called for 1:00 AM. Extra 5055 North was the official designation of what the crews always termed "a boat coal train". These trains could be anywhere from 125 to 200 cars in length and would never have more power than they needed. This day would be an exception as the train has normal power, but only 128 cars. The crew would jokingly agree that the horsepower/tonnage ratio would surely shorten the hills. Also, as they were under 140 cars they could traverse the Chicago Terminal at 40 MPH instead of the 30 MPH called for in the special instructions of the current timetable. It wasn't a big deal but it was a plus.

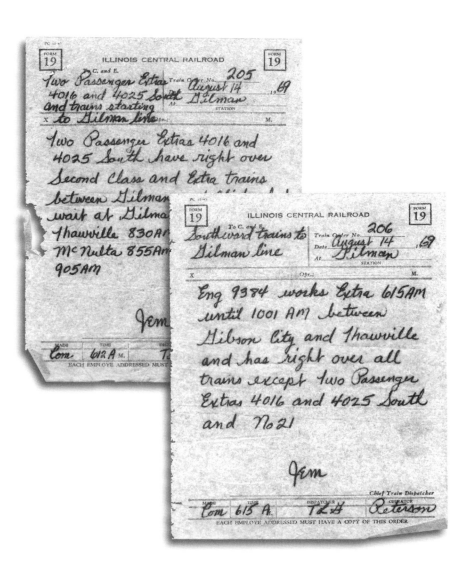

Running orders August 14, 1969.

The major drawback would be the 1:00 AM listing time (starting), not exactly the optimum best time for a pool crew to be going to work. Freight pool crews went to work when their number came up and the number of crews were determined and regulated to work seven days a week. No regular days off. A man would have to make a choice, either a decent lifestyle or the money. It was interesting work and the hours were normally short. A four hour trip or less was common, but it came not without a price.

The terrain between Champaign and Kankakee is predominantly level with a 23 mile stretch between Rantoul and Buckley that the "hoggers" always referred to as "hill and dale" country. A coal train always had enough power to make the hills, but seemingly, just enough. A train would struggle through Rantoul and then begin to roll once it started downhill. The longer trains would roll by their selves in throttle two or three. When the head end of the train was moving uphill, the hind end was rolling downhill and pushing you. The slack in the train was doing two different things. You didn't want to use the air if it could be avoided, and when you felt the slack change, you would back off a notch and by the time you got the train back on the flatland you were usually in the second or third notch and it was time to slowly come back to throttle eight. With only 128 cars the Extra 5055 North would not have to worry about "throttle modulation".

This particular crew had worked 13 hours and 30 minutes on the night before. That was an all-night affair. They would put off duty close to 1:00 PM and then go to the hotel, get their rest, and await the call for duty. They would officially have 11 hours and 55 minutes rest when they were called. It was a pretty standard layover as layovers go. One of the problems pool crews encounter is the lack of adequate information as to when they would be going back to work on the northward trip. It would have been a great advantage to have a good general idea as to when you would be working again. The company had the technology for it, I mean they had telephones, didn't they? Why couldn't a more accurate system be in place? A freight train is a very large commodity, why couldn't they be more reliable about telling crews where and when these trains might show up? After working 13 1/2 hours or all night, the first thing a crew will do is go to bed. As each member awakes, the first act of the day is to call the caller, inquire as to how many times out he is and ask what trains are coming. Half the time, you don't get an accurate picture, at times you may even be lied to. I have heard crew callers proclaim that there was absolutely nothing coming and then along with a shift change (different caller), a ghost train suddenly shows up. That happened a lot and I think that is what happened to the crew of Extra 5055 North.

The engine crew of the coal train didn't think that they would go to work until much later and had had more than enough alcohol by the time they were called. I am not making excuses for them, but you have to remember that these crews are human and cannot be expected to operate like robots. One of the major problems is the regulation of sleep. Guys simply don't sleep on command. Alcohol consumption is a problem that can be dealt with, as is the provision of adequate information. Sleep regulation (or lack thereof) is one of the unsurmountable pitfalls that pool crews are subjected to. The only way to approach the situation with viable results is to run your freight trains at the same time along with the same crews. That will never happen.

Extra 5055 North leaves Champaign without fanfare. They are having a good trip as they roll through Gilman and Kankakee. Leaving Kankakee the train will almost immediately encounter the first of the long hills. For the next 25 miles this train will be moving predominantly uphill. Once Indian Oaks is gained the train will roll fairly well. Now Peotone is behind them and the train is now on the side of an almost eight mile hill. If an engineer or brakeman is having trouble staying awake, this is where it will happen with intensity.

That is what I think happened to the crew of the Extra 5055 North. I have been there myself, many times. If you are short on rest or are simply not ready to come to work, this is where it will get you as the harmonic roll of the train and the repetitive, yet noisy drone of the diesel engine rocks you to sleep. Once the train finally reaches Steunkel Road someone had better wake up as the situation changes in a hurry. The periphery of the railroad makes a radical change and drops downhill for almost 18 miles. It starts to level out at Kensington. This train would not get that far.

As it passes Steunkel, the coal train doesn't acknowledge the southbound train waiting for a signal, nor does it blow the whistle for the road crossing, the radio goes unanswered. The southbound crew would attest to this at the investigation. It was said that this train was out of control when it passed the Harvey yard office. Witnesses estimated that the train was moving at least 70 MPH. The frantic radio contact would be to no avail. By this time, it was later determined, the entire crew was in the arms of Morpheus.

A yard job was ahead of the 5055 and was in the process of going into Wildwood yard with 13 loaded auto racks. It was on the bridge that the coal train would collide with the yard job as it stood on the Little Calumet River waiting for a switch to be lined. The conductor and flagman of the yard job were not aware of the impending collision which would kill the flagman and maim the conductor as they occupied a demolished caboose. Their train would be moved 185 feet before it came to a stop again. The entire train-full of automobiles were no doubt written off as damaged, and the IC probably had to buy the entire 156 car lot. The last five rail cars were heavily damaged. Five of the six trestles that constituted the bridge were rendered severely damaged and out of service for a considerable time. The smaller bridge that spanned both the B & O and Penn Central was heavily damaged with wreckage and coal blocking the Penn Central.

The engineer and brakeman of the coal train were probably killed upon impact. The 5055 (U33C) was totaled and the pair of trailing GP9's suffered heavy damage. The first 66 cars of the 128 car coal train derailed. 65 of these cars were destroyed.

For a long while, the head brakeman of the 5055 could not be found. Only after wreckage crews began to watch the flies did they determine the presence of his body.

Track one was the only track that stayed clear of the wreckage and IC would solely rely on that track for its commuter operation.

For the investigation the IC would have to rent a major portion of a local hotel-motel and also secure one of its huge banquet rooms. Witnesses from Champaign would need a place to stay. The witnesses were comprised of bartenders, waitresses, hotel clerks and fellow rail workers.

Both the conductor and flagman of the Extra 5055 North stated that they estimated the speed of their train to be between 30-35 MPH as it approached Riverdale. I wonder if they had a straight face when they said that.

For this wreck I hold both the train crew and the establishment (the company & the unions) responsible and hopefully something good can come of this most incredulous and very tragic of accidents.

This otherwise eventful year was filled with grief. IC would have to dig deep within its coffers to cover its losses.

Five days before Christmas I was set up. Two days before Christmas Eve I made a trip on CN3. This was a day job. We had three big GP40's and flew into Champaign. Coming by Indian Oaks I looked over at the wreck site. That accident had happened almost a year ago and nothing was left to indicate that a tragic event had occurred here. It wouldn't be very long, I mused, and the memory of the men that died here would be lost. We worked a little over four hours and put off duty a little before noon.

We would lay over in Champaign just short of 24 hours before we were called for NC4 at 11:00 AM. We were there long enough to rack up seven hours and fifteen minutes alimony. I didn't mind the long layovers, as it gave me a chance to get caught up on my sleep. Our northbound trip was a good one as we were only four hours on duty. I was hoping that that would be all the work I would get until after Christmas. It was not to be. On Christmas Eve they decided to put on an extra transfer job at 4:30 AM. We would take a single 1200 switcher and go to Congress St. yard from Harvey, round up a bunch of cars and bring them back to Markham. I was home before 11 o'clock. Merry Christmas! The year would at least end on a good note.

[1] When "setting out" a train leaves or delivers cars to a particular point on the railroad. [2] While the authorized timetable speed was 79 MPH, train 25 may have been early enough or on time and would be running cautiously due to the fog. 25 was a mail train and would enjoy a more or less leisurely schedule. [3] "Set up" means being raised in elevation from fireman to engineer. [4] "Run through" is a term used when two railroads pool their power to create a "run through" train. [5] "Soybean" brake shoe was a euphemism for brake shoes made out of something other than the same metal that the regular shoes were made from. [6] The "dead man" was a pedal on the floor of a passenger locomotive. The engineer would exert a minimum of foot pressure to keep the pedal down. Taking ones foot off the pedal while moving would cause an application of the brakes. [7] Mr. Williams got tagged with "Jughead" because of his initials "J.H." [8] At one time the stationmaster's office was well endowed with glass. Hence: Glass house. [9] Charlie Selsor was the Illinois Division traveling engineer, which is a salaried position in the management scheme of things. [10] "Alimony" is a term used to describe "held away from home terminal in excess of 16 hours". After 16 hours, crews will be paid the time consumed until they are called to work, but not to exceed 8 hours. After 24 hours the process begins again.

Chapter 9

1970

On January 1st, 1970 a major change in national railroading became effective. The hours of service law is repealed. Instead of it having a sixteen hour limit, it would now be reduced to fourteen hours. The law was written in two parts and would change again. It would go from fourteen hours to twelve hours effective 1-1-73. Giving the railroads three years to adapt was felt to be adequate. There were mixed emotions within the rank and file. Some welcomed it, others were threatened by the decrease in income. For the railroads it may have been a blessing in disguise as they would have to alter the efficiency level in some areas. Conversely, by 1973, it might mean more jobs, which was good for the brotherhoods, whose brainchild it was to begin with.

On January 7, 1970 the northbound "City of New Orleans" struck a gasoline truck loaded with 2,000 gallons of gasoline at Hammond, La. It was a near miss and miraculously there was no explosion and without injury. The driver of the truck cavalierly stated "another foot and I would have made it".

Later that same month would be another gasoline truck accident. This time, the accident would be more exacting and would take four lives as the engine hit the truck squarely and with high impact. The date was the 24th of January. Illinois Central train #1, the southbound "City of New Orleans", would strike a gasoline truck loaded with 800 gallons of fuel at Loda, Ill. at about 9:25 AM. This day would not begin routinely as Newell C. Brown, executive assistant to the IC president, would be taking his first cab ride. To facilitate Mr. Brown's trip would be Traveling Engineer Jim Zagorski. The engineer was Tom Clarke with fireman Royster. Royster was back on the third and last unit troubleshooting and was as far from the point of collision as he could have been. It was to be a godsend as he mercifully would survive unscathed. The three men in the cab would perish as would the truck driver. The Illinois Central Railroad would encounter yet another horrific tragedy.

One account of the accident claims that the train was moving in excess of 80 MPH. I would have to dispute that for more than one reason. I am not saying that it couldn't happen, however I feel that it is unlikely. There are factors to take into account. After running an engine for 37 years, I feel qualified to further examine the alleged infraction. First of all, speeding is a precept that was almost always overlooked (until something happened). Tom Clarke, while having 33 years under his belt, had only recently begun running in through passenger service. He didn't know Brown or Zagorski and I doubt that he would have taken the liberty to "exceed" with two company officials in the cab. Mr. Brown, I'm sure knew the authorized timetable speed to be 79 MPH, however being the "new kid on the block" so to speak, probably would not have said anything. Jim Zagorski on the other hand was a young guy with a lot of years in front of him and knew Brown to be privy to President Alan Boyd. I doubt if he would have jeopardized his career by condoning excessive speed. It is my opinion and experience that with two strangers riding the engine, the speed limit was adhered to.

Another factor that should be looked at is that when a train moving at that speed and its brake system is put into "emergency", for a split second the train will experience a surge ahead and the speed on the odometer will increase. Also what with the explosion of gasoline may have caused an erratic wheel slip that would have altered the speed indication on the odometer. Crossings are also known to be a little greasier due to fluids emanating from vehicles. It is also impossible to keep a train at exact speed.

February would bring delivery of twenty 2000 HP GP38's from General Motors. Surprisingly, they came equipped with dynamic braking. It was as though they were invisible, as they were largely ignored at first. The IC provided little or no information on them. The north end of the IC was pretty much a flatland railroad and "stretch braking" was the preferred technique to slow a train. When using dynamic brakes, the "bunch braking" method had to be used. To properly use the latter technique, the slack must be carefully gathered until the entire train is against the engine or pushing it. That is time consuming and had no place on the Illinois Division. Dynamics were great if you had heavy grades, not so hot on the flatland.

I asked one engineer his thoughts on the 9500's (new GP38's), his reply was: if you have three of them, you may as well have two, they don't seem to do any better. In two words another engineer summed it up quite sardonically with: "beats walking". Some guys thought they were sluggish compared to a geep (GP9 or GP10) although the GP38 had more power. They were reliable, however. These units were immediately placed in the Chicago-St. Louis pool upon delivery to lend substance to IC's bid to handle the General Motors automobile business with the "hot" connections at E. St. Louis. The forty GP40's would now be assigned to the mainline exclusively.

In March of 1968 IC would begin a program to rebuild 164 GP7 and GP9's. The most noteworthy change would be an increase in horsepower increasing RPM's by re-setting the injector racks. Rebuilt GP7's would now be rated at 1600 HP instead of 1500. GP9's would also be increased 100 RPM's to now be rated at 1850 HP. I had two of them one day on a northbound extra. They had just come out of the shop at Paducah and it was their first trip. We had 67 cars and those units really gave a terrific account of themselves as they walked away with that train. I don't remember the load vs. empties ratio, but for that train to run the way it did, the majority of the cars must have been empties. Hats off to the boys at Paducah!

In 1970 I was "set up" (on the extra list) about seventy percent of the time. There would be no rest for the wicked so they say. Not knowing where you are going to be from one day to the next isn't conductive to a good family atmosphere. When it was tough on me, it would reflect on my wife. I didn't begrudge her a bad day. We had a new home and she worked hard around there. We would get through it.

From January 17th, 1969 through January 24th, 1970, the Chicago and Illinois Division seniority list would suffer fourteen deaths due to tragic accidents or ill health. These unexpected developments would accelerate my climb up the seniority ladder.

The next story describes how I spent one summer weekend waiting for trains that never came. It was to be an unplanned additional "paid vacation".

Of course the movement of trains is always first and foremost on any operating departments agenda. The actual operation of a train is only a part of the forces that are responsible for train movement, however.

More than one factor comes into play when the running of a train is contemplated. First you have to have the train itself. A train has to be made up of cars available that are basically meant for a specific place or area. A train may have three or four or more blocks of cars that are set out of the train en-route to its final destination. Conversely, the process is reversed when a train picks up cars at these same locations en-route to its final destination or terminal. Switch engines are needed to place these cars into proper alignment. Ultimately the train is "made up". Once this is done, the yardmaster wants to run the train from point A to point B and that means power is needed. Power is a definite factor as a train cannot move without locomotives. Now that power has been provided, manpower enters the equation. Crews and power go hand-in-hand as you cannot move a train without either element. Both need to be in the right place at the right time. On that note, we get into the text of our story: Deadheading.

"Deadheading" is a railroad euphemism for moving a crew or person from one point to the other. Quite often there would be a shortage of crews at away from home terminals. A train could be at Champaign ready to head for Chicago, however, there would be a shortage of rested crews and the train would have to sit. The Chief Dispatcher would have to determine well in advance if an imbalance of trains vs. crews was impending. On great occasions one or more crews would be deadheaded from one point to another because they then would be rested and in position for a train movement. The following story is presented to you and is a true example of the non-glory part of railroading. The following story tells of how I once spent a weekend as a guest of the Illinois Central Railroad.

Through freight service on most railroads are manned by pool crews, i.e. "first in first out". For example a crew would bring CN5 (Chicago-New Orleans) into Champaign[1] from Chicago and be eight times out upon arrival. That means that seven crews would have to be called for work before CN5's crew would be called to bring a train back to the home terminal (i.e. Chicago). This rule may be circumvented when there is a train to run and no rested crews, then the deadhead crew would upon arrival be eligible to take the train. The average layover for a trip in pool freight service would be 12-14 hours, occasionally exceeding 24 hours.

These "deadheads" were almost always on a passenger train of which IC had many. Once in a great while, usually while at Clinton, you might get called to "deadhead" on a freight train for lack of a passenger train.

I should take time to briefly explain the "hours of service" or "hog law". If a crew came close to exceeding 16 hours on duty, arrangements would be made to "die" at a location without blocking the mainline and tying up the railroad. The hours of service would apply to a "deadhead" crew in the following manner. You are called to deadhead to Champaign on #3 (the Louisiane). Almost always the entire crew would entrain at Homewood. Roughly it would take one and one half hours from there to Champaign. Upon arrival the crew would call the yardmaster and he would apprise them of the situation. If there was a train for Chicago and no crew available, the deadhead crew would have about 14 hours to work and would have plenty of time to get the train over the road. I should further explain that the hours of service have since gone from 16 to 14 hours and subsequently to the present 12 hour limit.

The freight business always intensified as the weekend drew nearer. By Friday or Saturday most loads pulled from industries are in circulation and en-route to their destinations. Couple that with the fact that the normal world had week-ends off and could attend weddings and other such social events that are held on weekends. If a regular engineer in the freight pool wanted off, he almost al-ways wanted to be off on the weekend. If a regular pool engineer was contem-plating a bout with the flu, it would surely be brought on by a call to deadhead. Deadhead pay rates for engineers were much lower. If there was a straw that broke the camel's back that would be it. The call board didn't encourage laying off on the call, but it usually happened when the regular man found out that he wasn't getting such a plum. If the regular freight pool was exhausted (no one available), the crew caller would have no choice but to summon an engineer off of the extra yard list. The call was always welcomed because I could actually get some genuine rest on the other end of the road. It also enabled me to spend the weekend away from the rigors of the Chicago Terminal yard extra board which at the time was moving every eight hours and had been for quite a while. There also was the thought in the back of my mind that we might just get on a waiting train and come back right away. We would have had time to bring back any train they gave us. In any event there was the possibility of handling a "hotshot" over the road. Any train on the road was a challenge and catching a trip out there was a welcome change of pace. I loved to run trains!

Our story unfolds with the ring of the telephone. My incredible adventure is about to begin. It's the crew caller and she is calling me to deadhead on #3 to Champaign. I asked her what the strategy was and she said that she didn't know the particulars. Of course my first thought was that we would jump on a north-bound manifest and be home in a few hours. It wasn't to be. We were told to check into the hotel upon arrival and of course we knew we would go to the bottom of the board, but would probably get out of Champaign on our rest (8 hours), as there must be a lot of trains in the northbound picture. It didn't work that way. We sat there for 24 solid hours wondering how and why they decided to deadhead us in the first place. Granted, I could have used the rest, but I would have preferred to have been resting in my own bed at home with my family. We originally deadheaded on a Friday night and now it is 10:00 PM Saturday and they want us to go by taxi from Champaign to Clinton (45 miles). Again our thoughts begin with like "are we gonna take a train home right away, or are we going to start this fiasco all over again"? Sure enough, we went to the bottom of the board and sat in Clinton another 25 plus hours. Amazing.

Champaign-Urbana is a college town and there are things to do if you are re-sourceful enough. Long layovers in Champaign can be productive. The Uni-versity of Illinois has one of the finest if not largest libraries in the world. Its campus is also endowed with more than its share of beautiful women. Clinton on the other hand is more of a "down home" farm town. It is located on IC's Chicago-St. Louis mainline or Gilman Line. The Illinois Central put Clinton on the map as seven main and branch lines radiate from it. Even though going to Clinton paid more (126 miles vs. 105 miles), most guys would prefer Champaign if they had their "druthers". We had spent plenty of time in Champaign simply waiting and now there was a strong possibility of repeating the process in Clinton. You have to remember that this isn't your normal road trip. You are a victim of the "breaks". Your luck is running out when you consider how long you have been away from home. Luck isn't the only thing you're short of when you look in your wallet. Eventually over the course of the day you realize that the ennui that is caused by company calculations made you aware of the fact that you can't make money any easier and then you realize that you can't make it any harder either. We were being paid the "deadheads" and also getting "alimony" or compensation for being "held away from home terminal in excess of sixteen hours". A crew would go on alimony pay for the next eight hours unless they were called. Rarely did anyone ever collect the full eight hours. Once you did get to eight hours, you went back off of it and then started the process over again until you were called.

We were four times out when we went to the bottom of the board upon our arrival in Clinton. We sat first out (next crew to get called) for a long time. Our conductor called the dispatcher to see what the plan was. The answer was: probably deadhead on #22 (the Green Diamond). We were astounded. Unbelievable! However, that was not to be the grand conclusion. #22 came and went (we weren't on it). An hour later we were called to deadhead on #62, a freight train instead of the slightly earlier, more convenient passenger train. Once again...we were victims of being in the wrong place at the wrong time.

Six or seven hours later our train was entering Markham Yard. After registering off duty, I called the caller and she informed me that I was two times out on the extra yard list and would get out on my rest or soon thereafter. The caller was right on, it would be nine hours exactly between when I put off on the deadhead and when I was called to work the 4:00 PM North Pulldown at Harvey (for straight time, I might add).

In conclusion I have to say that even though I was often bored to extreme and suffered from lack of funds, there was no lack of rest. The bed may not have always been the best but I couldn't say I wasn't rested. Usually when you think back about your railroad experiences, it's the bad trips that first come to mind and although we never turned a revenue wheel, I cannot remember a worse trip. One of the good points was that my vocabulary expanded when someone mentioned the word "ennui" and then explained its meaning.

The aforesaid is a part of railroading that doesn't get talked about but is very much a part of it and needed to be told. It was a paid vacation that I would have rather worked. It didn't do the Illinois Central any good either as we didn't generate one nickel's worth of revenue for them.

As long as I can remember, the West Pullman job always went to work at 10:30 PM. On regular nights it would leave Markham Yard with cars for the Blue Island branch, usually tying up at around 4 AM. A good job if you had the seniority to hold it even if it was nights.

Labor Day came and went and as usual would upset the railroad scheme of things what with jobs being pulled off as the companies would avoid paying big bucks to employees working the holiday.

The night of 9-8-70 was no different. The West Pullman was pressed into doing "charity work". It would have to first deliver cars to the Indiana Harbor Belt and thereafter do its regular work. The crews weren't exactly enamored over the prospect of having the extra work piled on them, but the holidays always screwed up the machinations of the operating department. The Labor Day weekend was no different.

The West Pullman left Harvey (Markham Yard) with 22 cars, 20 loads, 1 empty, and a caboose. The train was being shoved north by the single unit 1218, a switch engine type. It would proceed approximately 2 ½ miles where it would encounter a semi-permanent red signal which was due to incomplete track changes. Its physical designation was "Highlawn" or IHB Junction. The red signal was called a restricting block signal. When the signal was approached by a train, the crew had to be in compliance to the rule which at that time defined the rule as "proceed prepared to stop short of train, obstruction or switch not properly lined and to look out for broken rail but not to exceed a speed of 10 miles per hour".

Although the crew on the caboose had control of the brakes, the engineer would usually slow down from his end of the shove. Also the "hind end" could talk (radio) the engineer to a stop. This night was no different. The engineer was shoving the train between 15 and 20 miles per hour and went to slow the train when its brakes went into emergency being applied from the caboose. The engineer could then see the rear end of his train begin to fall down the embankment and realized that a serious accident had developed.

What had happened was that an Indiana Harbor Belt transfer job was crossing over from the IHB lead to track #5 for a movement with 36 cars to Markham Yard. The IC steel caboose knifed into the engineer's side of IHB 8717. The engine was backing the train to Markham. Ironically the crew wanted to run the engine normal or to the front. It didn't happen and the engineer was killed because he literally had no protection. He was surrounded by glass and that surely didn't enhance his chances of survival. He was later found dead in the wreckage. The IHB "headman" suffered serious injuries, but survived. The IC conductor died shortly after the accident. The IC flagman was seriously injured.

Alcohol, this time didn't enter into the picture. The absence of the white light displayed on the caboose was a strong indication that there was a lack of focus. Complacency can and will get you killed.

Throughout the last five years the IC went from one of the safest railroad companies to, unfortunately, one of the most dangerous.

[1]Champaign, Illinois is the first division point south of Chicago on the Illinois Central Chicago-New Orleans route. It is touted to be the "Mainline of America". It is also the first crew change point going south. Conversely, Clinton is the only crew change and division point between Chicago and St. Louis on the Gilman line.

Chapter 10

1971

I would be on the extra list through the holidays. Not only did I get to spend Christmas away from home, the New Year would also be spent on the road. New Year's Eve wasn't as important to me as Christmas, and wasn't a big deal. I was called for SE-1 (southeastern merchandise). SE-1 was the "hottest" southbound train the IC ran for many years until they recently inaugurated the all piggyback #51. We ran 70 MPH with the newer, heavier SD40's. They had six axles and rode "rough". On the return trip, we were called right on our rest (eight hours off duty). It was a rare day when that happened and we weren't complaining. We would get #50 the northbound counterpart to #51. The only bad thing about it was because of the holiday, we would have a Markham set out before we continued our journey to IMX (intermodal facility) (I still haven't figured out what the "X" stands for). Once we yard our train at IMX we would run the three units back to Woodcrest. It was time consuming but a big payer. This day we would have a pair of GP40's along with a GP9 for power. The four axle GP40's tracked better at 70 MPH. Because we had the GP9 in the consist we were held to 65 MPH, as the geeps were geared for 65. My wife and I would celebrate the New Year when I got home that day.

Although we didn't know it at the time, there would be more than enough time to celebrate as the extra list "died". When this happens, the list is cut a few numbers. Two or three guys would get set back to firing. In this case nothing was done. This went on for five days before they set anyone back firing. The "powers that be" sat on their hands and did nothing. The explanation for this never came. I remember one time when I was on the extra list and had just talked to the caller and was advised to go have a "few pops" as I was thirteen times out. I eagerly accepted this anomaly and complied. Two hours later the phone rings. The night shift caller had just come on duty and he was calling me for some job. I wasn't about to go to work as I was feeling no pain. The caller didn't have time to explain what had happened as he had to find somebody to fill that job. It's either feast or famine on the extra list and I just provided two examples of what does and what doesn't happen. Your heart and soul belongs to the railroad. You will find yourself saying hello to yourself as you pass on your way to work or on your way home. Every time the telephone rings will bring a note of antipathy into your life! All of this erraticism does nothing to enhance a marriage, I might add.

AMTRAK becomes effective on the 1st of May and we would see subtle changes. During the initial period, I was set up and wouldn't see any passenger service until the middle of November. By that time 27th St. was no longer used for anything and was slated for the wrecking ball. IC would sign a contract with AMTRAK and would maintain their passenger locomotives at Woodcrest. When the smoke cleared, Central Station would be nothing more than a landmark. The IC main offices would now be "downtown". All through trains would be using Chicago Union Station, and IC enginemen would be afforded five jobs to operate four trains (two each way). On a good note - now that the IC maintained AMTRAK's power, almost every day there would be an engine transfer. These jobs were considered "plums" as they could be a one hour job or a twelve hour job depending on what needed to be done. If you started at Woodcrest, the engine or engines were usually ready. When you got down to 16th St. (ex-Pennsy engine house), you had to keep your fingers crossed and hope that there was nothing to go back. If there was something, more often than not, that power would not be ready. You never went to work at the same time, and never did the same thing twice at the same place. The average time on duty was only four hours, however and of course we were paid for eight.

Sometime during the summer, the new suburban equipment began to trickle in. At first they looked out of place when your eyes were used to seeing the battle tested war torn 1926 trains. The new cars were built by the St. Louis Car Company and were not compatible with present equipment. Wouldn't that have been a sight to see? If you were already qualified on the old cars, it was no big deal to break in on the new cars. The major internal difference was the brake system. You had three major components blended into a conventional brake application - electric, hydraulic and dynamic. Use of the dynamic was preferred but optional. It would fade out at 10 MPH. You didn't want to come against a bumper post thinking that the dynamic was going to help you get stopped because under 10 MPH you didn't have one.

I recently caught a trip on CN5 and would like to take this time to tell you what goes through any young engineers mind when he gets called for the road. Train CN5 is about to conclude its air test. The car inspector has acknowledged that its brakes are released and the train may proceed, when ready. This is happening at Illinois Central's Markham Yard on a beautiful October evening, on the southern outskirts of Chicago. CN5 is the symbol for "Chicago-New Orleans" and the 5 is just a number. The train crews refer to it as simply #73. My engine consist is made up of three 3000 class GP40's. These engines are fairly new to the IC and I looked forward to running them. IC had well over 400 GP7's and 9's and was probably the last railroad to explore turbo-charged engines, when they purchased forty GP40's. My train information tells me that I have 77 loads and 30 empties for 8700 tons. No restricting cars and no pick-up at Kankakee. Good. A perfect match for the power and the train should run at 60 MPH in most places. We wait for clearance from the yard, the trainlister, and lastly, our conductor. Once this happens, all we need is the signal permitting us to enter the mainline, vicariously through the train dispatcher. I acknowledge our collective "highball" and notify all concerned that we have the signal. All that is left to do is to pick up the conductor and flagman. Once the crew is safely aboard the caboose, I'll wait for the conductor to tell me when the train is through the crossover and entirely on the main. #73 is leaving town!

Once this happens, my thoughts begin to mull over operational stumbling blocks such as where #3 (Louisiane) is going to get around us. Our departure time is 7:40 PM. #3 leaves Central Station at 7:30 PM. He'll definitely go into Champaign ahead of us. Hopefully, the dispatcher can keep us moving. In those days, the IC had a lot of passenger trains. When you add the Gilman liners (St. Louis trains), the dispatchers had their work cut out for them. The St. Louis trains branched off the mainline at Gilman and ran over 81 miles of the 128 miles of the Chicago division. Almost all of the track between Stuenkel road and Gilman was signaled for "Centralized Traffic Control". Once a mainline train left Gilman, he was governed by "RULE 251" or "trains will run with reference to other trains in the same direction by block signals whose indications will supersede the superiority of trains". Northbound trains ran on the northbound main. Everybody stayed to the right and could not enter any of these tracks without signal indication. If you ran "wrong" you needed a train order from the dispatcher.

The dispatcher put us over from track one to track two at a place called Otto and we knew that #3 would probably get around us at either Ashkum or Gilman. As luck would have it, we really never did have to stop and followed #3 out of Gilman. Clear signals the rest of the way!

The train is rolling at 60 MPH in throttle seven. We're by Rantoul and I see no reason not to start thinking about stopping this train with aplomb at the "crew change" point, in one piece without much fanfare or embarrassment. Milepost 122 is coming up and now I have to make a decision-when to begin braking this train. Of course the engineer always makes the initial brake application with a minimum reduction of seven pounds. By applying a light application of brakes, yet still pulling the train with major throttle allows the train to settle or so the old timers told me. They also said that you could feel what a train is doing by the seat of your pants. With all of this in mind, I elected to pull the throttle back to notch "eight" and simultaneously make that minimum application of seven pounds we talked about earlier. Pull the train, let the brake shoes heat up and at the same time the train will settle. If I start my braking at the correct location, I should prevail. It should take one more small application of air to stop this train and when I decide to do this-the outcome will be decisive. Judgement becomes critical. Now I have to balance the momentum of the train with the power that is pulling it. If I get nervous and begin shutting the throttle down in haste, it could get ugly. No two trains are alike, you have to remember that. They don't always do what you want. We didn't get train profiles in those days you had to rely on good old fashioned experience (if you could get it). Every engineer has a basic mark with which he uses as a guide to either begin braking before or after the mark depending on how the train is running, which way the wind is blowing, etc., etc. I once stretch broke an empty coal train simply by slowly shutting down the throttle notch by notch, due to a very strong southern wind. The empty coal hoppers acted like sails.

One factor in my favor was that the lay of the land coming into Champaign was nearly perfectly flat.

We're now at 61 MPH in throttle eight and I elect to make my initial brake application at MP 124 (Leverett Jct.). The brake exhaust quiets and nothing seems to happen. Typical. My thoughts went from "it's a good thing we had a clear signal to-are the brakes ever going to grab?" Seconds go by along with a sigh of relief as the train is beginning to drag a little. We're now at 55 MPH and I'll shut off a notch and hold it. When I began to brake the train, I had exactly two miles to bring it to a stop. I can see MP 125 in the distance and the train is at 50 MPH and coming down nicely. Should I shut down another notch or should I draw off another three pounds from the brake pipe? I draw off the three pounds as we go by MP125 at 45 MPH. Better go to throttle six, these units have power I'm not used to.

When stretch braking a train the engineer should be in at least throttle one when the train comes to a stop. I want to be sure that I don't run out of amperage, so I try to shut the throttle down in a proportionate manner.

We're now at 35 MPH and I can see the yard office. Next to the yard office stands a block signal showing "approach". We want to stop this side of that signal. It is time to unload another notch going to throttle five. We are getting close at 25 MPH and is time to drop to four notch. It doesn't look like I'll need to draw off any more air off the brake pipe, but I still can if I have to. I am mindful that most train separations (knuckles, drawbars) occur during this particular phase of train braking I.E. under 25 MPH and shutting down on the throttle too quickly. At the same time I am thinking that too much throttle at too slow a speed could cause a wheel slip, which could affect a "run-in" which could easily result in a train separation or "extraction". This train is handling well and I go to throttle three. We're right at 15 MPH and it is starting to look like I may have to draw off more air. The train played a slight trick on me, as it bogged down like it should have, but now as we are very close, it wants to stay at a constant 15 MPH. We are near enough that I can go in and use all of the brake pipe air that is left. The cab becomes very noisy what with the entire train-line venting into our ears. I shut down to throttle two...then one... and I'm stopped. The throttle is officially in idle. I briefly reflect that while I may not have gotten a textbook rating for that stop...I'll bet I did get a 95. It was a good stop.

Getting off and approaching the outbound engineer, I comment that the train started to "creep" while I made the stop. No problems otherwise. He retorted, "Yeah they'll do that" as he climbed aboard. I thought...the guy must know what he's talking about as he probably had thirty years on me.

All in all we had a good trip. I felt that the dispatching was excellent and the train and the train handling was above par. I had yet to run by the "crew change" point but I knew a couple of other young engineers that did and they sure got teased about it!

The other day the wife and I got involved in a rather heated discussion. Sometimes anger can be constructive if you learn to channel it that way. From this argument emanated the conclusion that we didn't have a lot in common. We didn't feel that that particular factor was harmful to our marriage. However, we had never given it any thought before. Of course the kids would always be the minions of our common interest.

As the year came to a close my time as a fireman was also closing as I was set up 90% of the time. Of course the old timers would always say and I was to find out that they were right that nothing is written in stone on the railroad! Don't count on anything!

Christmas came and the new year wasn't far away. The road men usually hide around the holidays and this year would be no different. I was called for CB9

(Chicago-Birmingham) at 7:40 PM on Christmas Eve. I had made a personal agreement with my family and myself to be "off" or at least home every other Christmas holiday. This would be my first year to work and I planned on being home the following year. The crew callers never knew that. The rumor had it that every crew would be scrutinized over the holidays for alcohol as a consequence of the accidents that occurred the previous year. I couldn't blame the company for being gun shy. As the trainmaster approached the engine, the brakeman yelled out the window "you don't have to come up here you can smell it down there". Knowing the brakeman, the trainmaster ignored his advice and climbed up on the engine. Through the dim light of the cab he squinted as he peered intently at the two of us. His comment was "you look bright eyed and bushy tailed". He then wished us a good trip and a Merry Christmas. "Merry Christmas" was our refrain.

The main topic of conversation in 1971 would be of the impending merger with the Gulf, Mobile & Ohio Railroad. Mergers are always good for the carrier and the stockholders, but held with acquiescence by the employee's. We would see.

Chapter 11

⟶

1972

The first two months of 1972 are spent firing AMTRAK. When I fired passenger I almost always worked with either Johnny Taksas or Joe Rivard.

One night I was called to "pinch hit" on a "WEPX" coal train that came out of southern Illinois. "WEPX" stood for Wisconsin Electric Power Co. We would pass this train to the Chicago & Northwestern at a place called Mayfair and they would take it to Oak Creek, Wi. It was always a long drawn out affair and you made sure you had a big lunch with you. This night would be no different. Once we got on the BRC (Belt Railway of Chicago), it would be an uphill climb all the way to Cragin Jct. In anticipation of this, I was charged with four units to move these one hundred or so bathtub hoppers wherever it needed to be moved. At Clark St. (Rock Island), we got a red signal. We have no communication with the tower man at Clark St. as he is on a different radio frequency. A half hour goes by and after several futile attempts at calling whoever wants to listen, the Markham general yardmaster (GYM) comes over the radio. He admonishes me to monitor my radio activity. These radios are nice, however they don't always do the job, especially when we are sitting between two ten story buildings, and don't hear anything, I answer. Now that the pleasantries are out of the way, the GYM informs me that due to a derailment somewhere around Belt Tower (where we usually gain access to the BRC), we would be going via the GM&O and would get on the "Belt" at a place called LeMoyne. I advised the GYM that I would need a pilot between Bridgeport and LeMoyne and then to Belt Tower. Over the years I have come to learn that the word "pilot" is a dirty word to the folks in control. That part of the rule book that they would like to see re-written or to forget altogether. The "old timer"" once said "you can let the book of rules work against you or you can make it work for you.

The trick is to thoroughly understand what you are reading". Good advice. And now because of radio inconsistencies, the Markham GYM is talking to the GM&O yardmaster and is vicariously passing this information to me. He says: the GM&O doesn't have a pilot. I ask does the GM&O even know what a pilot is. Twenty minutes go by and the signal at Clark St. goes to a more favorable indication. About that time the GYM comes back and tells me to take the train to Bridgeport and wait for a pilot. When it comes to a pilot my thought was that had Casey Jones had had a pilot (did he ask for one?), he wouldn't have become posthumously famous. You have to remember that he wasn't working his normal seniority territory and probably didn't know where he was at.

We sat at Bridgeport for over an hour and my pilot shows up. They may as well have called out Donald Duck or even Goofy as I would find out when I nearly ran by the "STOP BOARD" at the PC-C&WI crossing. The board is situated on a curve and can't be seen until you are right on top of it. I'm not sure this guy even knew that he worked for the railroad. I don't think they called the pilot in the spirit it was intended. This guy turned out to be a young GM&O switchman and may or may not have ever been over the pike we were currently running on.

Once we shoved the train around the wye at LeMoyne, we could proceed north to Mayfair and deliver the train to the CNW and then head for home with the light power. The "big lunch" surely came in handy as we racked up well over twelve hours overtime.

By the end of February I couldn't even hold a passenger job and was firing freight. One engineer would always comment when he knew he was going to be bumped off of his passenger job "come Monday mornin I'll be out amongst the coal cars".

The turns (pool jobs) were staggered and the firemen would work with a different engineer each time he was called. You would get a variation in operating techniques that way.

The brakemen and conductors would always "rate" the engineers in their prowess as being smooth. A brakeman once told me that the three best engineers out here are brakemen! The overall consensus of trainmen rated the three best engineers as Jim Callahan, Bill Bates and Ken Connelly. The trainmen were on the road the year round and were more than qualified to assess the capabilities of these engineers.

I was called for #51 with engineer Jim Callahan. I hadn't worked with Callahan a lot over the years, but I would welcome the call. #51 was a big payer and was the "flagship" of the southbound "hotshots". We had three GP40's and that should have been sufficient enough to move the "pigs" at 70 MPH. Callahan was known as a fast engineer and as far as I knew, he always ran his own engine. Callahan commented that we weren't rolling the way we should be. We all agreed. The brakeman noted that the wind was coming out of the south earlier and that may be our problem. Callahan opined with: I think we have a sick engine as he put on his gloves and at the same time motioned for me to run the engine. We were at Rantoul and there wouldn't be enough time for Jim to go back and troubleshoot, and be back in the cab in time to bring the train to a stop at the yard office in Champaign. I would have to stop the train.

Piggyback trains were a little tricky as they didn't brake very well. Some guys thought that it was due to the style of brake shoe that was used on these flatcars. "Soybean brake shoes" was what we jokingly referred to them as. Whatever they were made of - I had to stop that train with the same adroitness and guile that Callahan would use to get it done. I had no choice. Seemingly the whole world would be watching. Yardmasters, trainmasters, car knockers, brakemen, they all knew who was running that train and if I screwed up, I would forever be banished to working the night north hump and Callahan's good name would be besmirched. There wouldn't be any practice I had to get it right and right at the crew change point.

As we approached the mark it looked like I would stop on the mark. The brakeman congratulated me and all I could stammer was "I had no choice"! The brakeman agreed when he answered "no.....you didn't". Once we came to a complete stop, Callahan came back up to the lead unit and grabbed his grip. Without saying a word, he then got off. Although I couldn't show it, I was riding high. Callahan paid me a fine tribute when he trusted me with that train.

During that trip, job insurance was brought up. It was something that I was kicking around but hadn't yet done anything about. One guy had the "big policy" and got himself into some kind of trouble. He got some time off and bragged to his buddies that it wouldn't be so bad because he had the "big policy". Well.....he had it, but he didn't have it because his wife hadn't paid the premiums for a couple of months. Callahan wryly commented that "if that had been me, I would have told her to find a job, peddle your ass, sell apples, whatever". Engineer Ralph King was our local job insurance agent and the next time I saw him we would look into insurance.

Back on the home front our marriage was becoming more and more like a roller coaster ride. At times we weren't on the same page or even in the same book. I remembered the guy with the "big policy" and my thoughts went to "that could have been me"! Although my wife readily accepted her role as the family bill payer - it didn't always get done.

IC was taking delivery of the new suburban cars in weekly two car increments.

They were sweet little jobs as these cars ran exclusively by themselves. The movement of those cars from St. Louis was almost 100% Illinois Central. We caught one of those trains out of Clinton for Woodcrest (Markham) and were on duty a little more than three hours, one engine and two cars.

On the 10th of August, 1972 the merger of the Illinois Central Railroad and the Gulf Mobile & Ohio Railroad became official. Railroad merger's, be it high in the corporate scheme of things or conversely, struggling on the bottom of some seniority roster are taken with mixed emotions. Everyone involved realizes that eventually the job force will be pared. Someone has to go.

What it meant to me almost always on the extra yard list would be more city driving, more railroad to learn and lastly to get to know yet another bunch of guys and to overcome any post-merger trepidations that I was to learn, always came with that particular territory. Intrinsically, the overall attitude that generated from each railroad was a world apart. The guys in the trenches would have to adjust to the whims of the current regime. If you didn't have enough seniority to stay where you were, you had to make the tremendous adjustment. So did your family. The new Illinois Central Gulf Railroad would aggrandize its new image with the old "we're one big happy family" trick.

On October 31st, 1972 the mettle of the two types of cars would, sadly, be tested. It was on a Monday morning, 7:27 AM to be exact, when two morning rush hour trains, both loaded with over 1,100 passengers collided at 27th Street. Both trains had originated at South Chicago and were running on the same track. The first train operated by Engineer J.A. Watts consisted of four of the new cars barely a year old. The second train operated by Engineer R.W. Cavanaugh had six cars of the 1926 vintage. These trains were standing room only, heavy with office workers on their way to the business district of downtown Chicago to begin their daily routine. As the first train approached 27th St., that routine would soon change.

The first train overran the platform at 27th St. In fact it might have completely gone by the automatic block signal located 142 feet north of the platform. The conductor immediately signaled with a buzzer that it was okay to back up the length of the platform and stop before he could open the doors. As the train backed, the trainman had one door open and was looking back when the headlight of the following train came into his view. In a split second the second train would be knifing into the rear of the train still backing up, thus intensifying the impact.

What probably happened was a sequence of events that if you tried to re-create, wouldn't come easily. The first train probably entirely cleared the block signal located north of the 27th St. platform when he overshot it. When he backed up and re-entered the block that he just vacated, if everything is working, the block signal at 31st Street should have gone from "yellow" to "red". At the very second that the first train re-affected the signal it just left, the second train was either very close to the signal at 31st St. or even by it and into the block.

As a train approaches a signal there is a split second when the engineer cannot see its indication because it is directly above him. The fact that it was daylight also obscures an engineer's ability to see a signal.

The circumstances for which this accident occurred may be difficult for the men that were there to accurately re-enact. These things happen so quickly and often are shaded, even blocked from memory due to a person going into a state of shock.

Overrunning a station stop is a normal occurrence, albeit frowned upon. It is accepted by the carrier as a "normal" mistake if there can be such a thing. Before the conductor "buzzed" the engineer to back up, he should have been on the rear of the train instead of midway. The time that it would have taken the conductor to get to the rear of the train, would have kept the train stationary and when the trains collided, it would have diffused the impact. The fact that the first train would be backing through a block signal that it just physically altered would have been another reason to stay in place. The previous block signal was at 31st St. and may have been "yellow" or "red" or in the transition of going from yellow to red. Some seem to think that the signal may have shown "clear", which would be a false indication and is almost unheard of in the industry.

The rulebook for which train operations are governed by states: Rule 285 describes a yellow block signal. *Indication-Proceed: Preparing to stop at next signal, train exceeding medium speed (30 MPH) must at once reduce to that speed, name-approach.* Rule 291 describes a red block: *Indication-Proceed at restricted speed. Name-Restricted proceed. Definition: Proceed prepared to stop short of train, obstruction or switch not properly lined, and look out for broken rail, but not exceeding 10 MPH.* In the current timetable "special instructions, this rule is amended to read *"But not exceeding 15 MPH."* The current rulebook was effective 6-1-70.

This writer is in no way trying to point a finger in anyone's direction. It is my intention to share what may have happened along with what did happen relative to my experience as a motorman. There is another point to make as to the efficiency of the brakes of both trains. A brake test is always given to a train at its point of origination. It is considered a routine matter and the condition of the brakes may not always be reported accurately. Another factor, having operated both types of equipment in all conditions, I knew through experience that the brakes on the "old" cars were more than adequate. In fact those brakes were that good that they caused guys to take chances. It was considered normal practice to go by a "yellow" block at fifty miles per hour.

Looking back 37 years, I can remember telling my wife and friends that I was very, very, fortunate to not have been anywhere near there. My mother called our house as soon as she heard about the accident and to her relief I was in bed and had no knowledge of the incident at that time.

In defense of both engineers-they were victims of circumstances. Up to that day and since 1926 the Illinois Central had had a stellar safety record, recording only one fatality in commuter service.

Something was learned this day, however unfortunately it took the lives of 45 people. Because of it, many other lives were affected. Not very long after the accident, Engineer Jim Watts succumbed to a heart attack and passed away. Engineer Bob Cavanaugh was to find out that after 40 years or so of normal life that he had only one kidney which was discovered on the operating table. Ironically, Watts was directly behind Cavanaugh on the seniority list.

During the 4 1/2 year period that I was subject to work in suburban, I more than once contemplated giving up my rights.

Shortly after the accident at 27th St., my wife and I were devastated after she had been diagnosed with cancer of the uterus. Earlier she had taken a routine pap smear through a local laboratory and was found to be clear of any problem. Later she would have an appointment with our family doctor and he insisted that she take another pap smear through the laboratory that he used. This time it came up "positive". Our doctor saved her life.

After extensive tests were taken, we were presented with the option of a partial hysterectomy which would enable her to bear children, however she would be on medication for the rest of her life and there would be no guarantees that she wouldn't endure a further resurgence of the cancer, or to undergo a full hysterectomy procedure which would erase any chance for childbirth and would fully eliminate the cancer and negate the need for medication. I can't remember if hormones were discussed. We opted for the latter. After all we already had two beautiful children. My wife's well being as well as our marriage would be predicated through the importance of her good health.

I didn't know it at the time, but 1972 would be the last year that I would work as a fireman on the Chicago Terminal or Illinois Division for that matter.

A PAEAN TO WAYNE JOHNSTONS ILLINOIS CENTRAL

I was introduced to the Illinois Central at the young age of 16. The year was 1959 and it was during the holiday season. We were part time help working on the mail platform and had just received our first pay checks. My friend and I were riding the elevator when some guy, in a suit, saw our checks and asked my buddy if he wanted to split it with him. We all laughed. We got off the elevator and one of the more tenured employees remarked - that was Wayne Johnston. "Who is he"? I asked. Only the president of the company! Unlike ourselves, Mr. Johnston had already had 41 years with the company and was president for the past 14 years. Over the years employees always referred to IC management as "under the clock" which comes from the huge clock that oversees the vast network of facilities around Central Station. Mr Johnston's office was under the clock.

I was later to hear that running into Mr. Johnston was not uncommon as he commuted on the IC electrics on a daily basis. As a rule Mr. Johnston would arrive before the usual starting time and would retire after everybody went home. His first question of the day was always: where is number 6? Is 6 on time? Number 6 was the northbound Panama Limited and flagship of the Illinois Central. Often as he came across the footbridge that linked the suburban platforms to the main IC offices, he would see the headlight of the Panama nosing its way into the train shed. Number 6 would be a few minutes early that day, its arrival time being 9:00 AM. The Panama was near and dear to Mr. Johnston's heart.

Mr. Johnston was at the helm when in 1947 the IC bought two new train sets from Pullman for the newly designated "City of New Orleans". The most unique and most obvious of changes would be the color scheme of orange, chocolate, and yellow. They were described as "Panama" colors and were a welcome departure from the olive drab of Pullman.

The Illinois Central was without peer when it came to meticulous track maintenance. IC's racetrack for most passenger trains was the Illinois divisions Champaign to Centralia segment. One hundred miles per hour[1] was the prescribed timetable speed for the 125 miles it ran. It was not uncommon for a train to leave Champaign 30 minutes late and arrive at Central Station "on time". Although an obvious and blatant infraction of the rules, exceeding the speed limit was always overlooked as it was common knowledge that the railroad was good for it and the Illinois Central and its employees took pride in their train operation and the bravado that went with it.

During Mr. Johnston's tenure, the IC dieselized and conversely took an entirely different avenue of approach when it came to freight engines. IC wisely elected to buy its power exclusively from GM-EMD. Early freight diesels would be both utilitarian and standard. The Illinois Central could have easily been "the standard railroad of Mid-America". When it was fully dieselized, there were over 400 geep's on the property. With the exception of passenger power, all freight engines were painted "coal black" with the "green diamond" on the side of the cab and the unit number in bold letters on the car body. A large horizontal white stripe was painted the length of the frame below the car body for flair. IC was a coal hauler and black was its color.

If you took a closer look at IC's power, you not only realized that the color black was cost effective, other factors or lack thereof would loom largely. All locomotives would be sans turbo-chargers, dynamic braking and without six axles. It was sparse to say the least. Wayne Johnston ran a tight ship. IC's power fleet would not see any modern accouterments until 1966 when 40 turbo-charged GP40's were purchased. A new era began as IC was one of the very last railroads to completely dieselize.

Mr. Johnston once referred to the Illinois Central as the "Mainline of Mid-America" and that became the IC's calling card.

When Mr. Johnston stepped down as leader of the railroad at the age of 69, he had 48 years of company service. He would yield to men brought in from other companies. These "business men" would begin to change the complexion of the company almost immediately. Once called by "Railway Age" magazine as an "authentic railroad man", Johnston loved the IC. Tragically, seven months after he relinquished his post as Chairman of the Board, Mr. Johnston was found dead of a massive heart attack. Some said that Mr. Johnston was saddened by the changes either made or proposed by the new regime. Others suggested that he died of a broken heart.

When I think back to those years my thoughts and emotions take me first to the passenger trains. To see and hear an IC passenger train moving across the prairies of the Illinois night would be enrapt with an aura of reverent emotion as the oscillating light, of the lead unit, would bounce off the grain elevators, ever searching, also resonating yet piercing the air were the poignant, shrill yet melodious sound that the Nathan P-5 air horn would make. All of this came at you at 80 miles per hour or better. And then it is, as fast as it came, gone. It is again-still. Indescribable. The freight trains were another source of captivating sounds. Some were operated with abandon, with the staccato roar of a set of two or three 567C's going through reverse transition in staggered unison at about 55 MPH[2] in preparation for stopping, would be for the titans to witness.

The din of a pair of GP9's struggling to gain Loda with some nondescript drag. Pulling for all they've got, sand flying, always making it. These were the sounds of the Illinois Central and they are the sounds that I have missed.

The many attributes that were brought about during the Johnston era are too many to speak of here. In closing I will say, looking back over the years, that when Wayne Johnston stepped down from Illinois Central leadership, it signaled the beginning of the end.

As we watch it fade into the misty past, I give many accolades to Mr. Johnston's Illinois Central.

As I sit here reflecting over what was......I conclude that the Illinois Central that I have just spoke of.....was also Bud Hoekstra's Illinois Central.

[1] Trains having cars that were equipped with friction bearings were restricted to 90 MPH. [2] The traction motors of a GP9 locomotive were designed to better utilize the current that they used by means of transition. Depending on the wheel radius the locomotives would go from series-parallel at 19 MPH to series-parallel-shunt at 28 MPH and then to parallel-shunt at 55 MPH.

Chapter 12

~~

1973

Two major changes beginning the new year would be the final phase of the hours of service amendment which would be effective 1-1-73. We went from working fourteen hours down to twelve hours. I would be able to live with that. The other change was one that we were more than disenchanted over. After the first of the year, the extra list would now consolidate with the GM&O side and their extra board. With that expanded board, we would now protect all jobs in the Chicago Terminal including Hawthorne, which came off of the Freeport board and the Chicago & Illinois Western, a jointly owned operation with only three jobs. The GM&O prior rights engineers would now have to protect the IC road jobs. In other words, instead of having two different boards, we would become one big happy family, except we weren't happy. In essence they seemed to be bent on alienating everyone, having us drive all over the city of Chicago. For this we were paid forty minutes. Our pleas for keeping the status quo fell on deaf ears. One example of how ludicrous it was came one morning when I was called to pilot a pilot. The Chesepeake & Ohio began running all the way into Markham. As this was new to them, they would initially ask for a pilot. The first guy out on the list or board was a GM&O man. He didn't know any more than the C&O engineer and so I was called to pilot the pilot. It was humor in an otherwise bad situation. I couldn't see how it was beneficial to anybody including the company. The old timer once said, "If it doesn't look like it will work - they'll make it work"! We accepted that with acquiescence.

The "new wrinkle" was just another fly in the ointment of life. Family life would be pretty much cast aside and the reality of it all was that maybe we should be looking for a new start somewhere away from the Chicago area.

"You'll make good money here, but you'll never get rich" was the sentiment echoed by senior engineers.

I was called for a road job and it was like going on vacation. I would temporarily be granted a respite from the extra list. It was pretty much a routine trip going down, one during daylight. We used to joke that the company didn't like to run trains in the daytime because they didn't want anyone to see them. The following morning I was called for BC4 (Birmingham-Chicago).

We were called for 8:30 AM and our train was coming up the main (mainline) when our cab pulled up to the yard office. By the time we got out of the cab, our train was stopped and its crew was getting off. I quickly read the bulletin board (nothing new) and headed for the power. The inbound engineer said that everything was fine and wished us a good trip.

The sheet that comes with the orders reads: 3037-3000-3055, three GP40's 66 loads 9 empties for 6,900 tons. This was a train to run with. Once the "hind end" was on we would go as we had the "high green" at Leverett Junction. It would quickly accelerate to 70 MPH. Seventy is only ten miles per hour over the authorized timetable speed limit of sixty for regular freight trains. The GP40's rode well and the track was good for it, and the brakeman never said a word. Go for it. Speeding isn't openly condoned, however rarely would anything be said unless something happened. Anytime I got behind the throttle, I had reservations. I would rationalize and then justify my actions by the conclusion of "it's what I do". We never encountered a yellow signal, our train came right up the passenger main and had the signal to come into the yard at Homewood. One track would hold our entire train and when I put off duty on the register the total time on duty was two hours and ten minutes to go 104 miles. It may be an un-official record.

From time to time the Electro-Motive Division of General Motors used IC trackage to test wheel slip relays. These jobs because they usually went to Kankakee and back would go to the freight pool. Quite often the regular pool engineer would "duck it" because it was a low payer and the job was open more often than not. Basically this equipment would coat the rail with a film of oil to promote slippage. Once that was done, the train would go the other way creating a dynamic resistance force, while they tested various "wheel slip" relays and their components. These EMD guys had been all over the country with this train. It was an interesting job.

Every division of every railroad runs a daily drag. A drag is a train that does all the pick up and setting out along the way and usually doesn't carry any time sensitive loading. 87 is no different. It had lots of cars and little power. 87 was another job the pool engineers avoided. The extra list was moving every eight hours and I was called for 87 which was a welcome change, as I could get caught up on my rest. This train always ran sometime after midnight. The night I caught it, we worked the full twelve hours. Once we finally put off duty and arrived at the hotel, I decided to take a long leisurely bath, soaking in the tub forever. I'll never get any awards for being an efficient sleeper, however this day I slept a full twelve hours, the longest I have ever slept at any time in my life. Later, I noticed my wedding ring was not on my finger. I was at the yard office when I realized that I didn't have it. I called the hotel and apprised them of the situation. They had no record of who the maid was, and no ring was found. I was in an awful predicament. Because of the extended bath, my fingers must have shrunk enough that the ring worked itself off. Sometimes the truth is difficult to accept and I would have to convince my wife into believing what actually happened. My wife acted like she believed me, but somehow, I don't think that she did. This incident was not good for our marriage although it was not mentioned again. I was sickened over it.

In late November I was called to pilot GM&O prior rights engineer "Babe" Anderson. The train would be good old 87 at 3:10 AM. They couldn't have come up with a worse time if they tried. I knew we were in for a long night when I saw the power. There were four units of the geep persuasion including the 8800 which might have been on its way to a museum somewhere. The 8800 was one of two GP7's delivered to the IC in 1952. They came with a purpose in mind as both were equipped with dual controls and steam generators. Twenty years later this unit was the same as it was when delivered except it was no longer shiny. When you had a combination of units that weren't exactly the same and in need of rest, you had a recipe for a knuckle or drawbar with a big train like 87. Mr. Anderson had no road or train handling experience to speak of. We would leave Markham with 182 cars. I asked him if he wanted to take the controls and he declined. I left the door open for later and he affirmed his original declination. I had to ask. We set out and picked up at Kankakee and received a message to pick up 22 cars of stone at Otto and set them out at Gilman (for Mr. Bogard?). That would give us 204 cars and would be the biggest train I had ever handled. This was not a normal train and couldn't be operated as such. Forget being in a hurry as this train had to be handled with "kid gloves". This type of train is always hindered by a plethora of cars that somehow escaped retirement and now we would have 22 loads of stone on the head end. You didn't want to use the air if it could be avoided. We were almost at 30 MPH and going through Ashkum when I went to throttle seven with the intention of slowing this train to 10 MPH for the siding at Gilman, using the engine brakes. That would give me about six miles to slow the train on a fairly level periphery. Once I finally unloaded the power, I would gingerly begin to start gathering the slack with the straight air (engine brakes). I was new to this particular game at this particular place and it showed when we headed into the siding switch at 24 MPH. It was only 14 MPH over the limit for this track. I had visions of stone cars lying on their sides when I elected to use the automatic brake valve (train brakes). If I use the automatic, I have to bring the train to a stop as there is no way that I'll get away with releasing 204 cars without separating the train possibly in a multitude of places. We stop and I release the air and wait a couple of minutes. Now the caboose should be released and the train should move. I can't get it to move, it won't budge. Finally the brakeman offers to walk the 22 car lengths to make the cut. We take the stone up to Gilman and come back and get the train. If the brakeman hadn't made the cut on the stone, we might still be there. Once we pulled the train into the siding and off the mainline, it will be time to eat. By the time we came out of "beans", the fleet would have gotten around us that being the two passenger trains numbers 1 and 53 (the Miami) and probably 71 the early "hotshot freight". We watched them all go by and then it was our turn. We would go into Champaign in good order. Our total time on duty was a hair over ten hours which wasn't bad for that job. Our lay-over was a little over ten hours and during that time I would show Mr. Anderson around town.

We were called for GC6 (Geismar, La.-Chicago). The crews always referred to it as the "bomb train" as it consisted of chemicals from around the Baton Rouge area. This train wasn't exactly an engineer's dream as almost always it would have huge tank cars (sloshers) on the rear end. It was usually a big train, but this day it was un-characteristically not a big train. That would be a boon to us as we would end up going into Markham with one unit out of three running. The middle unit was a GP40 that had put in a terrific performance. The lead unit was dead and when I "stretch broke" the train to a very quiet stop, it was different. I asked "Babe" jokingly if he was considering taking a road job on the IC side. He looked at me and muttered "I'm not going anywhere". It sounded like he was making his first and last road trip.

With every road trip I would make, it became more and more evident that the ICG wasn't as aggressive with its track maintenance program as it once was. Years before, we never had much power, but we had the track to run on. The railroad was always in "tip top" shape, the finest in the land. The situation was going the opposite way, as we now had plenty of power, but good track was slowly becoming scarce.

For a while SE1 was a 70 MPH train. It always had the newer, heavier SD40's.

These engines didn't ride well and if the track was less than perfect, they would bounce violently, the footboard of the engine quite often would make contact with the rail. Some engineers took it upon themselves to keep the train at 60 MPH with those particular units and it worked well.

I will have to refer to 1973 as the "year of the pilot". Along with C&O crews would now come Penn-Central crews. ICG was now implementing a jointly operated train with the PC. A PC Elkhart crew would bring their entire train into Markham and we would conversely run an entire train into Blue Island (Indiana Harbor Belt) with a Champaign road crew. When you considered the engine transfers (AMTRAK) and threw in the Pilot jobs, they really helped take the "sting" out of working that Chicago extra list. 1973 would also be the first year that I would be "set up" 100% of the time.

My wife tells me that she loves me but she doesn't like me. I thought about it for a minute and then agreed with her. We didn't like one another. What stage are we in?

Someone said that with the new orange and white paint jobs on the re-built power came the belief that now that they spent all of that money on paint that they would pull more cars. Sardonic humor prevails.

Chapter 13

⟋⟋

1974

I had made my miles by the 29th of December and so with a little luck I would be off over the New Year holiday, also. The way it worked out, I would be off four straight days which didn't make me mad.

Our marriage needed some quality time together and we enjoyed it. The kids were getting big.

The 11 o'clock north pull was open and I decided to jump on it for as long as it would last until someone would "bump" (seniority move) me. It was during this short period of time that it became known to me that the second unit of my double unit consist was providing a convenient service to a gang of thieves. They would load whatever it was that they were stealing on to the running board of the second unit. I wasn't aware of it until one night we were doubling one track to another and made a rough joint (coupling). When this happened, I noticed something fall off the side of the second engine. It was "time out" as I thought at first that we had damaged that unit. It was then that I discovered that it wasn't attached to the engine at all. Somehow a box of contraband had fallen out of a boxcar and onto my engine. At least that was pretty much how the head man (switchman) explained it to me. I wasn't happy about it but I said nothing. Later, the head man would ask me if I needed a couple of lawn chairs. At that time it was ten below zero and the last thing I wanted was a lawn chair. I am being put into a precarious position. These characters were always up to no good and working nights was right up their alley. One way or another, I'm a bad guy. I wasn't going to risk losing a job that played such an important role in my life. I chose to ignore it and to this day I don't know whether or not they continued breaking into cars and using my engine for a "goat" or not. I would later become aware that theft on the railroads in general, was rampant.

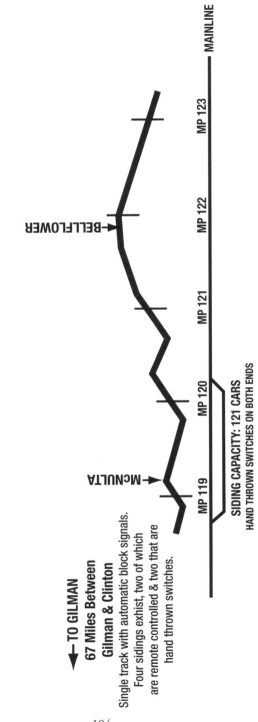

TRACK PROFILE MAP
ILLINOIS CENTRAL'S GILMAN LIME
MILE POST 118 TO 123

MAINLINE

MP 123

BELLFLOWER

MP 122

MP 121

MP 120

SIDING CAPACITY: 121 CARS
HAND THROWN SWITCHES ON BOTH ENDS

McNULTA

MP 119

TO GILMAN
67 Miles Between
Gilman & Clinton
Single track with automatic block signals.
Four sidings exhist, two of which
are remote controlled & two that are
hand thrown switches.

104

The Chicago & Illinois Midland Railway was controlled by Chicago based utility Commonwealth Edison. C&IM would generate coal which normally would move by barge on the Illinois River to Edison's Chicago facility. Every few years the river would freeze over negating any barge movement. This traffic would then be shipped by rail. The C&IM would give the coal to the IC at a place called "CIMIC" (guess how the two roads arrived at "CIMIC"?) Much of the C&IM fleet of hoppers was about ready for retirement because of deferred maintenance and the fact that many of the cars simply sat for lack of use. The cars that were in constant service ran less than 150 miles round trip from the mines to the barges at Havana. If the coal was interchanged with the IC that mileage diminished drastically to less than 40 miles.

Of course this upturn in business always took place during the coldest part of the winter and had a bittersweet effect. The IC had gained additional revenue and it created more road turns at a time when IC business was traditionally at its annual nadir. The down side of it was the challenge of getting these trains over the road without any unwanted fanfare (i.e. knuckles, drawbars, etc., etc.). The Gilman line was not conducive to moving coal regardless of the equipment used. It wasn't exactly a polished art by any means.

As a young engineer working the yard extra list, we were required to protect any road work that became available as a result of a shortage of road engineers. These trips were relished even though the thought of a coal train, especially one of those C&IM trains over the Gilman line, wasn't anyone's first choice. I was hoping for a more mundane challenge to my skills. It wasn't to be.

The call came for 2:30 AM. I personally cannot think of a worse time to go to work, nor to do anything else for that matter. The roundhouse (starting point) was located just short of a mile from the hotel. If the roundhouse had been situated over a mile from the hotel, then per union agreement, the company would have had to furnish transportation to the starting point. Most times, especially with inclement weather, a company representative would drive us, however at 2:30 AM there was no one available. We would walk that short mile carrying our grips and plying our way through the thick fog that morning. Luckily it wasn't cold, which was unusual for a February. Fog is never welcomed by any engineer and it intensifies when you take into consideration that I was a young engineer off of the yard extra list, with little experience on the Gilman line. Now the brakeman mentions that a young "hogger" off of the yard extra board caught a similar train out of Clinton the week before and got four knuckles somewhere around McNulta. I couldn't fathom a time on the railroad when the odds were more stacked against me, and began having thoughts of "should have stayed in school" etc., etc. We had one plus, it wasn't cold!

The train make up would consist of three units in various stages, differing in age, horsepower and paint jobs. Tucked behind the drawbar of the third unit would be 122 venerable, loaded C&IM coal hoppers.

We have our orders, the dispatcher gives us the signal at East Junction and the conductor is on the hind end. All were in accord the only dissenting element was the fog. Our train orders indicate that we will have to "meet" at least one train somewhere on the line. We are hoping that it will be Gibson City, as there are no switches to throw. We have clear signals at Farmer City but the order board is red. The dispatcher fixes a meet with not one but two southbound trains and at McNulta of all places. Our opposing trains are long trains of auto parts and are "hot". They won't fit into the siding at McNulta and the order specifies that we will take the siding.

Now this is a pressure situation. First of all, there is the fog. The fog will affect the performance of all three trains. Secondly would be my lack of experience. I would be running against two of the best engineers in the pool. The siding at McNulta lies in the middle of "hill and dale", or undulating territory not conducive to the handling of ancient coal hoppers. McNulta holds 121 cars. We have three units, 122 cars and a caboose. I'm wondering out loud if maybe I should simply stop the train and get off. The brakeman reminds me that there is no cab service around here as we are out in the middle of nowhere.

Rule 1210 in the timetable reads: Siding capacity is based on cars with average length of 50 feet and allows for four diesel units and caboose. Trains made up of cars less than 50 feet in length may be able to get more cars in sidings than shown in station column.

We would fit in the siding, however there would be very little margin for error, it would be a tight fit. For now I have to concentrate on stopping for the south switch or siding switch. If I run by the switch, it would be considered a technical head on "collision". First, 65 is just coming through Gibson City and wouldn't yet be at the switch to throw it for us. Forget about making any kind of textbook stop, just bunch it up, get it under control and stop this side of the switch. If the brakeman has to walk a few car lengths - so be it. If only I can see through this fog. My thoughts go to "they use McNulta about once a year for meeting trains, why me, why here with a train like this"? (but of course I was being facetious). In the fog? I will definitely give Ralph King, the job insurance guy, a call when I get home.

It was an accurate stop, the brakeman didn't have to walk far at all, I kept the train together, despite the old and rusted equipment. I considered myself lucky. As we began to move into the siding, the headlight of first 65 was showing up. I also heard the voice of the engineer of second 65 talking to the towerman at

Gibson City. By the time our train would be compactly tucked into the siding, both trains would have arrived. When our conductor announced that we were in the clear on the siding, we had about four car lengths of room on the north end. Hearing that, I drew a tremendous sigh of relief. We did it! We met two "hot" auto parts trains without a hitch. At a remote place called McNulta in the fog with a coal train of antiquated equipment and it worked. I was elated, relieved, but yet I was going to give Ralph King a call anyway. By the time we got to Gilman, the fog had pretty much lifted. We were complacent with the knowledge that we had just dodged a bullet.

My wife, since she was a little girl, has always wanted a horse. I would tell her that once we were out from under our bills and could finally see our way to financial freedom, she would get that horse. That time had come and she was promised a newborn filly by the name of Teja-Zane-Assad. That was a big day in our lives. Once "Teja" was old enough, we would show her. She was in two shows and produced four ribbons, including two for first place.

If you were to select a type of freight car that would be the most dangerous to work around, the flat car would win hands down. They are most cumbersome to get on and off of, they are extremely difficult to ride as they offer nothing to hold onto with any leverage whether you use the stirrups (footholds) or simply stand on its flat bed. Flatcars because of their low profile can be extremely hard to see. A crew may go into a track thinking that the boxcar they are looking at is the first car on the track. There may be one or two or more flat cars in front of it, however. Nothing should be taken for granted. One night we were doubling a cut of cars into another track and in one fell swoop I was knocked to the floor of the engine, after bouncing off the window. Up to that time, that was about the most violent impact I would experience. My "field man" was giving me radio car lengths and all the while concentrating on a boxcar that had seven flat cars in front of it. When he saw the flatcars, it was too late to stop me via the radio as he only had time to jump. Luckily there were no injuries or derailments and everybody walked away from it, a little smarter. "They don't call 'em widow makers for nothin'", one old timer quipped.

Union meetings were held monthly. I would go once or twice a year. The one meeting that always comes to mind is one where they were looking for blood donors for a certain retired engineer. One guy stood up and said that he would donate a "pint of cold piss" to the guy. I'm thinking, how did they come to call this a brotherhood?

I finally cornered Ralph King and went with a more extensive insurance policy. The policies would cover most rules violations, however Rule "G" (drinking) and insubordination were not.

Sometime during late summer of 1974 we decided to pack up the family (including my sister Kathy) and take a three day weekend. We would go up to Fond du Lac, Wisconsin, which sits at the foot of Lake Winnebago, hence the name "Fond du Lac". The family would have a diversion, as would I, and I also would be scouting around for a new job. Soo Line had extensive facilities here. Train crews worked both north to Stevens Point and south into Chicago. I was able to talk to the general roundhouse foreman and he said that he would hire me if I came back Monday morning. That was too easy. I chickened out. If I only knew then what I know now. It was an interesting vacation, however.

AMTRAK was toying with a turbo-train that they brought over from France. AMTRAK used the old GM&O coach yard as a maintenance facility. I was called to pilot the train from Brighton Park to Union Station. It was interesting. I was on duty for 45 minutes, the time consumed to get the train downtown. A guy needed a good day here and there.

Only a few days after the "turbo-train", I played a major role in causing $12,000 in damages to a switch engine. I had a fairly new head man. The yardmaster at Harvey told us not to use a specific track as there were engines "in the foul" on one end of it. It was our last move, getting to the "oil track". I don't think the head man quite understood what the yardmaster meant and by the time I realized what we were doing, it was too late. We had just sheared off the battery box of a 1200 type switch engine. Two weeks later we have an impromptu meeting with Eddie Enzenauer. Both the local chairman and Enzenauer are urging me to take five days off and to waive the investigation. I would be the only crew member to be subject to discipline because "I knew better". Sign right here. Enzenauer tells me that I could start the five days anytime I wanted. I would be getting seven days off as I had my miles made and coincidentally, my job insurance would "kick in" for those five days. I was also fortunate to have increased the coverage. I often wondered if Enzenauer ever caught on? I took an additional four days at the beginning of September and had a total of eleven days off. I went up north, fishing.

The phone rings very early one morning. I am being called for the "sludge train" at 3:10 AM. That means thirty-six cars of liquid fertilizer, a by-product of "you know what", from the Chicago Sanitary District for the fields of southern Illinois. We wonder why they can't run a train of this nature at a more conventional time, after all there isn't anything particularly "hot" about this train. The brakeman opined that maybe they don't want the "normal" world to know what they're hauling. We laugh. We would come back on GC6 (the bomb train), being on duty five hours. We made the round trip in less than 24 hours.

Anytime a crew can make a road trip, including the layover in less than 24 hours, they have done well.

Right before Thanksgiving I get a call from an irate Ralph King. You will remember that Ralph sells job insurance. He begins by berating me with the fact that he had just gotten off the phone with some insurance executive and he told him that I had pulled a fast one on him and that they couldn't combine the two policies again. As they had already paid me five days, they would let it ride. Ralph didn't appreciate my "duping" him. I said nothing. Whatever I did was completely by accident, but if he wanted to think that my business mind was sharper than his, so be it. I beat him at his own game and wasn't even trying. Ralph also mentioned something about me "hitting" on his wife. Bear in mind that over three months had lapsed since I last talked to Ralph. He lived fairly close to us and so I drove over there to sign the insurance papers. I was introduced to his wife who was probably 25 years my senior. I may have said something a little on the flirtatious side. I liked to "schmooze", but it was all in fun. Ralph, in so many words would more than admonish me to stay away from his wife. No problem.

Chapter 14

1975

The first three months of 1975 were spent firing AMTRAK with either Johnny Taksas or Harold Falkenthal. I would also work the early local with Joe Rivard.

I was set up for good in April. Our anniversary was the 16th of April and on that date I would catch #50, the northbound counterpart to #51, the all piggy-back manifest. This day #50 would be a very short four cars plus the caboose. For power we had the standard three GP40's. Speed would not be our problem today, stopping would. Short little trains don't break so easily, especially piggy-back flatcars. We had more than enough power and so the engines would be a hindrance because of their weight. I'll never forget the fog that day. Always a bane to any engineer, it was as thick as I had ever seen it. Leaving Champaign I couldn't see the home signal at Leverett Junction until we were right on top of it. The signal was clear and our train accelerated to 75 MPH in a hurry. I was apprehensive to say the least. Forget seeing anything sitting on a road cross-ing. A signal could not be seen until we were right there! And I thought "if I get a yellow signal-put the brake valve into emergency" other thoughts went to "why not keep it at 50 MPH" to "it's what I do" We were lucky enough to have all green signals and the fog mercifully lifted around Kankakee. I would run that train at 75 MPH almost the entire way. As I sit here writing this, my thoughts go to "would I do it again, the same way?" I'm much older now, and I know from experience that as you get older you get wiser. I might also have a little "shit" in my blood along with everything else I'm not supposed to have in it.

It wasn't much of an anniversary, especially with the prospect of having to go back to work right away.

Ever since the hysterectomy, my wife wasn't really herself. Instead of being friends and lovers sharing a common goal we became adversaries. If it hadn't been for the kids, our marriage would probably have ended a long time ago. The railroad deserves to be mentioned because of the overall anomaly that it contributed. I will also blame myself. When you put these three factors together, nothing good happens.

One beautiful summer day, late in the afternoon and during the rush hour, I would grace the Chicago Terminal with 145 loads of coal destined for Lake Michigan and beyond. As I came across Steunkel Road, I initiated a minimum reduction of the train line. We had over 140 cars which meant that I would have to maintain the 30 MPH for coal trains of 140 or more cars on the terminal. I drew off the seven pounds of air and then notched down on the throttle. From Steunkel it is predominantly downhill. Regulating the speed of a big, heavy coal train is not an easy task. After pulling this train with the brakes set for five miles or so, we began to see smoke trailing from the train. As we passed the Flossmoor Station, our train was smoking profusely. The IC big shots were coming home after a hard day at the office and couldn't help but notice the smoke. Before we hit Homewood, the Markham General Yardmaster came over the radio announcing that someone had just called him and said that a coal train coming through Flossmoor had "sticking brakes". Answering him, I professed that I was the culprit and that the brakes were sticking by design. I then thanked Illinois Central management for their assistance.

Over the summer, I discovered the G.I. bill, and managed to use it for a year. I would attend a class on Tuesday and Wednesday evenings. They paid for the books and tuition along with a bonus check for $192.00 per month. With my hours or lack thereof, I didn't think that I would be able to complete the courses. I was lucky as it turned out, I only missed three classes out of a total of four courses. I was catching the right jobs at the right times. I remember working engine transfers three days in a row for an average of just over three hours each day.

It was at school, that I confirmed what I already knew-that I wasn't cut out to sit in a classroom. I was determined to make it work and I passed all four courses, two of them by the skin of my teeth. Alas, school would soon be out for me as I neglected to use my G.I. benefits when I should have. You had seven years from your release from active duty before the time lapsed. Looking back I realized that I couldn't have gotten the maximum out of it as I wanted to be an engineer, and the railroad would provide the only education I would get.

It was at this time in our marriage that we both realized that it was over. There were times when I didn't come home, leaving lipstick smeared filter cigarettes in the ashtray. I would be spending time in one of the bars, which railroaders frequented, with one of my female classmates. My wife saw the writing on the wall. She was a cocktail waitress and it wouldn't take her long to find a boyfriend. We were being cruel to one another. It was time to go. One day she screamed at me for tracking mud into the kitchen. I had just dropped a railroad tie on my foot and was hurting. I received no sympathy from her. She pushed the right button-I moved out. It was all over but the shouting. The kids were old enough to understand that our relationship worked out better if we didn't have one.

By this time our championship horse was losing her importance. My wife would use the four ribbons to entice the services of some local lawyer. The horse was half Arab and half quarter. There is a competition class for half breeds and our horse had "shown" well. Everybody found out later (especially her lawyer), that once you leave the show ring, a half breed horse isn't worth feeding. When the attorney saw those ribbons, his eyes must have had dollar signs in them. He was duped.

All the while this was going on, my wife assured me that I wouldn't need a lawyer, if I "played ball". When I would catch a suburban job during the week, I would sometimes get three or four hours off during business hours. I would use that time to sit in on divorce proceedings. Always the woman's lawyer did the talking and the guy's representative would simply stand there. I felt that I could do that and do it well, and for the price of a three piece suit and a briefcase with a comic book and a ham sandwich in it, I would look quite capable.

I wasn't in my new apartment very long when I realized that I had lost my mouthpiece. I would have no one to lie for me. There was no one to tell the crew caller that I wasn't home. I would have to invent a voice (my own voice) for this purpose. A high falsetto type female voice would suffice. This worked for close to a year when finally one day one of the smarter crew callers queried, "Bud, is that you?" I couldn't control myself and busted out laughing. That particular ruse would no longer work. The thought of being single and on the extra list was depressing. The normal world played on the weekends but young engineers with little or no seniority, went to work.

We would go to divorce court on the 11th of November, 1975. The divorce was granted and we agreed to the afore mentioned stipulations. The judge had no time for me as I was representing myself and of course because of biased laws which always ruled in favor of women. We were both happy that it was over and rode home together with her girlfriend. I looked good in my three piece suit.

It was about that time that pilfering was approaching astronomical propor-

113

tions. One night I was working a south pulldown job at Markham. Someone had broken into a carload of expensive baseball gloves. It looked like spring training around there, everyone had a glove.

I thought that sooner or later the well is going to run dry. This can't go on much longer. It wasn't very long after that that the IC gumshoes (cops), set up a sting. Apparently they rigged a car so that its door was ajar. Someone told me that the car was made to look like it was full of television sets. Sure enough, here comes the ringleader and he takes the bait. As soon as he stepped into the car, it was lights, camera, action , and you're under arrest. The guy ratted out 22 fellow rail workers that somehow aided, abetted, or simply bought the stolen items. There is no honor among thieves.

April of 1975 was another month spent on the extra list. I randomly selected this month because it was a typical month for working everywhere. I will talk briefly about each day in an attempt to enable the reader to better understand what working the extra list was about.

April Fools' Day brings a call to work an "Extra North Pulldown" at Harvey. Any job at Markham was relished as I only lived eight miles from there. It was a 4 o'clock job and because it was an extra meant that we could and would be doing anything. We were tied up before 10 o'clock and so it must have been a good day.

The following morning the phone rings at 5:30 AM the caller wants me for CM1, a road job. Road jobs were always welcome as it was fun to run a big train at speed. It also was a change of pace and was a good opportunity to get caught up on sleep. CM stood for Chicago-Memphis. Apparently it wasn't a good trip as we were almost ten hours on duty. We were well rested as we laid in Champaign almost nineteen hours. We caught BC4 (Birmingham-Chicago) and did a little better working six hours.

By the way, I should let you know that all of the details are coming out of a time book. There isn't room for particulars, and I kept no diary. This all happened almost thirty-five years ago and isn't easy to remember.

Friday morning comes early. I am called for an 8:00 AM extra job at Hawthorne. We made 30 minutes overtime and I got to drive in heavy rush hour type traffic both ways. My luck doesn't change as they call me for GM&O job #7 which is a strict transfer job from Glen to Markham and return. We worked the full twelve hours. Of course there would be that long drive home, but it would at least be Saturday traffic. As I am driving, I am contemplating laying off for a day or two. But no, I'll wait maybe get my miles in early. I don't know how I did it back then. It was a good thing I had the wife at the time, to make sure I got out of bed. Sunday morning, it's 3 AM and the phone rings.

I'm hoping it'll be a road job, but alas the engineer on the 5 AM Chicago Produce Terminal job lays off. I hated those CPT jobs. I'm gonna spend the whole weekend in the car. Another long drive into the city for a lousy 30 minute quit. That night I would get called for 87 at 10:40 PM. It would also be my second start for the day. For straight time I might add. You can't get time and one half when going from yard service to road service or vice versa. 87 was the division drag that always ran in the wee hours picking up and setting out at Kankakee and Gilman. They always made sure you were at capacity when they added sixty or seventy empty coal hoppers to the hind end of your train. In spite of all that, we did pretty well being on duty only 5 hours and 15 minutes. We were off duty a little over 15 hours. We were called for a 7:00 PM Inland Steel coal train. It wasn't such a hot job as we were on duty 10 hours. I did get caught up on my rest in Champaign though. Tuesday afternoon I got called for another 4:00 PM Extra North Pulldown. We had another good day on it, tying up before 10:00 PM. Wednesday morning brings a call to work the 8:00 AM Relay job at Randolph Street. I hated working any relay job. A relay engineer gets a switch list from the yardmaster and he makes couplings or un-couples cars specified on the list. You were a walking switch engine. The relay man has to stay the full eight hours as he is also their ace in the hole should another engineer not show up or gets sick. It was boring. At least I could ride the train downtown and it would be "time and one half on account of working in yard service twice within 22 1/2 hours". After working that relay job for time and a half I'm thinking that I deserve a day off. Thursday would be an R&R day.

I didn't get called until Friday night. The engineer on the Hawthorne Transfer was a GM&O prior rights guy. He didn't like working seven days a week and so he would lay off quite often. It really burned me up. This guy doesn't have anywhere near the railroad seniority I had, but I had to drive all that way to be his replacement. He didn't know shit from apple butter about running an engine either. He must have had pictures of the caller performing an obscene act because they always let him lay off. We made two hours overtime. The weekend is upon us - so what.

At 3 AM the phone rings. This time the caller beckons me for the 5AM Clearing. As you probably know by now, clearings are transfer jobs and depending on the crew, can either be a quit job or an overtime job. This day I had the overtime variety and we worked the full 12 hours. Come Sunday afternoon It's the 4 PM Extra North Pulldown again. The last three times I've caught this job we have tied up at 9:45 PM. A rubber stamp. I tally my mileage for the month and I am at 1772. Remember a day's pay constitutes 100 miles and I am allowed 3200 miles for the month. It looks as though unless the list really slows down,

EXAMPLE OF A TYPICAL MONTH ON THE CHICAGO TERMINAL EXTRA YARD LIST.
THE FOLLOWING PAGES WILL GO INTO EACH TOUR OF DUTY IN DETAIL.

MONTH OF APRIL 1975

DATE	TRAIN #	PLACE	ON DUTY	OFF DUTY	PLACE	TOTAL TIME	DAY
4-1	EX NORTH PULL	HARVEY	4:00 PM	9:45 PM	HARVEY	5'-45"	TUES.
4-2	CM1	WOODCREST	7:40 AM	5:25 PM	CHAMPAIGN	9'-45"	WED.
4-3	BC4	CHAMPAIGN	12:30 PM	6:35 AM	WOODCREST	6'-5"	THURS.
4-4	EX VARIOUS	HAWTHORNE	8:00 AM	4:30 PM	HAWTHORNE	8'-30"	FRI.
4-5	GMO#7	GLEN	7:00 AM	7:00 PM	GLEN	12'-0	SAT.
4-6	PRODUCE TERM.	CPT	5:00 AM	12:30 PM	CPT	7'-30"	SUN.
4-6	87/CP1	WOODCREST	10:40 PM	3:55 AM	CHAMPAIGN	5'-15"	SUN.
4-7	INLAND COAL	CHAMPAIGN	7:00 PM	5:00 AM	WOODCREST	10'-0	MON.
4-8	EX NORTH PULL	HARVEY	4:00 PM	9:45 PM	HARVEY	5'-45"	TUE.
4-9	RELAY	RANDOLPH ST.	8:00 AM	3:30 PM	RANDOLPH ST	7'-30"	WED.
4-10	LAID OFF						THURS.
4-11	HAW. TRANS	HAWTHORNE	10:30 PM	8:25 AM	HAWTHORNE	9'-55	FRI.
4-12	EX CLEARING	HARVEY	5:00 PM	4:59 AM	HARVEY	12'-0	SAT.
4-13	EX NORTH PULL	HARVEY	4:00 PM	9:45 PM	HARVEY	5'-45"	SUN.
4-14	LAID OFF						
4-15	CM1	WOODCREST	9:45 AM	4:55 PM	CHAMPAIGN	7'-10"	TUES.
4-16	50	CHAMPAIGN	5:00 AM	11:05 AM	WOODCREST	6'-5"	WED.
4-17	EX NORTH PULL	HARVEY	8:00 AM	3:15 PM	HARVEY	7'-15"	THURS.
4-18	ENGINE TRANS	WOODCREST	12:00 NOON	1:30 PM	LUMBERST	1'-30"	FRI.
4-19	ENGINE TRANS	WOODCREST	1:30 PM	3:30 PM	LUMBERST	2'-0	SAT.
4-20	WEPX	WOODCREST	12:30 AM	6:50 AM	CHAMPAIGN	6'-20"	SUN.
4-21	LAKE COAL	CHAMPAIGN	1:25 AM	8:25 AM	WOODCREST	7'	MON.
4-22	CLEARING	HARVEY	5:00 AM	2:20 PM	HARVEY	9'-20	TUES.
4-23	LAID OFF						THURS.
4-24	SOUTH PULL	HAZELCREST	10:30 PM	5:00 AM	HAZELCREST	6'-30"	FRI.
4-25	CN5	WOODCREST	8:40 PM	8:00 AM	CHAMPAIGN	11'-20"	SAT.
4-26	DF	CHAMPAIGN	10:30 PM	4:05 AM	WOODCREST	5'-35"	SUN.
4-27	NORTH PULL	HARVEY	3:30 PM	9:30 PM	HARVEY	6'-0"	
4-28	OFF, MILES						
4-29							
4-30							

116

I'll get a few days off and so I take Monday off. "Laying off" must have changed my luck as on Tuesday I get called for CM1 at 9:45 AM. It was a mediocre run as we were on duty seven hours and ten minutes. On the rebound we caught #50 the hot piggyback train. It was a good run being on duty only six hours and five minutes, when you consider that we take that train to IMX (intermodal exchange). IMX is located in Bridgeport, which is in the city. Once the train is yarded, the light power is returned to Woodcrest-25 miles. We were flying as #50 is a 70 MPH train. Thursday morning brings an 8 AM Extra North Pulldown which worked a little over seven hours. Nothing to write home about.

On Friday I stand first out after the day board has been called. Quite often they will put on an engine transfer around noontime. Yep, sure enough, I get the call for an "engine transfer" at Woodcrest for noon. We took an engine to Lumber Street (the old Pennsy passenger engine facility taken over by AM-TRAK). When we arrived there the foreman said he had nothing and to go back, so we grabbed a cab to Randolph Street and rode the IC suburban train back to Woodcrest. That was a good day at only 1 hour 30 minutes on duty. That helps me to forget some of those bad days. My good luck continues as I get called for another "engine transfer" on Saturday. This one is called for one thirty. We do the same thing we did the day before, only we're on duty a little longer at two hours. I guess it all balances out. Nine hours later I get called for a road job (straight time). There are empty coal hoppers coming from Wisconsin Electric Power (WEPX) bound for the mines of southern Illinois. The train was delivered to the IC at 67th Street and we got it there, hence the 136 miles. Once we got on the train we went right along. The layover in Champaign was just short of 19 hours and we got plenty of rest along with two hours and 35 minutes alimony. Alimony is another way to say "held away from home terminal in excess of 16 hours". That is all pretty much covered in another chapter.

The return trip would be on a "boat coal" train. These trains go to 94th Street. The latest contract negotiation stipulated that the road crew would deliver its train to the BRC (Belt Railway of Chicago). We lucked out and didn't have to deliver it. Seven hours on duty for a boat coal train isn't bad. On Tuesday morning the phone would ring bright and early for the 5 AM Clearing. Usually an overtime job, we made an hour and twenty minutes. I'm getting tired and I'll have my miles in early and so I decided to lay off Wednesday. I wouldn't work until Thursday night on the 10:30 PM South Pulldown at Hazelcrest (Markham). The "South Pull" jobs make up the southbound road trains. We had a good night tying up at 5 o'clock. Friday night brings the call for the road again on CN5 (Chicago-New Orleans) at 8:40 PM at Woodcrest. My records are strictly basic facts. I took no notes, however the time off duty tells me it wasn't a good trip as we worked nearly 12 hours. As a rule this train rated three GP40's. This night it was given two GP9's and a GP38. CN5 had quite a drop in status that night. They used to say that the revenue collected from CN5 for one trip would pay the IC payroll for a week. Our layover in Champaign was 14 hours and 30 minutes. We were called for a "Dead Freight" at 10:30 PM. A dead freight was just a fancy word for "drag". These trains were ran for many reasons. We had good power and went right along being on duty only five and a half hours. I would work one more day and have my 3200 miles in. The call came for the 3:30 North Pulldown and that is where I will spend my Sunday afternoon for the next six hours.

That being completed, I will have the next three days off and beginning on the 1st of May the entire process starts over.

Frequently when business is good and there is a shortage of engineers, the company along with the unions blessing, will waive the mileage, and we get to work the entire month. Sometimes it is an option left to the individual.

Probably more than any other location, I worked at Markham Yard and it would be a good idea to say something about Markham.

Markham Yard is divided into smaller yards. Trains with northbound loading coming from the south will enter into "A" yard (north receiving yard). "A" yard is the smallest yard with eleven tracks of which the longest track only holds about eighty cars. Trains are "humped" into the 64 track "B" yard. North pulldown engines will couple, double and pull these tracks into "C" yard, the northbound departure yard.

The process for southbound loading is reversed. Trains from the north will enter the 22 track "D" yard at Harvey. Cars are "humped" into the 47 track "E" yard. Once cars are coupled, they are doubled up and pulled into "F" yard, the southbound departure yard. The rip track has eleven tracks. "Rip" stands for "repair in place". If you count the humps, Markham has five starting points and is one of the largest freight classification yards in the world.

At this time I would like to discuss two rules in the rule book, Operating Department Rules 106 and 107. But first I will explain the circumstances that led to the following letter. One day in May I was called for NC6 out of Champaign for Chicago. NC 6 was a hotshot and we had less than ninety cars, some of them empties and good power, two GP40's and a GP38. We had a good running train. Coming into Kankakee we heard AMTRAK #381 call the operator at KX Tower advising both him and us of his location. Of course it would have been a sin for us to stop this big freight train for that dinky little passenger train. I knew it would be close, but I thought I could make it without delaying him. I guess I did delay him a little bit when you figure the many exaggerations that a conductors pen contains. Both the conductor and engineer on #381 may have forgotten about their days out on freight. Basically it wasn't a misjudgment on anyone's part. It had the same effect that a driver experiences when he approaches an intersection and the signal goes to "yellow". Does he keep going or does he come to a screeching halt? In other words—it could happen to anyone!

The bi-product of this event is that not only did I receive a letter, but my conductor also received one. We both were chastised for an event that occurred on the head end. He shouldn't have received a letter, he was a mile away.

I will now extend to you the letter:

Kankakee, Illinois
May 20, 1975

Engineer A. L. Hoekstra
Conductor W. B. Olmstead

Gentlemen:

It has come to my attention that on Friday, May 16, 1975, while you were working as crew members on train NC-6, engine 3061, you delayed Amtrak train #381 at Kankakee for six minutes account you had him blocked from station platform.

Operating Department Rule 107 states as follows:— "Trains or engines must not pass between a passenger train and the platform at which traffic is being received or discharged, except where proper safeguards are provided."

Unnecessary delays to Amtrak trains such as this will not be tolerated and, in the future, you should use your radio to ascertain if a due Amtrak train is getting close to the station at Kankakee or Rantoul and, use your good judgment so as not to cause any future delays of this type.

Any future violations of this rule, on your part, may result in formal handling.

A. L. Phipps
A. L. Phipps
Trainmaster

Obviously you have read the letter. Now allow me to quote the rule or rules that generated the letter.

We will start with rule 107. "When a passenger train is receiving or discharging traffic, a train or engine must not pass between it and the stations unless safeguards are provided".

And now let's go to the tumultuous rule 106. "The conductor and the engineer are responsible for the safety and protection of their train and the observance of the rule's, and under conditions not provided for by the rules must take every precaution for protection". It goes on to say…."The general direction and government of a train is vested in the conductor (if more than one conductor, when trains are combined, the conductor with the most seniority), and all persons employed on the train must obey his instructions, except they will not comply with any instructions which imperil the safety of the train or involve a violation of the rules. Should there be any doubt as to the authority for proceeding or safety the conductor must consult the engineer who will be equally responsible for the safety and proper handling of the train".

More egregious doctrine follows…. Conductors and engineers must know their subordinates are familiar with their duties, ascertain the extent of their experience and knowledge of the rules, and instruct them, when necessary in the safe performance of their work. Another beguiling distraction to this rule reads: When the conductor is not present, trainmen must promptly obey the instructions of the engineer relating to rules, safety and protection of the train.

Other crew members, after carefully reading track warrants and track bulletins must keep them in mind and assist in their observance, call attention of conductor or engineer immediately to any apparent failure to observe their requirements, to clear the main track as required, or to comply with rules and instructions.

When safety of trains and observance of rules are involved, other crew members are responsible to the extent of their ability to prevent accident or violation of rules.

When the conductor or engineer fails to take action to stop the train, and emergency requires, other crew members must take action to stop the train.

Conductor must advise engineer and dispatcher of any restriction placed on equipment being handled.

MAXIMUM SPEED: Conductors and engineers are jointly responsible for ascertaining the maximum authorized speed for the operation of their train or engine and such speed must not be exceeded. Passenger speed is applicable only to trains consisting entirely of passenger equipment.

When possible to do so, employees must promptly advise the train dispatcher of any known condition that will delay or prevent train from making usual speed.

Rule 107 is a very practical rule, you don't want to cut out a passenger train while it is loading and unloading. There are baggage carts and mail trucks pulled up to the train and possibly fouling the other tracks and most importantly, there are people coming and going. This situation is almost always avoided when the engineer of the passenger train knows there is a freight train approaching the depot, he will lay back a little and avoid stopping in the depot thus preventing the doors from opening and nobody can get off. It didn't work that way in our case. I'll bet that passenger train may have left Kankakee a bit late but I'll also bet that he left Champaign on time.

Those things are usually covered up by the crews, in this case it wasn't. Our conductor, 90 cars away was the scapegoat. I never got a chance to apologize to him. It wasn't fair.

Rule 106 has probably been the most controversial rule in the book. It has always been the source of dissension between engineers and conductors. For crews that always worked together, it was never a problem. This rule has been written and re-written several times for a myriad of reasons. Both management and labor have shared mixed emotions when rule 106 was brought into the picture.

Crews have always tried to keep their business to themselves. However, the way Rule 106 is written, it expects the crews to run around whining about everyone and everything.

Now that almost every road crew is down to two men, both in the cab, a lot of the egregious crap will take care of itself. That almost makes me sound like I'm for cutting jobs. I'm not.

Chapter 15

1976 - 1979

The 9th of March 1976 brought me to Joliet Yard. Joliet was a "satellite" yard and formerly a GM&O property. Someone mentioned the fact that they needed another engineer. There was a very strong possibility that I just might be that engineer and it would be my ticket away from that Chicago extra list. I called the "call board" and planted the seed. The list wasn't moving very well at that time and that would be one for my side. I didn't work the following day and after the call board officials mulled my request over, the call came on the morning of the 11th. "Okay Bud you're zoned in to Joliet. For now you'll have to work the 3:00 PM yard job as the engineer on a vacation vacancy, also because you're the youngest man, you will have to protect any extra work on the weekends. When there is no engineer work, you can fire the job of your choosing". Okay? Of course it was okay! I began to worry....that was too easy. It was definitely a reason for exuberance. I would have some consistency in my life. I would have only one starting point, no more stifling traffic, just 22 miles of country roads between Richton Park (my home) and Joliet. No more exasperating suburban combinations to decipher. It was a win, win situation! There was a down side, however, there would be no more big road freight trains to handle at speed. It was a small price to pay for some semblance of normalcy. Joliet would have four jobs counting the "plug".

The regular engineer on the 3:00 would be on vacation for another week and then I would move over to the other side when he came back. We worked together for a week and then I didn't see him again. He was having some health issues. In a few days I would hear that he retired. The job was mine. You don't like to see anyone endure physical hardship, but sooner or later everybody has to quit for whatever reason. That's how the seniority game is played.

The 3:00 was almost always an overtime job due to the Montana coal trains we would get for the Commonwealth Edison plant down on the river.

Joliet handled anywhere from one to three coal trains on a daily basis. The trains originated at Cow Creek or Decker, Montana. While these mines were quite near one another, interestingly, they ran over different routes. One of the routes coming via the Twin Cities while the other came via Galesburg, Illinois.

These trains would ultimately come into Eola (BN-Aurora) and would be turned over to the Elgin, Joliet & Eastern (EJ&E) for the twenty four mile trip to Joliet. The "J" would give us those trains at Collins Street and we would eventually spot them at the power plant officially located at Plains, Illinois out on the Pequot line. That line is owned and operated by the Sante Fe and gives the GM&O (ICG) trackage rights between Plains and Pequot, which is near Coal City. Plain's is three miles south of Joliet.

A typical day on the 3:00 would be to bring the yard engine down to the yard office and await further instructions. Usually we would switch cars for an hour or two and then depending on how the coal train situation stacked up, we would grab the BN road power and go down and pull the empties, deliver them to the "J", come back to the yard by taxi cab and finish our switching and then go to "beans". After lunch we would run our engine up to the south end of the yard and get on another set of BN road power that was attached to a loaded train delivered earlier that day. One track wouldn't hold an entire 100-105 coal train and so a 30-35 car double would have to be made. Coal wasn't in the picture when they laid South Joliet (official timetable destination) out. Once the double is made and all requirements are met, we would then proceed to the power plant. Once the train is pulled down in its entirety far enough so that we can get around it, we cut off and run around the train on the mainline.

Now we are going to tie on to the hind end and shove it into the Edison yard in four pieces or cuts. Once our "field man" is picked up, we head for the yard office. We'll either "tie up" or wait for another coal train. We don't care, we're on overtime. The yardmaster puts the phone down as we're walking into the yard office. "Coal train at Collins Street at 1:15 AM you'll have to take it and store it on the main, set the overflow over to #3 track". Our foreman jokingly tells the yardmaster that he hopes that that will be all because there won't be any time left we'll be close to the 12 hour limit.[1] If that train falls down anymore, "someone's gonna have to eat it".

An interesting aspect to changing from one power consist to access another (single unit is a consist) was that a few years back the IC and the BLE signed an agreement which stipulated that "when an engineer changes power for the convenience of the company, he or she will receive 15 minutes compensation. If a second change is performed, 30 minutes will be paid. For a third change, one hour will be paid, and one hour will be paid for each change thereafter". When I first read the agreement, I didn't think it would ever apply to me as we rarely ever changed power once much less two or three times. Another reason for not claiming the changes would be the fact that the GM&O engineer didn't have that agreement and I was working in a GM&O yard. One thing for sure, I reasoned, I definitely won't get it if I don't claim it. Nothing ventured, nothing gained. We would see.

Of course what makes any job a good job, are the people around you. Working in harmony with people you like, sure helps take the sting out of those long hours. On the 3:00 I was working with the best crew on the GM&O.

Payday came and sure enough the engine changes were paid. Some nights I would get as many as five changes. That translates to 4 hours, 45 minutes extra pay. Also the heavier coal power elevated the daily rate to a higher scale.[2] Factor in the overtime that went 15-20 hours a week. Add an occasional day off worked for time and one half, and I was riding high. Coal was definitely my favorite tonnage commodity. Always as an afterthought - I would hope that my ex-wife wouldn't get wind of the sudden surge of financial security that was coming my way.

About the same time that I came to Joliet, Gerry Harmon was promoted to Assistant Trainmaster and became the supervisor in the Joliet scheme of things. I knew Gerry from his brakeman days out of Markham. Gerry was a good guy to work with and a good guy to work for. I don't know how true it was, but Gerry supposedly had a bet with an EJ&E official that I would get an empty coal train to Collins Street at a certain time. I had no idea that there was a wager in the works. Harmon won the bet.

Eventually I would get "bumped". The day guy wanted to make some money. We changed jobs. Now I was the regular engineer on the "day job". I got bumped and actually moved up the ladder. Working the 7:00 would better fit into my plans as a single man. I would be on that job for almost a year. I knew sooner or later, someone with "prior rights" GM&O seniority would want my job and when it happened - I wasn't surprised. I simply moved from one side of the cab to the other and became the fireman. It would be a smooth transition as the new engineer was a good guy.

I remember a coal train we were bringing from Collins Street to store in the yard. I was running the engine and had stopped many a coal train short of the signal. At Joliet tower this day the towerman was letting a Rock Island commuter train go and the signal was red. I began preparing to stop where I always did but this train didn't respond. I finally had to put the train into the "bighole"[3], and when it stopped we had to get off the engine to see what side of the signal we were on. It looked to me like we were very close, but I think we got by it. The towerman said nothing and was able to give us the signal. As we went across the diamond we looked over at the tower and there was no indication that anything was wrong. I mentioned to Mullins that maybe we had better stop at the tower on our way home and try to smooth it over. I told the towerman what happened and I don't know if he was kidding, but he said that when it happened there was both a Sante Fe and Rock Island superintendent in the tower. When they questioned it, he simply told them that I may have left the sanders on and that is what "shunted" the signal. Whew! We thanked him. I have found that during the course of my career simply telling the truth always worked better than trying to come up with some story out of "left field". One Sunday morning (my day off) the phone rang calling me for an extra job. It was probably a coal train. I took the call and went back to bed. When I got to work Monday morning the yardmaster reminded me of what happened and said that "Bonner" wants you to call him. Ken Bonner was the superintendent and was known to be a fair and just man. Bonner answered the phone, I told him exactly what happened and his comment was - "being that you fessed up", we'll let it go this time. Bonner was a gentleman.

I had already been at Joliet well over a year when the fireman's position on the "plug" came open. The plug was a three car commuter train that ran from Joliet to Chicago Union Station and return. The engineer would be my old friend C. T. Anderson. About four years prior to this, on the IC side, I would pilot[4] "Babe" on #87, the longest train I would ever have. Now our roles were reversed. "Babe" was a prior rights GM&O engineer. The plug (nos. 16 & 17) started work at 5:35 AM and would not be back to Joliet until after 7:00 PM. It was a long day. I was glad that the job was only open for a week. It was to be a prelude of what was in the future.

My next job would be on the 4:00 PM "Blockson" industry job, another prelude to future events. This job was to put it into a word "egregious" to my lifestyle, but still far better than that Chicago extra list. I would work that job for close to six weeks before the regular guy came back. The job worked almost 12 hours daily and at least the pay was good. Olin Chemical owned the plant. It was a grotesque place to say the least.

I would pretty much finish out the year firing the 7:00.

1978 would bring about a drastic change. I would be the fireman on the plug until further notice.

I've been working with "Babe" for a couple of weeks now. When you work with a guy here and there, it isn't long enough to get under one another's skin, but after a period of time, you start to notice things. Every day our civility toward one another got more and more tense. My first clue that this guy was a jerk was one morning when we stopped at the bumper post at Union Station and he got off the engine in a big hurry to get into the concourse where he could greet his passengers and let them know that he was the engineer. When I stood next to him, he moved away. He didn't want to share the spotlight with me. I'm not exactly Clark Gable, but apparently I threatened the guy. He was a throwback to the fifties what with constantly combing his black greasy hair and the ducktail. I think that maybe part of it was that he resented me because I was an IC man working in GM&O territory. Some guys will hold on to that for a long time. He had no reason to feel that way. The IC men got the short end of the stick in the merger negotiations.

One day he casually announced that—"tonight you can run the train back to Joliet". That was fine with me. Splitting the work is a good way to go. That night I'm sitting in the engineer's seat and "Babe" enters the cab through the engine room after visiting with "his women" on the train. He says; "Bud I'm in a hurry tonight so I'll run the engine". No problem. My thoughts went to the time when we had over 200 cars on a freight train and he wouldn't run the engine to how important he became running this little three car passenger train. I'm not "throttle happy", but I wasn't exactly enthralled with being the crux of one of his ego games. He pissed me off! A few days later he asked me if I wanted to run the train and I declined. That's when the shit hit the fan. All of the bottled up tension began to come out. He threatened to kick my ass, and I admonished him to "bring a big lunch", because it wasn't going to be easy. He finally shut up when I made the vindictive comment that "I forgot more about railroading than you'll ever know"! We didn't talk for about a week. Time has a way of healing old wounds and we eventually began to become amicable, although I felt that we both would have been happier if I had gone elsewhere.

One early morning "Babe" doesn't show up. We're between a rock and a hard place. We had two ways to go, either sit tight and let the "powers that be" dictate our moves, or keep it quiet. After all, I was a qualified engineer and had been on the job quite a while and yes, was running the engine on a daily basis by then. The conductor said that he could put the flagman up front to be the fireman. We elected to go with the latter. All was going well until we stopped at Willow Springs then who should climb up on the engine but the "west end" traveling engineer. As long as I had been on the job, nobody has ever ridden up in the cab with us - until now of all times. The first thing he says is where's Babe? All I could say was, I don't know. He then launched into a tirade which led me to believe that I was the bad guy and that he wasn't focused on the catalyst of our problem. Our next stop was Summit and if he didn't cool down by then, there would be another reason to keep quiet. I asked him, what would you have done? Nothing was said. He apparently didn't take it any further, although I'm sure he had a word or two to say to Anderson. Babe fumbled twice that morning as he not only forgot to come to work, but he also forgot to go home to his wife. They didn't call it Romeoville⁵ for nothing. Babe was a Vietnam veteran and he used to keep the "dollies" swooning by showing them pictures of dead Viet Cong that he carried around with him.

Shortly after I started working at Joliet - Connie came into my life. We dated for a while and shortly thereafter I moved up to the second floor. Connie was a social worker for the state and of course worked a normal day job. After six months had gone by, I began to toy with the idea of buying a ring. Summer came and went and alas, our relationship began to sour. I bought a town house and moved out. It was a mutual split. See ya.

Meanwhile back on the railroad. I was working the 3:00 for a couple of weeks and on one of those days while I was cheerfully jumping from one power consist to another, the yardmaster comes over the radio and tells me to stop at the yard office when I had the chance. Later we went to "beans" and I asked the YM what he wanted. When I saw the sly grin he was trying to hide, without success, I knew it wouldn't be good for me. Now he is exuberant and tells me that he just talked to someone in accounting and that person told him that because I was an IC man working in a GM&O facility, I no longer was authorized any engine changes. I wondered what took them so long. It was hard to believe to begin with. At first I was hedging on incredulous but he was having so much fun with it, that it must have been true. I congratulated him on his ability to project humor and deigned that he have a "nice day".

One summer day I was running the 7:00 and we were switching from the "bottom end" (south end) which we rarely did. Here comes Eddie Enzenauer driving the superintendent, as he usually did when he wasn't operating radar somewhere on a speed trap. You remember Enzenauer from the "air car days"? Bob Morgridge relinquished his traveling engineer's job and went back to Freeport, running an engine. This created the opening that Enzenauer relished. Enzenauer was not one of my favorite people. The Chicago Terminal was split in half. There was the "west end" (Glen, Joliet, Hawthorne & C&IW) and the "south end". Bonner had one side, and Bob Mills ran the other, which was at Markham. Suburban service was separate. They were referred to as "terminal superintendents". The guy Enzenauer was with was the "superintendent" period. He ran the whole show. He was the big boss. This day Mr. Biscan is driving and Mr. Enzenauer is his radio man. I notice as they drive by. We are making a six car double to another track with one guy relaying sign's on the radio. Enzenauer's voice comes over the air. He is trying to call Joliet and is oblivious to our radio transmission. It was slipshod radio procedure by the big shots. I should have stopped the engine then and there but we worked through it until I was thrown off my chair and into the window. Now I'm pissed off. The same guy that was always writing "chicken shit" notes about some petty violation of the rules was now showing us how it was done. It was a violent impact, but only my feelings were hurt. We went to lunch when we finished our work on the bottom end. I was still mad. I went into the yard office and told Enzenauer what I thought about him "walking" on our radio communication while we were working. I also mentioned that he should practice what he preached. By now I'm getting the feeling that I've said too much. Biscan was talking on the telephone, but I knew that he was trying to monitor my exhortation. Enzenauer is sitting there hearing me out. His facial expression told me that I had better get out of there. Biscan had a reputation for having a short fuse and I can see that his neck was very red and all of that blood was heading for his forehead and I wanted to be out of there before it got there. As I swung the door closed, I can hear Biscan slamming the phone down and bellowing "what did that man say"? And again, this time a little louder, "what did that man say"? Right then and there I knew that I hadn't exactly enhanced my career and if Enzenauer or Biscan ever had the chance, I would be looking for work elsewhere. Another rolaid moment. I would have loved to have been a fly on the dashboard of that sedan when they drove back to Markham, though I wonder if Biscan let Eddie drive.

We had a basset hound that used to hang around the yard office. Either we adopted him or vice versa. The guys always said that he would be a big dog if he had longer legs. They would poke fun at his genitalia and would wonder how he kept it from dragging on the ground. The poor pup took the brunt of many a joke and while I'm on the subject, I think it's time for "animal stories".

One fine day we were waiting for the "J" to show up at Collins Street with about 105 of those black diamonds. A young lad of about ten and his dog (a young beagle) came over and sat down. The kid told us that he had to find a new home for the dog because his parents wouldn't let him keep it. I didn't think that I could keep it either, but I thought that I could find someone that could provide a good home for him. That was good enough for the kid and then the train showed up. Have you ever tried to climb up on a locomotive with a wiggling, squiggly beagle in your clutches? It ain't easy.

We managed to get the pup into the cab and the first thing he does is to jump up on the engineers seat. My sense of humor immediately took over. How would the good citizens of Joliet react when they espied this 14,000 ton behemoth being operated by a beagle? The pup stayed in the seat, I stayed back and pulled the throttle out, getting the train to move. Now all I had to do was pull out the bell button and the beagle was on his own. He stayed right where he was as if he was getting paid to run that coal train. Coal trains weren't real popular around Collins Street, but if anyone forced to wait for our train had seen that pup up there sitting in the engineers seat, he would have laughed until he cried. It also didn't make us railroaders look too smart. I mean if a dog will do it for nothing why should they pay us the money they so vehemently contest. By the way, the pup went home that day with our very capable chief clerk - Amy Nelson. A good home indeed!

And of course we can't forget the owl. We were handling a coal train one fine day, as we did almost every day. Thirty to thirty-five cars would have to be doubled into the yard someplace. The cut could have been made in four or five places, depending on the guy that makes the cut. As the switchman stepped between the cars to turn the anglecock, he steps away as he hears this unexpected "hiss" emanating from a most unusual source. It was a great horned owl perched majestically on the drawbar sill of a coal car in a train that originated in Montana. Somehow the poor bird broke a wing and rode between those coal cars from wherever it happened, all the way to Joliet. Everyone had a theory as to how the bird got there. The operation at South Joliet was on hold until the animal people got out there and threw a net over it. I later heard that the bird would be released into the environment. Would a Montana owl be at home here in Illinois? This would not be the final owl story, it seems that railroads are magnets to animals.

For the next three months, I would be bouncing around between the 7:00 AM, 3:00 PM, or 4:00 PM as either the engineer or the fireman. Remember they kept me around Joliet as their one man extra board. It was looking like I would finally end up on the 4:00 PM Blockson (or Olin) forever. The word had it that the regular guy was beginning to realize that there were better jobs and that he had the seniority to hold them. My only recourse would be to either work the Blockson job or go back to Markham (Chicago extra list). The lesser of the two evils would be to stay at Joliet. Another factor that was slowly beginning to rear its ugly head, of which I hated to think about, was that at the time of the merger the GM&O had five or six guys on their engineer seniority roster that had very little overall seniority, but because of prior rights, it didn't take much to be older than me. These guys were getting a taste of the Chicago extra list and were probably being badgered to break into suburban. That would cause anyone to start looking for greener pastures. It happened, and in all honesty, I have to say that I didn't blame them for coming down to Joliet. It was survival of the fittest or in this case, the one that survived would be the guy that bene-fitted the most from the merger agreement. It's called prior rights!

When all was said and done, the dreaded 4:00 PM would become my new home. After Connie and I split up the thought of having to work the "Blockson" was right up there with a trip to the dentist. It definitely would stifle any pro-jected adventures I had as a single man. The Blockson worked long hours and that would leave only the weekends, provided I didn't get called for a coal train. It was a bleak picture. I would have to suck it up and take my poison. That was more than just an exaggeration. After all, it was a chemical plant!

While I was in the process of accepting this radical change to my lifestyle, we had an influx of new people. The switchmen's list needed new blood due to a retirement and an injury or two. The first kid was the son of a superintendent down south somewhere. I mentioned to him that I remembered his dad when he was at Kankakee. The next kid was the son of a west end engineer working at Hawthorne. Shortly after that they hired two more kids from around Joliet. The Blockson job would have a new look. Having a new and inexperienced crew would be frosting on the abjective cake. My thoughts of having to switch Blockson each night for the next 10 or 12 hours was not without poetic over-tones. One day I comprised this poem:

With antipathy these men of stygian darkness go,
Each night with sordid regularity, into this plethora
of uncertainty, into this maelstrom of hot gasses, chemical
mists and potions kept secret.
Into the dark, dank and rancid network of acrimonious
parameters go these brave men each night, into the
sounds of asperity and with temerity only to emerge from
this abyss of vapors, to come in from the cold, the rain and
this workplace called Blockson.

I couldn't have written this poem without the help of Dan Webster, Olin Chemical Co. and J.R.R. Tolkien. Edgar Allen Poe was also thought of.

I have to admit that for new guys these kids caught on easily. I had been toying with the possibility of having a fireman. Now that I was officially on the 4:00 PM, there was no one to take my place as the Joliet "extra board". I mentioned that to Gerry Harmon and he wondered if maybe Bruce Hartman would be interested. You remember that back in 1972 Hartman along with Harmon, made a trip to Clinton with me? Even if Hartman liked the idea of coming down to Joliet, there was no guarantee that he would mark up on the 4:00, however, he would be available for the weekend coal trains and such. I called Bruce and he said that he would think about it. He didn't think about it for long, because the next day he was at the roundhouse when I came to work. Good! That would take a lot of pressure off of me and make the job a lot more bearable.

The way the job worked was that we would bring the engine out of the round-house, tie it on to the track we were made up on, and get an air test. Once the air test was completed and everyone was in compliance, we would shove the train down the Pequot line a distance of less than two miles. Someone on the caboose utters "ten car lengths to the switch", following up with additional commands until the switch is gained and our train is stopped. Once we enter Blockson, it is time to see the "list man". The list man is an Olin employee that acts as a liaison between the switch crew and the plant. It is also a good time to take a coffee break. Our foreman studies the switch list and ponders the work load. Most days there is enough work to more than simply "burn the midnight oil". On occasion everything looks like it will fall into place and we try to finish early. There are nights when it can go either way, depending on the weather, our foreman's frame of mind, etc. etc.

National Lampoon would have gotten a few ideas from watching our crew. They were a wild n' crazy bunch and I often wondered when the Olin higher ups would make an appearance and put an end to our shenanigans. That never happened, however our "liaison man" disappeared one day, replaced by a relative of some Olin official. And then the weather went bad. I remember on one occasion we couldn't get out of the yard because of the snow. Olin began to complain to the ICG that they weren't getting any productivity out of their work force, because they couldn't get a proper switch. Now we were getting two units. One night Bruce and I were having a discussion over the merits of the GP9 versus the 1200 HP switcher we now had. Our ordinary power was always a GP7 rebuild or a GP9, usually a rebuild. This day we decided to put the engines to the test. My money was on the geep. Bruce put his fiver on the SW7. The geep would have 1750 h.p. and the switcher had 1200 horses. The switcher won and Bruce pointed out that the SW7 was geared lower. I wanted to make sure that everyone knew that the geep was pulling up hill and pleaded no contest but to no avail. Luckily we were in a place where we couldn't easily be observed. We quickly coupled the units back together making sure all hoses were re-connected, when someone came over the radio and wanted to know our location. Had ICG management been exposed to our little motive power contest, this story would have ended right here. Bruce would always say - "relax, they're short of engineers".

One night we had an unexpected visit from an ICG official. Bruce Hartman was on vacation and I had an engineer trainee. The trainee was running the engine and I sat on the other side, critiquing him. The guy wasn't readily absorbing the myriad of knowledge that I was plying him with. Finally our "visitor" climbed up on the engine and more than admonished me to "run the engine". That was the only time anyone ever showed up that we knew of.

Our foreman had friends in high places. Quite often we would "tie up" earlier than the time slip would indicate. We would be headed for home sometime after two o'clock and the foreman would make it four o'clock on the time claim. This made me nervous as I was equally responsible for what was on that time slip. My rationale always would be: "they're not gonna fire me, because they sure as hell aren't gonna fire him". Time for a rolaid.

One bright sunny day, after the snow had finally quit, the aftermath of it was left in huge stacks. In some places it was piled in the middle of the highway. When Bruce and I worked together, we usually had lunch in New Lenox. I had bought a Volkswagen Rabbit with a diesel engine in anticipation of the many long country drives I looked forward to. The car was brand new. We finished lunch and headed for Joliet. I was leading the way and going about 50 to 55 MPH when my bright sunny day went to darkness in a hurry in the form of a dark blue van. Some dodo came out from behind one of those giant snow piles and simply pulled out in front of me. I didn't have even a split second to react. He was there! His wife was watching for trucks and busses but not necessarily for little VW Rabbits. It was a new version of roulette. Bruce was directly behind me and saw the whole thing. He told me that he had me scratched off the seniority roster even before my car stopped spinning. The driver of the van didn't even get a ticket. I got a bruise on my right knee and my ego sustained a setback as I wasn't too thrilled about living 22 miles from my workplace and not having a car. I was tickled to be alive, however. Let's hear it for German engineering! That car was designed to take an impact such as what I had just walked away from. Luckily I hit him behind the passenger door in about where the sliding door was. Had I hit him in the passenger door, he would have been looking for a new wife. I rode with Bruce to So. Joliet and we had a conference with the yardmaster. It was decided that one of the guys would drive me to the hospital and then home. I checked out okay at the hospital. The job would work short-handed and the fellow that drove me home after the hospital visit would also go home once his mission was completed. Nothing was said to anyone about the accident and no further legal action was taken. The accident happened and then was put to rest. I was damn lucky that I had a ride available because it took a good six weeks to get another new car also Bruce let me use his van. I didn't relish walking the 22 miles to work, nor did I want to transfer back to the Markham or Chicago board. This occurrence would be the harbinger of a long string of bad luck events. That same night the guy that drove me home ran off the road and did some damage to his vehicle. There was more on the way.

Bruce's van had a few quirks that took some getting used to. It was a column stick shift. It seemed as though you could only go from neutral to first gear if the van wanted to, as if it had a mind of its own. Sometimes the lesser of two evils was to walk. Many a Saturday night went in the dumpster because I was leery of the van. However, it beat walking and always got me to work. I was lucky to have it.

One Saturday morning I drove over to my ex-wife's house to pick up the kids. It was the usual time on the usual day. I got no answer when I rang the doorbell. I looked inside and the place was empty. Somehow they sold their house, packed up lock stock and barrel and vanished. I am devastated. Words cannot describe how I felt that morning.

A few days later, I came to work and one of the guys met me in the parking lot with more bad news. Rich Holly, one of our newer guys, was found dead in his van early that morning. He was a young guy with a wife and a couple of kids. It was another very sad event.

When we weren't encountering any particular setback, we always had the weather. It was one of the worst winters I could remember. Most days it was very cold and everywhere there was a thick blanket of snow. There was many a time during that long, lonely winter when I thought....if I can get through this, I can get through anything, and I didn't mean the weather exclusively. All the long winter we tried to overcome our abjective dilemma with idiotic behavior and sheer lunacy. During these beleaguered times if there should be a lull in the depression, one of the guys would taunt me about getting bumped out of Joliet. Maybe one of the GM&O kids would make a seniority move and I would be on the bus heading for Markham where Mr. Enzenauer could keep an eye on me.

Spring finally and mercifully came. I became a big fan of melting snow. We had just come through a winter that had everything - and it was all bad!

My new car had arrived and the world was fast becoming a better place. "Beef" Anderson came on the job. Beef was an older head GM&O engineer that up until lately had worked what was called the "oil job" that switched the industries between Glen Yard and So. Joliet. Beef was a character.[6] He used to always say to me in his "down home country twang" "that Enginehouser fellers gonna get you". Beef was an okay guy, but after working with him for three weeks, I decided that he would be even better if he was on some other job. Not mine. As luck would have it, we were both able to kiss the "Blockson" goodbye. Beef went back to the oil job and I jumped on the 3 o'clock.

All that summer I bounced around. The Regional Transit Authority (RTA) was a recently formed agency that monitored commuter operations in the Chicago area. They were experimenting with a new train. The "plug" (16-17) always ran into Union Station at full capacity and there was a demand for a second train. That would create two more jobs for enginemen at So. Joliet. Once they finally came to a regular starting time, it might not be a bad job, but until then I avoided it when I could.

I was able to work the 7 o'clock job for three weeks in July. I always entertained thoughts of retiring off that job, but that was a dream. Sometime during that period we had an incident occur that would have had dire consequences had I not been vigilant. One fine day we delivered one car to the Rock Island over on the east side of Joliet. They had a small yard with about ten or twelve tracks over there. This day there was only one car in the entire yard and that was the car we had just delivered. The Rock Island had an engine working or at least on duty. We cut the car off, tied the hand brake on it and came out on to the ladder track and headed for home. We stopped to line the switch back and now have the adjacent track fouled. I look up and I see their engine, an ALCO C-415 with a center cab come trundling down that track, just as pretty as you please, and he wasn't stopping. If I hadn't leaned on the whistle, he would have broadsided us and almost assuredly turned us over. That crew was oblivious to our presence. The yard was empty, what could they possibly have been thinking? I don't think there was much thought given to railroading. Nothing was said and we left. That was our last move and would have been an odd way to end the day - turned over on our side. How would that one have been explained? You have to stay on your toes when you are dealing with massive machinery. Even the most minute error can result in tragedy.

Babe Anderson would be going on vacation for three weeks and I would take his place. Babe may have had some wonderful qualities, but running an engine wasn't one of them. He was, to be blunt - a lousy engineer. The plug made nine station stops between Joliet and Chicago Union Station. Each stop had a desired "mark" to stop the train. Babe was so engrossed in stopping the train at the precise mark, that he never gave his technique much thought. As long as the train was stopped at the mark, he was an ace engineer. It didn't matter how he stopped. Had we much more than three cars, I'm sure somebody would have gotten hurt. Even a three car train has enough slack to affect the quality of the ride. He would shut the throttle down and use the independent (engine brake) along with the train brakes, once he would see that he was going to stop short of the mark, he would sometimes release the brakes and open the throttle or simply pull out the throttle and literally drag the train to the stop. He would be either standing people up or sitting them down or any combination of the many tricks he had at his disposal. He had such a tremendous ego, that he couldn't ask anyone what their thoughts were concerning his train handling prowess. He was the best!

They say that vengeance is a dish best served cold. If ever there was a chance to shatter someone's ego, it would be during the next three weeks. I wasn't preoccupied with embarrassing him, but this was extremely hard to resist.

I never had to work too hard at train handling, as it came easy for me. I was also willing to learn and had good teachers. These people needed a taste of what smooth train handling was like.

Every day we would pull into Union Station and I made sure that the passengers could see who was the engineer and who wasn't the engineer. As soon as we stopped, I would quickly head into the concourse so that the passengers could see why they were able to nap or read the paper, or maybe simply enjoy the smooth ride. One guy said; "It looks like I can put the neck brace away". Another stated; "I thought all trains were jerky and hard to stand up on". A woman said that she is once again learning to relax so that she can take the nap that she was once accustomed to. All of that was good for my ego. I would have loved to have been there when Babe came back off vacation. I'm sure he was expecting the passengers to breathe a sigh of relief when they saw that he was back. I later heard that he was the brunt, both openly and candidly, of their sarcasm. It wasn't too far in the distant future and Babe would be looking for greener pastures. After much conjecture, the RTA would officially establish a second train complete with designated times. Actually the second train became the first train as it left Joliet 30 minutes earlier. 5:05 AM was a very early time to be going to work. We didn't tie back up in Joliet until 6:30 that evening. The routine was the same as the plug except the times were different. We went on duty thirty minutes before we left So. Joliet. Once we left the depot in Joliet we would consume one hour and five minutes to our destination (Union Station). Once the passengers were unloaded we would have to vacate that track, shoving the train the ten miles back to Glen. At Glen the train would be serviced both inside and out and the crew would be released and would be on their own until 3:50 PM when the process would be repeated in reverse. Within that all day layover there was almost nine hours to kill. The GM&O provided a bunkhouse that was in disarray. About all it had was a washroom and a place to flop but it was home. You became an expert at "time utilization & consumption". As soon as the train was secured at Glen, the fireman and I would walk up to Archer Avenue and have breakfast. Archer Avenue was one of the few streets that ran into Chicago at on angle. It would roughly parallel both the

GM&O and Sante Fe all the way to Joliet even though at times they were miles apart. Archer was a busy street and had many shops. It was about a mile from Glen yard give or take a foot or two. I got to know it well and it became my "one stop" place to shop. If you wanted lunch, you could do it again or dine at the little tavern not far from Glen or wait until you got back to Union Station to sample faster cuisine. Once you received the "highball" from the conductor, all that was needed was the signal, which we referred to as a "pot". In the rulebook it was called a "low home signal". The "pot" now shows lunar (white) and we can proceed cautiously to the next signal, which indicates that we will be crossing over and soon will be on the GM&O (ICG) mainline and everyone will be heading for home.

Unbeknownst to me at the time, was that trains 18 & 19 would be the last job I would ever work on the Illinois Central Gulf. I was growing more and more despondent over the loss of my children. It had been nearly ten months and I hadn't received as much as a forwarding address. For all of the things my ex-wife was....the one thing she wasn't was a bad mother. I knew that she would take care of them wherever they were. Over the last few years I began to wonder about leaving the Chicago area. The two reasons that I stayed, was the fact that I would soon have 20 years of service on the railroad and of course the kids. The kids were now out of the equation. All that was left was this lousy job that had me by the throat. There would be no more opportunity for one of their officials to fire me, I would no longer be under the gun, I would beat them to the punch, they could take their job and shove it. The more I talked about quitting and hiring out on another railroad, the more I painted myself into a corner. I would ultimately have to quit because of my big mouth. That was provided that I landed another job somewhere. I would soon be going on a three week vacation. We would see.

Horace Greeley said...."go west young man" and west I went. Found out in the western plains would be the long divisions of the Union Pacific, Santa Fe, and the Burlington Northern. On these long divisions enabled a guy to make a lot of money and do it fast as they ran their trains at 60 to 70 MPH. That was for me. I could see myself passing a long string of semis with some 70MPH hotshot. Bring it on!

My first stop would be Omaha, Nebraska, home of the Union Pacific. There I would find out that all of the hiring is done through the Nebraska Job Service. I wasn't a resident of Nebraska and was told that the UP wasn't hiring anywhere. Someone had heard that the Burlington Northern was looking for engineers at Lincoln, Nebraska's capitol. Remember, I'm on vacation, and driving all over places I've never been is what I enjoy doing, so I will happily head for

137

Lincoln. My stay in Lincoln wasn't for long. I talked to a roundhouse foreman. He also told me that the hiring was done through the state. He also volunteered that the guys that could steer me in the right direction were out of town. He hadn't heard of any hiring going on anywhere on the vast BN system. I was beginning to feel relieved. If I struck out, I wouldn't have the heavy burden of having to make this momentous decision.

I would make one more stop and that would be in Minneapolis at the Soo Line building. The Soo Line had a good reputation and I thought that I would look good running one of their SD40's that we would see on the many transfer jobs they had around Chicago. I wasn't very optimistic and I felt that if I make this last stop, I can honestly say that I went job hunting. With the thought in the back of my mind that I wasn't going to be there very long.....I parked in front of the main entrance, you know the one that always has an assortment of signs prohibiting everything except breathing. No this, no that, no nothing. One hour later when I came back down, there was a ticket on the windshield of the VW. A new adventure is about to begin. I never looked back.

---

[1] Our crew wouldn't have time due to the "hours of service" to handle the train. Either the BN or the EJ & E would have to hold it somewhere on their property.

[2] Enginemen's pay scales are determined by the total weight on the drivers of the locomotive consists they are operating.

[3] Bighole is only one of the many terms used to describe putting the train brake system into emergency.

[4] Rules & Regulations of the Illinois Central operating department define "pilot" as an employee assigned to a train when the engineer or conductor, or both, are not fully acquainted with the physical characteristics or rules of the railroad, or portion of the railroad, over which the train is to be moved.

[5] Romeo or Romeoville was a station stop for 1 & 17 and had a nightclub or two.

[6] Not to be confused with Babe Anderson.

Chapter 16

Sand

At this point in our venture, I would like to talk about "sand".

QUOTE: Rule #144 in the Illinois Central handbook for train handling states: *Sand should be used to prevent slipping, but not used to stop slipping. When necessary use it without hesitation; if not necessary DO NOT USE SAND.*

Soo Line goes a little more in depth as stated in their Air Brake, Mechanical and Train Handling Rules. Rule 511 entitled "Use of Sand".

QUOTE: Rule #511.
A. The use of sand increases the adhesion between the wheel and rail and is beneficial when properly used. However, excessive use of sand can increase train resistance or lateral forces. During operations under which high lateral over vertical force ratios may be generated such as when heavy dynamic braking forces are employed in curve territory, the use of sand should be held to an absolute minimum. The use of excess sand will also cause increased maintenance costs due to damage sustained by exposing certain components to an abrasive substance.

When stopping a short train, it can also result in failure to shunt the signal circuit thus indicating that the block is clear.

The normal use of sand is to prevent wheel slip while the locomotive is in power. Improved wheel slip detection and correction equipment on locomotives built after 1985 has eliminated the need for manual sanding at speeds above 5-7 MPH.

Sand can be useful when braking to avoid sliding wheels where the rail is slippery due to rain, snow, dirt, or oil.

B. Sanders must not be used over the movable parts of a power operated switch or spring switch.

ONE NIGHT ON A COAL TRAIN

Most railroads powered their coal trains with just enough locomotion to keep the train moving, hence the crews termed these trains "drags". Illinois Central was not different. Sometime in the fall of 1969, I caught a trip off the extra board in pool freight service. We worked to Clinton and Champaign, Illinois; this particular trip took me to Champaign.

Well rested, after a layover, we stood for a northbound "boat coal" train. We were called for 2:45 PM and the caller was right on the money with his estimate. Callers and dispatchers are notorious for giving bum information. You learned that that was part of the game.

Our train was sitting on the northbound main when our taxicab pulled into the yard. That was always a plus. I also noted the 5053 in the lead and a pair of GP9's behind. The 5053 is one of ten GE locomotives with six axles and 3300 HP. They were new to the IC for two reasons: up until recently IC never owned a powered six axle locomotive and they were exclusively GM-EMD all the way. Apparently an obscure monopolization law forced the IC to purchase a total of sixteen locomotives from GE and six from Alco.

Coal tonnage spends much time on the long hills of the Illinois Division. Behind our three units were 153 loads of "black diamonds". This proved to be a challenge on the hills for the power. It was raining and that can often be the straw that breaks the camel's back. Our sanders were minimal due to the dampness. I was told by the "old heads" that "you don't need a lot of sand, just enough sand". With that thought in mind, I crossed my fingers and hoped for the best. Rain isn't conductive to good traction, either.

Once the engine inspection was completed, it was time to get permission from the yardmaster to pull the train down to pick up the flagman. Having accomplished the aforesaid, we wanted a favorable signal indication at the north end of the yard; that would be a "high green", and it was.

We wondered out loud on how the dispatcher was going to squeeze us through the gamut of opposing passenger trains, not to mention the one that was scheduled behind us. The conductor said something like "that's what God made CTC[1] for". Dispatchers don't like to stop coal trains and the dislike is more intense when it comes to passenger trains.

We were leaving Champaign on the northbound main and would reach CTC territory at Gilman, 47 miles away. Our major concern was the three hills that would truly test our locomotives. The first one started near MP112 and was the ruling grade on the Chicago District. The hill is two miles in length and we would get a slight run at it passing Rantoul. Once we got over "Ludlow", we would be in hill and dale territory and the train would more or less roll on its own.

Let's take a minute to evaluate the train. One hundred fifty-three cars make the train about 1 1/4 miles in length. Our power consist represents 6,800 HP and should be enough to complete the mission.

When these coal trains are put together in western Kentucky, no room for error is left. Economics and efficiency worked hand in hand here. We got over Ludlow in good shape and now it was time to ease up on the power output as this train was now picking up speed and working a full throttle might result in the extraction of a knuckle or drawbar or possibly a multiple combination of both. The slack in the train was "bunched" on the head end and "stretched" on the rear. If somewhere in the middle of the train, the slack action suddenly decided to go in two directions, working a full throttle would be detrimental. My rule was to reduce the throttle one notch each time I felt the slack change. Ultimately, once the train got over the hill and dale terrain, you would be in throttle two or three depending on how your train ran.

After we successfully negotiated the 20 miles or so of hilly profile it was time to begin gradually bringing the throttle back to the "8" position or full power. We were approaching Gilman and hadn't seen a yellow signal yet. We noticed, as we headed north, that the sky was getting darker and darker and the rain was probably not going to let up. This night the conductor chose to ride the head end in order to help expedite the train movement once we reached the Chicago Terminal. Anticipation was synonymous with good train handling and my conductor and I were doing just that. Our chances of being stopped were becoming more and more possible as we got closer to Kankakee. We wondered out loud about the whereabouts of numbers 5 and 9, the southbound Panama Limited and the following Seminole.

As the scenario unfolded, we realized that if we had to stop due to either train sitting at the depot loading passengers, would not be a good thing as we needed all of the momentum we could for the four mile hill that starts at "KX" Tower. We approached the home signals at Otto and neared Kankakee. It would be a good idea to ask the operator at "KX" as to the location of number 5. Good news! The Panama wasn't by Manteno yet and we calculated that we would have plenty of time to get by the depot. It also looked like we would slide through Kankakee with all green signals. Normally, the speed through Kankakee was 25 MPH, but this day we had a 10 MPH over the K&S Diamond and it was at that exact location where our biggest challenge started, the four mile hill over Indian Oaks. If we could get over Indian Oaks then we would be okay on Monee Hill which is identical to Indian Oaks in grade.

The rain was now driving hard as we nosed over the K&S Diamond as number 5 passed us. Then number 9 came by. Now the train was on the hill and my thoughts went from "if the dampness hasn't clogged the sand hoses we should be all right" to "I'd give my right arm for another unit about now". We were now at the "flip of a coin stage" and were down to 12 MPH with yet another mile to go. I noted that this 5053 I was running was sure earning its keep. The speed recorder was now showing between 9 and 10 MPH. The conductor yelled over the din of hard pressed machinery something about not wanting to double the hill in this rain. About that time, I wondered if, with the windshield wipers continuously being used and the air operated sanders on continuously, if this critical moment would somehow remotely deplete the train line air causing sticking brakes. It wasn't in the book, but we were at the stage where a trick of any kind was better than no trick at all. The conductor shut his wipers off. I did the same. The head brakeman walks up from the rear unit. More good news! He said the rear unit was only loading 150 amps, not much we could do about that then. We could only keep our fingers crossed and ride it out. Suddenly, we saw a flash and then we heard a "whoosh". That would be number 8, the Illini. He was doing a little better than we were. He was going close to 80 as he passed us. We plodded on, slow but sure. We topped the hill and the needle on the speed recorder began to slowly go the other way. With any luck at all, we would get our speed up to about 25 MPH before we begin to feel the rigors of Monee, the next hill to be encountered. I breathed a sigh of relief. If all went well and our sand held out, we would make it over Monee and onto the Chicago Terminal at Steunkel Road. Steunkel is at MP31. Old timers used to say you could kick a boxcar from Steunkel and it would roll all the way to the Chicago River.....and with that I had a new dilemma-keeping the train at or under 30 MPH. There is a 30 MPH speed restriction on coal trains on the terminal as duly noted in the special instructions of our timetable. The topography changed and so did my train handling technique. Cresting Monee, I decided to set the air (train brakes) at about 18 MPH while half the train is still rolling uphill. With the first service reduction I made on the train line, I could now begin to gradually reduce the power. The train rolled easily for the next ten miles or so. Train handling on the terminal was challenging. Any time you used the air on 153 cars of coal could be risky business. All it took was a leak in the train line toward the rear of the train and you had the recipe for a knuckle or a drawbar or worse. Many factors come into play.

IC had just begun looking at dynamic braking at that time and it would take years for the crews to familiarize themselves with its operation. Using dynamic braking correctly took time and preparation and the "north end" wasn't really conducive to it. Our engineers had been handling all types of trains for many years and pretty much had a technique of their own that worked pretty well for them.

The rain subsided and we yarded our train at 94th Street. A yard crew will later deliver this train in two cuts to the Belt Railway of Chicago and they in turn would take it to the Rail to Water facility for loading on a boat.

It was a good run even though we had problems with our rear unit. Once we rolled at Champaign, we never stopped, green signals all the way! The train crew never felt a drop of rain, I might add.

The Illinois Central was a class railroad run by good men-with good men. My final thought came again to sand. I would say that we had "just enough sand" and of course we will never know about the windshield wipers.

WORK TRAIN

One early summer morning I was called for a "work train" that would start out of Illinois Central's Woodcrest Shops and would tie up at Gilman, 60 miles south of Markham. We would be there a week or five days. This day I would have a fireman. I inspected the engine, a GP9 that met the prescribed requirements. It was only a little after seven o'clock and already it was hot. We went up to Homewood to pick up our orders and the balance of the crew.

Bill Olmstead was the conductor. That was good as Bill is always good to work with. We had a good crew, always important especially on a work train. Olmstead had a message that read "pick up your caboose and go directly to Gilman and report to J.D. Bogard, section foreman". Down to Gilman we go. Stopping at the depot for further instructions we encounter Mr. Bogard and about ten of his men. They were ready to go to work, but we didn't have the cars of stone that they needed. We were supposed to pick up 25 cars of ballast at Otto. We shot through Otto at about 60 per. Bogard was clearly in an agitated state while he was trying to explain to Bill that we were supposed to get the rock at Otto on our way down. Bill showed him the message, it said "caboose hop" to Gilman.

Bogard has been a section foreman since before time. He ran a crew back in the days when the foreman would pay his men according to what they had coming after he deducted the money for shoes, gloves, rotgut booze and female companionship. It was your one stop place to shop. That was pretty much how it worked all over the system. Some of those guys didn't get paid, they owed the "company store"!

It is time to call the dispatcher for authority to run to Otto for those cars we didn't have. Bogard wasn't a happy camper, however the guys in his crew were happy, they were all catching an extra curricular siesta, lolling in the shade of the depot. We had to retrace our steps going back the 20 miles or so to Otto, get the cars, test the air and return to Gilman. This would take well over an hour. One of the problems with work trains, especially our situation is that the train crew started work at a much earlier time than the section men. This imbalance could not be avoided. The two different crews would have conflicting agendas and did little to generate "good working harmony".

Once we returned with the cars from Otto, it would be time for lunch. By now Bogard is livid. We ask him about lodging. It was his responsibility to provide both transportation and a place to stay. The timing for this request wasn't the best for this, I noted, as I studied Bogards face. Mr. Bogard told us that he would fix us up with a motel within walking distance of the depot. That would be fine.

Lunch is over and it is time to collect our cars, get our air test and shove the train 12 miles north to the work site around Clifton. We were going to spread stone at about 1 1/2 to 2 MPH. This is where these section men earn their money. It is bad enough working in good weather but the temperature was over 90 degrees. There weren't many obese section men.

All in all we probably dropped stone for about 2 1/2 hours. It wasn't an optimum performance by any means. J.D. wasn't going to pay his crew any overtime and so we would be heading for Gilman to tie up. During the course of events we ran out of sand. There is not a good way to determine how much sand you have, but you assume that the roundhouse forces would fill it to the top, when they service the engine. This wasn't the case, with a full tank we shouldn't have run out. It should have lasted the five days we were going to be out there. Now I have a dilemma, should I bend the rule and try to work without it, or should we head for Kankakee in the morning for a re-supply of sand.

That decision would be made shortly after we found out that Bogard never did talk to the motel people. Instead of staying at a convenient location we would have to walk over a mile out to the crossroads motel. We were carrying our grips and we were tired just from the heat, and we weren't happy with Mr. Bogard. Tomorrow would be different. It was now a game of us against him.

We went to work at seven the next morning. It would be another hot one. Because there was no transportation available nor was any provided, we didn't leave the motel until seven. By the time we arrived at the depot, it was well after seven. Now the bulletin board had to be read, and then we would have to walk over to where the engine was parked. It was a good distance. I want to point out that not once did Bogard offer us a ride, not even in an effort to speed up the operation. It is after eight by the time we get the engine inspected and authority to enter the mainline and proceed south to the depot. We inform the operator that we were going to breakfast as soon as we could cross over and duck into the storage track at Standard (restaurant). The dispatcher said that we could do this as soon as NC6 (New Orleans-Chicago hotshot) got by us on the northbound. That would be Extra 3011 north and we see a headlight coming through Onarga. NC6 clears and it's our turn.

After breakfast we all climb on the engine, contact the dispatcher, enter the main and head for the depot. We have yet to talk to Bogard this morning, and he doesn't know that we have to go to Kankakee in order to replenish our sand supply. Once that was sanctioned we grabbed the caboose and proceeded to Kankakee. It would be a 50 mile round trip.

The operator at the tower (KX) crosses us into the east side of the yard and we line a few switches and enter the locomotive service track. It was clear and of course we were ever mindful of "blue flags"![2] I go into the yard office to make sure that it is okay to fill our sand tank at which time we will head back to Gilman. The trainmaster shows up and wants to know "who the hell are you"? We now have sand and it is flowing freely through every pipe. We get the signal and enter the main pointed toward Gilman. The signals at Ashkum are "all red" and we have to wait for #10 and a northbound "Gilman liner". We won't get back to Gilman until almost noon.

As we near the depot, pulling the caboose we see the section men standing on the ready with their picks and shovels and whatever else that is appropriate. Bill goes in and talks to the operator and then tells Mr. Bogard that we are going to lunch. I'm glad I wasn't there for the ensuing reaction that came forth. We're okay to head down to Standard and to cross over to the storage track. Standard is a huge truck stop that gets really busy around noontime. Today would be no different. It wouldn't be till almost one o'clock before we could come out of the storage track and start gathering our cars for today's intended operation. By one-fifteen we have our train made up, the section men are loaded on the caboose and we shove it and five loaded cars of stone to Clifton for another day of spreading ballast. It is two o'clock when we drop our first rock. At two thirty we stop. Bogard doesn't want to pay his crew any overtime. He didn't care about us, however. We must have been from a different budget. After we put our train away, we went down to the depot. I don't know what was said, but I'm sure Bogard was extremely agitated. I went into the washroom and when I came out, I saw Bogard's got Bill Olmstead by the throat bent backwards over a desk. A couple of the section guys separated them. I was laughing so hard, I thought that maybe I had better go outside. Olmstead came out with a big grin on his face. At that time I heard Bogard telling someone on the phone in a more than persuasive manner: "don't ever send this crew down here again" as he slammed down the receiver.

Bill went back into the depot, a few minutes later he came out and announced that we were relieved. We hopped a caboose to Markham. We would have to agree, Bogard had people working for him all those years, but he never had to work with anybody. We also realized going away, that our railroad suffered from a lack of communication. We never heard a word about our experience at Gilman.

SAND IN A PIGS EYE

Non locomotive types such as yardmasters and a few officials didn't put much stock in the concept of sand. Apparently the pipe fitters at the roundhouse didn't either. Locomotives must have a full supply of sand that flows freely through the pipes and directly on to the rail. The purpose for this has already been stated in the beginning of this chapter. Without a doubt the sanding apparatus can and is difficult to maintain. Quite often the sand element is overlooked by both the roundhouse and the engineers themselves. Hence, it gets swept under the rug, ignored until some engineer complains. Once that happens, someone from the roundhouse has to take a look at those pesky sanders, and a temporary "fix" is applied. Part of the problem is due to moisture and condensation which acts to clog the various passages for which the sand must flow, which is a never ending struggle.

Newer yardmasters could not understand why an engine could be bad ordered because of sand. After all it wasn't in the Yardmaster's Handbook........

One night I was on a transfer job with road power out of Pigs Eye.[3] The engines were spotted very near the superintendents window at the yard office. The "head man" was cutting the air in and the trainline must have had a hole in it, because it "dumped".[4] I reset the "PCS" (pneumatic control switch) in an effort to recover the air, however it is still blowing somewhere in the train. When a trainline goes into "emergency" it activates the sanders on the engine. The only way to stop it is to reset the "PCS". I did this, but apparently air is still blowing out of the front sanding hoses. I don't hear this because of the air blowing from the automatic brake valve. Air is blowing and sand is piling up and is becoming a source of irritation to the terminal superintendent. Next I hear someone shouting from down on the ground. I look out the window and it's him. I open the window and he queries, did I know that my sanders were on? I retort: "No, I didn't"! After looking at the control stand, I further went on to explain that the sanders are "off" up here. By now he is up in the cab giving me the evil eye. Knowing this man's history I make a mental note that went something like "this could get ugly". His tone of voice became altered when he asked me "well, aren't you gonna do something?" At that point I calmly called the roundhouse and advised them of the problem. I then got up and got down to the front of the engine, looked at it, and climbed back up on the engine and sat down. By now the guys face is beet red. Now I get: "Well, what are you going to do?" I reply: "I already did, I called the roundhouse, and they're on their way". He stared at me and finally all at once stomped off the engine.

This guy was expecting me to cower, when I didn't, that threw him into a rage that was better controlled in private. Right from the "git go" I knew I was down a few points as I was a Soo Liner and this was Milwaukee territory all the way.

Later I was to find out from a very good source, that he once made the comment: "see that guy (pointing to me), I'm gonna fire him someday"! This man was a most fastidious person and lacked the people skills that helped bring the Milwaukee Road to it's knees.

---

[1] CTC is an abbreviation for "Centralized Traffic Control", a signal system that enables trains to run on the same track in either direction.
[2] A blue flag is displayed on or around equipment that may have men working. Defective equipment is referred to in railroad jargon as "bad order".
[3] Pigs Eye is a euphemism for St. Paul Yard.
[4] When the air is "dumped" the trainline air pressure escapes to the atmosphere. This will also trip the PCS or Pneumatic Control Switch. The PCS will unload the power when the air is dumped.

Chapter 17

Lunch Counter Jack

No book about a young man's career, in the sixties, on the Chicago Division of the Illinois Central, would be complete without a story of the exploits of "Lunch-counter Jack". Jack had retired in 1971. He and his wonderful wife, Pansy, moved to her hometown of Opdyke, Illinois, where Jack spent his remaining years being happily married. My wife and I were on a road trip which included a stop in Opdyke, as I knew that any information that existed would be found in that place. Probably the best source of information in a town such as Opdyke, is to talk to the postmaster. She in turn made a call and then directed me to the business of one of the "city fathers". I introduced myself to Steve and explained that I fired for Jack

Jack's favorite engine.

ILLINOIS CENTRAL RAILROAD

Locomotive No. 2500
Wheel arrangement 4-8-2
Size of Cyl. 30" x 30"
Diameter of Drivers: 70"
Steam Pressure: 240 lbs.
Tractive Effort: 83,500 lbs.
Weights: Drivers: 280,500
            Total Engine: 409,500
            Tender: 225,500
Capacity of Tender: Coal 24 tons
                     Water 11,000 gallons

Note: No. 2500 rebuilt by the Illinois Central. Original number 2953
       Central-Freight built by Lima works in 1921, wheel arrangement 2-10-2.

and was interested in writing a story that would ultimately be connected to a book. He paid me a compliment when he countered that I didn't look old enough to have fired for Jack. He then told me that Pansy was 92 and he and others watched over her. After dialing Pansy's number and explaining that a guy was here to talk about Jack, he mentioned that I had my wife with me. Pansy then assented and said "in that case send them down to the house".

We were greeted by a most vibrant 92 year old woman. We could immediately tell that she had nothing but love for her Clarence. When I walked in, I had a pad of paper for notes. We exchanged pleasantries, looked at many pictures, and chatted with a lovely lady.

Jack often commented that "someone should write a book", and so before Jack died Pansy had put together "The Story of a Remarkable Man".

I have one of these books in front of me, which makes writing this story both enjoyable and nostalgic.

Clarence Oppelt was born February 1st, 1906 in Aitkin, Minnesota. You might say that he had been around the block more than once, having already lived in four states when at age 12 he accidently discharged the shotgun, he was carrying, blowing off his left thumb.

At age sixteen, he and a friend flipped a train which would take them to the world they had often wondered about. No stranger to work and always friendly and talkative, Jack (we will now call him Jack) landed himself a coal passer's job on a steamboat plying the great lakes. He did this for a year and finally decided it wasn't for him. He came to Chicago and stayed with his stepsister and her husband. Jack had known sister May's husband when the family lived in Loda, Illinois, which is located on the Illinois Central mainline. He'd seen many trains go through Loda and greatly admired their engineers. At the time of Loda, sister May was courting an I.C. engineer by the name of Henry Escarraz. Henry took a liking to Jack and got him a temporary job, at Christmastime, on the I.C.'s mail platform. On Christmas day he was laid off. Four days later he was hired by the Master Mechanic at Burnside to be a locomotive fireman. A legacy was in its infancy.

It was always an understanding, an unwritten agreement between the men and the company, that in yard service, when the work was finished, the crews could tie up (go home). Usually within six or six and a-half hours you were on your way home. Once in a while it didn't work that way and crews would pout and "pull beans" (go to dinner). The standard agreement for the yard service lunch hour was only twenty minutes. Depending on the yardmaster, you usually would get a little more time. Most of the guys wanted to do the work and tie up, without officially eating.

In road service it was almost unheard of. If you went to "beans" on the road, there was always the danger of getting "run around". The crews are working in a pool and getting run around would mean that a crew that went to work behind you at Markham would go to work in Clinton or Champaign ahead of your crew. That meant spending more time away from home. Getting run around going north wasn't so bad, but nobody wanted to have it happen going south. There were a few guys that had girlfriends, but they were a definite minority.

Jack was one of those rare individuals that wanted to eat once the sixth hour approached (within guidelines of the agreement) and he stuck to his guns. The dispatchers hated the idea that any train Lunchcounter Jack was running would always go to beans at Gilman, provided his crew was on duty long enough to justify a meal period. Unlike the yard agreement, which specified "20 minutes", the road agreement was much more liberal and "a sufficient amount of time would be allowed for the purpose of eating".

One trip Jack was refused the right to eat by the dispatcher. The power switches around Gilman were remote controlled by the dispatcher. At the time Jack's train was in the west siding at Gilman, waiting for a passenger train to go by. When Jack's train finally got the signal to enter the mainline from the siding, the dispatcher meant for the entire train to come out. Only the power came out and headed up to the depot to again talk to the dispatcher. The answer was "no, you can't eat, get back on your train and go". The crew tied back on the train but never took the signal. The dispatcher displayed the signal for a good hour before he had the operator drive down to the engine (there were no radios then) and inform the crew that the dispatcher was going to take the signal away from them and to wait for the Kankakee trainmaster to show up. When the trainmaster arrived, after talking to the crew, he decided to pull them out of service pending investigation. The investigation was at the time, the most controversial of confabs ever held on the Illinois Central.

Jack had set a precedent, as a result of the investigation. He only lost one trip and was immediately re-instated with full pay for time lost. Jack once related to me what he told a dispatcher that wasn't happy about his crew going to eat. He said; "We either eat or I'll be sitting on Wayne Johnstons lap come Monday morning". Jack would be the benefactor of the "meal issue". Lunchcounter Jack would be known from Chicago to New Orleans. When the dispatchers were fixing a meet on the Gilman line, if Jack's train was in the picture, it wouldn't leave Gilman until the opposing train arrived.

Jack, more often than not, would draw the 2500 in the early fifties when the Korean War was raging. IC was taking delivery of as many GP7's as it could get, but because Jack was working a long haul, maid of all work, local he rated a steam engine. The 2500 was one of the biggest engines IC employed. Because of dieselization the steam engines were bumped down to more menial tasks such as the Markham-Clinton local of which Jack Oppelt was the engineer. Jack ran the 2500 enough times that he referred to it as his sweetheart. He had nothing but disdain for the diesels. He really loved steam. One time at the roundhouse, I asked Jack if he ever ran the 3600 class engine they had parked there. His reply was "that was one engine I avoided". After his retirement Jack found out that the 2500 was donated to the city of Centralia (Illinois). Jack and his wife Pansy lived in Opdyke, which was only forty miles from Centralia. Quite often they would drive over to see the 2500 for something to do. Once in a while they were able to sit up in the cab of the 2500. If Jack didn't have a tear in his eye, I think that maybe Pansy did.

The brakemen knew when they came to work that they would not go hungry on any job that Oppelt worked. One brakeman said that he liked Jack but he liked him even more when he was running around Jack's train as it sat in the siding somewhere. The rail world was a world of hand signs and the most prolific of signs was and still is the thumbs up. This is used to indicate either "tying up" or "go to beans", and is always a good thing. The standard reaction from a crew running around Jack's train, as it sat in the siding, would be either the conductor or flagman of the overtaking train, to stand on the rear platform of their caboose, and give Jack the "bean sign", except the thumbs would not be up! It was a kind of sardonic jab at Oppelt as he only had one thumb and also part of a finger was missing. You had to be there, it was more than funny. Jack would always laugh. He liked the "lunchcounter" tag. Jack worked a passenger job when he could. He didn't quite have the seniority that merited holding down a regular passenger job, year around. I remember one Sunday morning we came in on the Seminole (No. 10) and Jack made the comment " It looks like come tomorrow morning I'll be out amongst the coal cars". That was Lunchcounter Jack.

In Champaign the dispatchers are changing shifts. When there is a shift change in the dispatchers office there is a thirty minute overlap for obvious reasons. The reigning "north end" dispatcher is contemplating a meet at Thawville between the Markham-Clinton local and a "hot" 62 with perishable out of St. Louis. The oncoming and more experienced dispatcher idly inquires as to "who were the engineers that were on these trains"? Both trains were steam powered and the more savvy dispatchers knew the engineers and their traits when he heard their names. He recognized both engineer's names and realized that each one of them had an entirely different milieu. Lunchcounter Jack Oppelt[1] was just leaving Ashkum with a huge "drag" and con-

versely Bill Egan[2] was out of Clinton with #62. The more knowledgeable dispatcher consummates a decision when he flippantly says "hold the drag at Gilman and let Egan go all the way across the line". His reasoning was that Jack Oppelts train would eat at Gilman anyway. Bill Egan could run a steam engine with the best of engineers and would get across the Gilman line without taking water and do it in a hurry.

The Story of Major Boles

E. W. Boles first went to work for the Illinois Central at Freeport, Illinois, probably in the late 20's or early 30's. The facts are sketchy however the story is interesting and should be told. The depression came, and the "Major" was laid off. At that time, personnel records were kept at the headquarters of the division you worked on.

The yard office at Freeport had a fire and burnt to the ground. Records were destroyed, including the Majors. It wasn't long after that, that business everywhere was beginning to overcome the long years of depression and the Chicago Division was suddenly short of enginemen. Chicago was looking for experienced enginemen and so the Major, ever being resourceful, showed up in Chicago in the latter part of 1936 with his son's birth certificate. Mathematically, that would make him about 18-20 years younger than he really was. It worked and the Major was afforded an additional 20 years or so of longevity on the railroad.

When I came out of the army, Major Boles was barely able to work any kind of passenger job. Before I went into the army I was forced on a Kankakee switch engine and would have to deadhead on the "Riley" (James Whitcomb Riley) to Kankakee. The Riley always had three geeps and this day I rode the third unit. As the train snaked out of Central Station through the interlocking at Weldon, I could see the Major with his heavy black topcoat and the wool chapeau he always wore. Let's not forget the ever present cigar that was always there. I can't explain it, but that is a sight that had a lasting effect on me. He looked like he belonged there.

After the army, I caught a job with Major Boles. We caught the "Green Diamond" together. 21 and 22 went to St. Louis and back. The Chicago crew would bring the train halfway (150 miles) to Clinton, Illinois. Another crew would continue on to St. Louis with the train. This day our leg of the trip or at least the southbound part of it would include Charlie Selsor. Charlie was the north end traveling engineer and you never knew when he would show up.

We left the city a few minutes late and I noticed that the speed recorder began to creep up to 82 or 83 MPH. At that time Selsor would reach over and shut the throttle down a couple of notches. This was always echoed by a short spell of pusillanimous laughter emanating from the Major. I happened to bump into Leo Deany Sr. a few days after that and shared that same story with him. Leo had been retired a few years. Leo said that had that happened to him, he would have punched Selsor in the nose. Engineers in those days had a tremendous sense of pride and nobody ran their engine nor manipulated any part of it. Major Boles was from the old school, but I think he took Selsor with a grain of salt. Hence, the story of Major Boles.

[1]Clarence Oppelt was a pretty good steam engineer himself.
[2] Like Lunchcounter Jack, Bill Egan also had a nickname, it was "Blue Eyes".

BOOK II

Soo Line Days

155

Chapter 18

Soo Line

I left my car out in front of the Soo Line Building in "no man's land" with the idea that with any luck, I wouldn't get a ticket because I wouldn't be in the building that long. I was distantly hoping that the Soo would also say no and I would be off the hook and could go back to the security of my present job knowing that in my haphazard way, I did look for a new beginning, but without success.

The employment office was up on the eighth floor. The receptionist was a fox. Maybe I do want to work here, I mused. I asked the lady if the Soo Line would be interested in hiring a locomotive engineer. She replied, yes we would, but only experienced engineers. Not counting my two years on the mail platform and three years in the military, I had about 15 years of running an engine under my belt. Was that experienced enough? She smiled and about that time a Mr. Larry Bell walked into the room muttering for all the world to hear "I would give my right arm for a couple of locomotive engineers about now". The lady commented while pointing me out.....this guy might be a start.

Bell took me back to his office and interviewed me for quite a while. Mr. Bell said, yes we are hiring engineers, and if I was interested, I could go to work tomorrow in either Superior, Wisconsin or Enderlin, North Dakota. I asked him the usual questions that a guy about to give up 20 years would ask......would I always work. Yes, you'll always have a job we are very good to our employees. I didn't want to sound too objective but yet I didn't want to come across as aloof either. The one thing I never did mention to Bell was that I wasn't going to Enderlin. I didn't have to, as Bell then asked me, "how does Superior sound"? Any guarantee I had from the Soo Line was verbal with the inclusion of a meaningless handshake.

Bell made a couple of phone calls and set me up for an interview with Soo's director of personnel and a complete physical, all on the following day. He also mentioned that I should get up to Superior as soon as I could as there were a couple of guys in their engineers training program that were almost ready. "Wouldn't want them to get ahead of you"! I told him that it would take upwards to a week for me to get squared away in Chicago. I owned a town house and had furniture to store. He recognized that it was a big move.

My first appointment, the following day, was with their personnel director. I found him to be taciturn and condescending. I wasn't comfortable. His questions were direct. "Why do you want to work here"? The only way to answer a question like that is to come back with the plain truth. This interview seemingly took forever, however, in reality it only lasted less than 30 minutes. This day I would be more judicious with my vehicle and parked it in an "all day" ramp.

The second appointment was at one o'clock and would be within walking distance. The Soo Line wanted to make sure that I was "mechanically sound" and so a complete physical "onceover" was in store.

Other than finding out that I had one leg shorter than the other, the doctor determined that I was fit for work. I called Bell and told him that the physical was complete with good results and that I would be heading for Chicago, to tend to some last minute business and as soon as I could, I would be heading for Superior, Wisconsin.

Of course I went over to my mother's house and told her the news. She tried to talk me out of it. "You're just going through a phase", she would say. I told her that I had to go, I had to make this change, that I wasn't happy and had to do something about it. It seemed that she was victimized even more than I when the kids left. I told her that a lot could happen once I got up there. I might even change my mind and come home.

I said all of my goodbyes, put my house up for sale and left. I didn't talk to the ICG , however. I wasn't happy with them either. Goodbye Chicago!

As I drove north I had a lot to think about. What lies in the future? Am I crazy? Am I really doing this? Once I nearly turned around. My thoughts were "if I turn around, and go back, I'll never know what might have happened and would forever wonder". At least by going through with it, I would have the future in front of me. Que sera, sera.

On the afternoon of October 23, 1979 I drove to the roundhouse at Superior, Wisconsin. I asked how to get to the callers office and reported for duty. The caller said that I could begin making student trips immediately. He said that I could work the 3:00 PM Stinson Switcher. All I had to do was drive to Stinson Yard and introduce myself to the engineer. The guys kidded me when they saw this over loaded Volkswagen Rabbit. I guess the rocker panels were barely clearing the ruts in the road. No wonder, everything important to me was in that car. Sometime that week I and two other guys would have to take a rules examination. They would let us know when. The Soo Line used the same rule book that all railroads that operated in the Twin Cities used, for obvious reasons. The Illinois Central Gulf used a different set of operating rules and so I was at a disadvantage. The other two people taking the test were off the Rock Island which was part of the consolidation of operating rules. They were helpful. Of course we all passed. That little stumbling block was eliminated. I was still staying in a motel and trying to make student trips. My life was suddenly and literally subjected to unfamiliar endeavors both on and off the railroad. Maybe I needed that. I worked all of the terminal jobs as a student, including Duluth. The reigning trainmaster at the time had a pair of General Motors yard engines painted up. One engine had Duluth painted on it and the other had Superior painted on it. They always worked in Duluth and were always operated in tandem. I was impressed. My new company was actually trying to be appealing to the public. I was more than optimistic about the Soo Line.

My first student trip on the road would be on #73 which ran from Superior to Bemidji, Minnesota. After resting, the crew would return on #72. Wesley Nelson was the engineer. Neither he nor the head brakeman was very talkative. You had to pry information out of them. They would be termed "grunters". The Bemidji job always had a single crew that would work Monday and Tuesday, have Wednesday off and then repeat the process working Thursday and Friday with the weekend off. It was a small wonder that the number one engineer was on it.

Business was approaching record levels and it was necessary to add another job. The mileage from Stinson (Superior) to Bemidji was 171 miles. The first 41 miles ran over the Brooten Subdivision to Moose Lake, Minnesota where the lines split, one heading in a southwestern direction toward Brooten where it joins the "Twin Cities" mainline. We would be running over the "Plummer" line which leaves Moose Lake in a northwestern direction for 103 miles to connect with the Burlington Northern Superior-Grand Forks line at a place called Schley. The final 27 miles would be run over the 40 MPH BN into Bemidji.

Somebody said that he was pretty sure that the Plummer line was pretty much comprised of "loon shit". About one third of the 103 miles goes across a massive peat bog. Minnesota has vast expanses of peat bogs. There once was a derailment and when the road bed was cleared off, the loaded grain hoppers were left to very quietly and very slowly sink into oblivion.

We were called for the return trip for 7:30 AM on a bright, sunny day. Nelson ran the engine to Schley and then turned it over to me. I ran all the way to Kettle River. There we picked up a car and then Nelson decided that it was his turn to run. Kettle River is about nine miles from Moose Lake. I would find out later that I would have been better off if he had allowed me to bring that train into Moose Lake. The reason for that will be discussed at length in the next chapter.

On the 31st of October I would establish my Soo Line engineer's seniority working a "helper" job. The Soo Line would receive an entire train from the Duluth, Winnipeg & Pacific (CN) on a daily basis. The bulk of this train was made up of lumber, potash and other heavy commodities. From Stinson Yard to Hillcrest is a grade that seemingly goes straight up. This hill went for 19 miles and almost always called for a helper. Occasionally there would be a second train and the "helper job" goes from a good job to a mediocre job.

This train that came off the "Peg" was manned by Stevens Point crews. They always gave us the impression that they were doing us a favor by letting us make up the train for them. The train was numbered 418 and the Stevens Point engineer was one of those old timers that thought he was the only engineer on the seniority list. He acted (over the radio) like he was babysitting me. I finally asked him over the radio whether or not he was afraid of it (the train he was operating). In this case the "helper" is always on the rear of the train.

The grain was coming out of the Dakotas as fast as they could move it and men and equipment were taxed to the limit. The Glenwood freight pool would have five crews in it. The Superior-Bemidji job would have two crews instead of the usual one. Duluth would have a switch crew around the clock and Stinson would have the 7:30 AM, 3:30PM and 11:30 PM jobs working until further notice. Before the rush, the usual requirements were an around the clock lead switcher and the "59" jobs which did the transfer work. They were called "59" jobs because they went to work at 7:59AM, 3:59PM and 11:59PM.

Now it was time for a trip to Glenwood, Minnesota. Glenwood lay exactly 200 miles southwest of Superior. It served as a division point for crews coming from Thief River Falls, Minnesota, Enderlin, North Dakota, Minneapolis and Superior. The Superior trains would enter the mainline at Brooten and go west 16 miles to Glenwood. Soo Line had recently spent much in time, money, and teamwork to bring the 140 miles of track up to an operating standard of efficiency. There was a bumper crop of wheat in the Dakotas and Soo was fortunate to see it coming, track speed was boosted from 10 to 40 MPH in places. The night I made the student trip, I happened to work with a good engineer by the name of Dave Denny. Dave was pretty laid back and talkative. Although it was difficult at times for me to stay awake, Dave would always have something to say. I was running the engine from Onamia into Glenwood. It had been years since I was on a road train and I was feeling that harmonious cadence that a guy had to get used to. At least that's the way it affected me. I don't know if

Dave realized that, but he was awake the whole time and stayed with me. It was on that trip that I saw what a blizzard looked like across the openness of Minnesota. We crossed the Mississippi River and it was frozen solid. As a matter of fact so was the bridge. A bridge made of timbers embellished in ice. By the way there was no signal whatsoever and the crossing was very close to the dam. These guys do it another way and I guess it works. I was a bit apprehensive going over the river. We had been going across open prairie at 25 MPH and then we came to a curve and suddenly we were going across the Mississippi River. It was cold and we could hear the timbers of the short bridge creaking in protest to our weight. We laid over in Glenwood thirteen and a half hours and we were called for 8:00 PM. A unit grain train of 75 cars. It would be a handful as Soo was very short on power and we would get a GP35 and an F7A. Up until recently the 2229B (F7A) was in moth balls. We were progressing nicely until Genola. Genola marks the start of a very long hill of about 20 miles. It would be close to two hours grinding up that hill at between 9 and 11 MPH. Luckily once we made Onamia and met #71 we would cruise right along. Dave mentioned that we were lucky to have made it within the twelve hour limit.

I was having an auspicious beginning and was looking forward to working for the Soo Line.

Chapter 19

The Wreck

I hadn't yet gained access to the apartment that I had on retainer. The people living there had very nicely asked me if I would wait an extra day or two while their place was being readied. I felt that I could handle the Uptown Motel a few more days. I would come to be friends with those folks that were still in my future apartment.

I was still living at the Uptown Motel when the phone rang. Who else could it be but the Soo Line? They wanted me for the Bemidji job. I asked the crew caller if I could have a pilot, he said no, if there were a pilot available, he would be the engineer and I wouldn't be needed. I told him that I'd only been to Bemidji once and the caller came back with "the crew will take care of you". Please do me a favor and go with it. I defied my own principles when I accepted the job, but at the same time I wasn't trying to piss anyone off. Not yet anyway. J.J. O'Brien layed off and they simply didn't have anybody else. I was it. I had been there once and it didn't seem to be much of a challenge. How can you get killed on a 25 MPH railroad? That was my rationale and away I went.

We were called for 11:00 PM with one unit, a GP35. I don't recall the details of the trip going west to Bemidji other than that, the time book reflects working 12 hours. We spent all night crossing the peat bogs, through the forests and ultimately into Bemidji. We made it in time.

Eleven hours and thirty minutes later at 10:30 PM we were called for our return trip. The 714 coupled to the 4400 would be our power. The 714 was a GP30 and the 4400 was a brand spanking new GP38. We would depart Bemidji with exactly 50 loads of grain. Along with our train orders was a message to pick up four flat cars at Rosby. Rosby sits between Bemidji and Cass Lake and is entirely located on the Burlington Northern Railroad and is thought by my crew to be exclusively the work of the BN and not our own. We went into the Potlach facility with intention of picking up four empty flatcars. After coupling to these cars there was a considerable wait. I wondered what the problem was and so wandered off the engine to contribute any mechanical wisdom I had. The problem was that they couldn't get the hand brake off of the lead flatcar which meant, if they didn't, the cars would have to stay at Potlach. I tried to talk the guys into leaving the cars, however, they had an ulterior motive - if they picked up these flatcars it would be a time claim against the railroad and the crew would get a day's pay. They eventually released the hand brake and now we had four empty flatcars and fifty loaded grain cars leaving Rosby.

We left Schley and headed out into the peat bogs in the middle of the night. It's eerie. If you ever wondered what being in the middle of nowhere was like, I was in it. This was a weird place at night. There's fog in there too. As we continued through that part of the world, the diesel malaise began to creep in. I had to hang my head out of the window into the November night. My brakeperson wasn't used to the drone of the diesel either. Being the new kid on the block and fighting the same situation she was, I decided to let her slide. We picked up a message at McGregor that stated:

> "No 70's train with engs MNS41 and MNS40 is ahead of you dead on hour of service on main track at Moose Lake you are to set out all of your grain on 3 north at Moose Lake bring your chips and potash, engs and caboose and 70's entire train into Superior No 70 had 80-3-7054 tons out of Brooten also condg Stroozas call Stinson Yard when you get to Moose Lake".

PFM

It was during the wee hours of the morning that we received that message. I passed it on to the brakeperson (she was awake) and she briefly scanned it and told me, "okay".

She had no idea of what was lying ahead of us as she was as naive as I. I radioed the caboose, told them of the message and received a simple-okay. Now my thoughts go to "it must be a regular type of thing, they do this all the time and there isn't much for me to worry about."

We left the town of Kettle River and I realized that we weren't far from Moose Lake. My lack of experience coupled with the indifference of my crew, were leading me into a death trap, unknown to me at the time.

The way I interpreted this message was that we were going to pick up that train and double to our train and go. Railroad communications are never to be ambiguous, yet this was. It wasn't a clear message to a crew that was new.

Moose Lake is in "yard limit" territory and I fully expected to live up to the yard limit rule (rule 93). It pays to be experienced in a situation like this as Moose Lake lies at the bottom of a hill. I'm fighting the subtle drone of the engine along with the gentle rocking of the train as it pitched its way through the early November almost fog like mist. My head is again out the window. The brake person has again succumbed to Morpheus and left her life in my hands. I have to fight it, I'm the engineer.

Before you encounter the grade that drops you into Moose Lake you have to go over a hump. I took a 7 pound reduction off the trainline on the wrong side of the hump. Now I'm going uphill with the brakes set. I have to release them or it'll stop the train and I'm a long way from the yard limits of Moose Lake. I can't remember if I was aware of the grade coming into yard limits or not. Hill or no hill I wanted to be coming into yard limits under control, ready to stop if need be.

Using the air in advance of where I should have, now somewhat depleted the effectiveness of my brake system. Remember I have four empty flatcars and 50 loaded cars of grain. That fifty loads would drop into Moose Lake like a brick.

It is now just after 6 AM on a dreary, misty near foggy morning. We cross highway 27 and the yard limit board comes into view. My train is going faster than I want it to. I have no idea of what the lay of land is like nor did I understand the configuration of the yard. I saw a caboose and my thoughts went to "it must be on another track, this outfit wouldn't do that to me" and yet all at the same time I put the brake valve into emergency. There was a train sitting 34 car lengths inside of the yard limit board and we hit it at around 25 MPH. The caboose on the other train was completely totaled. Our lead unit GP30#714 was totaled. Second unit, the brand new 4400 went by us taking its right side handrails off and the four flat cars acted as a buffer stacking up to cushion the shock and spared our lives. Had we left the flatcars at Rosby, you wouldn't be reading this. After throwing the brake valve handle into the emergency position, I pulled the brake person from her slumber and threw her on the floor. I then threw myself on her, to protect her. There is no other way to describe what just happened, although it sounds a bit racy, it can't be, we were staring death right in the face. As I lie on this woman, waiting to die, I think of a million reasons why I want to stay alive. Your thought processes react quickly when you are near death. I explicitly remember the initial impact and saying to myself "here comes the nose (as the fire extinguisher flew over my head), now the glass and we'll be next and then it all stopped. The lead locomotive was understandably on a more or less 30 degree angle. Everything was in positive and cataclysmic disarray. What was more than okay was the fact that my brakette and I were able to crawl out of the wreckage and get away from the possibility of an explosion. Once I realized that we were home free, I began to realize how lucky I was and a euphoric state began settling over me. I was damned glad to be alive.

Once we managed to navigate around and over the wreckage, we walked along the side of the train until we met our conductor and flagman walking up from the caboose. The conductor flew into a rage when I told him jokingly that I thought we could re-rail the whole works and nobody would be any wiser. He threw his lamp at the side of a covered hopper and yelled over and over "you're nuts, you're nuts"! I replied with "I might be nuts - but I'm alive"! Our train had route 27 hopelessly blocked. To add insult to injury it was the first day of Minnesota's deer season. Walking across highway 27 our attention was called to by an irate motorist that demanded that we move the train and do it now! No amount of words could convince this guy that the train couldn't be moved and wouldn't move for hours. Luckily this guy was separated from our flagman by the drawbars of a couple of grain hoppers and they exchanged insults until the guy walked away. I told the flagman that maybe we should get the hell out of there because the guy probably had a deer rifle and was mad enough to use it. The company would enlist the aid of two D-9 caterpillars to shove whatever cars and the caboose off the crossing. It would take hours for this to happen.

Our boss gave the brake person and I a ride to the Moose Lake hospital at his insistence. There was nothing wrong with me and I saw nothing wrong with her other than her feelings may have been hurt. Our trainmaster took our statements at the hospital and was quite civil about it, considering we have tied up his railroad for a few days in the middle of the heaviest grain rush they ever had. I also found out how you could get killed on a 25 MPH railroad.

We rode back to Superior in a crew van. You could cut the silence with a knife. Of course I weighed my fate and the chance that I might get fired. I honestly didn't think they would come down too hard on me as I asked for a pilot, I was new, the crew I had with me wasn't experienced on that district. They were short of people. It all added up to a slap on the wrist to me. I wanted to keep my job.

The wreck occurred on the fourth of November. Sometime later that day I was given a "notice of investigation" to be held on the sixth of that month. Only two days. That didn't seem to me to be much time for either party or parties to get ready. The investigation was cancelled and re-scheduled for the eighth of November.

Shoreham (Minneapolis) Mn.
November 4, 1979

SOME PEOPLE ARE SO INDECISIVE THAT THEIR FAVORITE COLOR IS PLAID.

★ Star-Gazette

SURPRISE SALE see advertisement elsewhere in this paper.

Vol. 84. No. 45   Moose Lake, Minnesota 55767   Thursday, November 8, 1979   16 pages; 20¢

Sunday train wreck, injures 2--heavy damage

At approximately 6:15 a.m. on Sunday morning, November 4, a train belonging to the SOO LINE railroad struck and damaged another train belonging to the SOO LINE on tracks just west of Moose Lake by Highway 73.

There were no serious injuries resulting from the railway mishap although the engineer and brakemen of one train were taken to Moose Lake Mercy Hospital. The two men were treated for their injuries and released later that day.

The accident and subsequent derailment of a portion of the trains caused a traffic backup on Highway 73. The highway was closed to traffic from the time of the accident until approximately 10:30 that same morning when traffic was resumed.

The accident occurred when one train carrying grain from Bemidji to Superior ran into the rear of another train that had been parked on the track overnight at the SOO LINE station.

The moving train rounded the corner on a section of track and came upon the rear of the parked train. The collision caused the derailment of both of the moving train's engines. In addition, the caboose of the parked train was derailed and crushed along with the derailment of four flat cars and one car loaded with grain. A section of track was also torn up in the accident.

Diesel fuel from the wrecked engines and grain from the overturned grain car spilled and emptied into nearby water filled culverts.

The reason for the lack of knowledge of the parked train on the tracks has not been released as of yet. SOO LINE officials have been unavailable for comment about the cause of the accident.

The estimate of damages to the track and train have not been released yet.

Work crews will begin to clean up and repair the damaged track and train as seen as possible.

Community
page 3

DERAILED SECTION of the SOO LINE trains that collided early Sunday morning.   more photos on page 16

---

more train wreck photos

THE SMASHED remains of the caboose of the parked train.

FLAT CARS that were piled upon each other during the force of the impact of the crash.

To A.L. Hoekstra Engineer

Please arrange to report to the office of terminal supt. Superior Wisconsin 10:00 AM November 8, 1979 for formal investigation to determine facts and place your particular responsibility if any in connection with the accident which took place at approximately 6:10 AM November 4, 1979 when extra 714 east struck the rear end of no. 70's extra Mns. 41 train, on the 5th subdivision maintrack approximately 34 car lengths inside the west yard limit board at Moose Lake Mn. 172 accident report filed 12:40 PM November 4, 1979.

If you wish representation please arrange.
Acknowledge receipt of this notice A-1

H.A. Peterson
Supt. Central Division

Shortly before I left the Illinois Central Gulf, I dropped out of the Brotherhood of Locomotive Engineers and had planned to join the United Transportation Union-Enginemen as soon as possible. In the meantime my life began to get complicated and I hadn't been able to re-join any union. I had the accident at Moose Lake and the BLE immediately went to my defense. I thought it prudent to keep quiet about dropping out. It was considered normal practice to jump from one union to the next. Quite often a member becomes disenchanted with his representation and uses his or her membership to exact some leverage. It was later brought to the surface that I had dropped out of the BLE and was technically a "no-bill". The record will indicate that I have always been a dues paying member and will continue to do so. When the wreck occurred I was simply between unions. At that time there was a lack of substance in my life, what with the new job, the new town, etc. I was not trying to denigrate the importance of unionism and would have re-joined the BLE as soon as possible. I felt that the BLE owed me at least that much.

Rule 93

Yard limits will be indicated by yard limit signs. Within yard limits the main track may be used, clearing first class trains when due to leave the last station where time is shown. Protection against second and third class trains, extra trains and engines is not required.

In ABS territory, information issued by the train despatcher, either verbally or by message, may be used to determine when delayed first class trains are due to leave the last station where time is shown.

In Non-ABS territory, in case of failure to clear the time of first class trains, protection must be provided as prescribed by Rule 99.

Second and third class trains, extra trains and engines must move within yard limits at reduced speed unless the main track is known to be clear. Not to exceed 20 MPH and be prepared to stop within half the range of vision.

Within yard limits when running against the current of traffic or on a portion of double or three or more tracks used as single track, all trains and engines must move at reduced speed.

Chapter 20

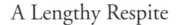

A Lengthy Respite

The investigation convened at 10 AM at the Soo Line depot in Superior, Wisconsin. It was presided over by a Mr. Hegquist. Hegquist would also represent the Soo Line. John Graves and Jack Peterson would represent me.

All in all there were thirteen of us in the room counting the stenographer. We knew it would be an all day affair - at least all day and hopefully we would finish in one day.

Once the formalities were met, the investigation would begin in earnest. Mr. Hegquist would often accompany a question with the word "inasmuch". Inasmuch as this and inasmuch as that, he sure liked that word. I mused to myself "Old Inasmuch", sounds like an expensive single malt scotch.

Once the facts were brought out and carefully weighed, we all felt that I had a good case and would prevail. There may have been some discipline awarded, but we weren't too worried, we were hoping for a fair and conclusive decision.

Less than ten days later, I received the following letter in the mail:

Shoreham-Minneapolis
November 15, 1979

Mr. A.L. Hoekstra, Engineer
1825 Baxter Ave., Apt. #14
Superior, Wi. 54880

Dear Mr. Hoekstra:

Referring to formal investigation conducted in the office of the Terminal Superintendent, Superior, Wi. at 10 AM Thursday, November 8, 1979, in connection with train accident that occurred at approximately 6:10 AM, November 4, 1979 when extra 714 East struck the rear end of #70's extra train on the 5th Sub Division main track approximately 34 car lengths inside the west yard limit board at Moose Lake, Mn.

Review of the transcript of this investigation clearly reflects violation of Rule 93 Revised, as contained in General Order #49 dated January 1, 1979, which provides that all trains and engines, except first class trains, must move within yard limits prepared to stop within one-half the range of vision but not exceeding 20 miles per hour, unless the main track is known to be clear by block signal indication.

The transcript of the investigation clearly reflects that you were proceeding, when past the yard limit board and immediately prior to that time, at a speed of 30 MPH and review of the speed tapes clearly indicate that your speed had increased in the 1 1/4 miles prior to the yard limit board from a speed of 19 MPH to 30 MPH at the point of collision.

With consideration to the fact, and your previous experience, that you were operating as a new engineer in strange territory, it is not conceivable that you would be operating in excess of yard limit rules, particularly in view of your just recently passing a Consolidated Code of Operating Rules examination held by Soo Line Rules Examiner and qualifying you as a qualified engineer.

This is to advise you that you are hereby dismissed from the service of the Soo Line Railroad Company, effective with your removal from service November 4, 1979.

You are hereby requested to return all company property in your possession to the Terminal Superintendent's office, Superior, Wi. The paymaster is being instructed to forward all monies due you promptly.

Please acknowledge receipt of this letter on copy attached.

Sincerely,

H.A. Peterson
Division Superintendent
HAP/dl

I hereby acknowledge receipt and understanding of the above letter -

It was difficult to describe my feelings after having read the letter. I was disappointed to be sure, but wasn't about to panic as I felt that we had a very good case and would somehow win if it got into the courts. Everyone I talked to agreed that I wasn't dealt with fairly and would eventually prevail.

The "QT" bar was sort of the Soo Liner hangout and is where before and after the investigation I met more Soo guys than I did on the railroad. I had many guys extend their support and after having talked, had many good words for me which I needed at the time as I will have to admit I was a bit despondent and needed reassurance. Most guys encouraged me to stay. I didn't know what to do, shit, I got fired from two railroads in less than two weeks!

I was most fortunate to have made quite a few friends in such a short time. Engineer Jack Peterson was kind enough to welcome me into his family. Jack did a lot of work on my case and I am forever indebted to him.

When I left the ICG, I had two job insurance policies in effect. These policies were through Ralph King (remember him?). Ralph represented a company in Michigan called CPA. I hesitated to talk to CPA and didn't want to talk to Ralph either (did he still think I was after his wife?). I filled out the forms that I had and attached a letter explaining what had taken place and that I hadn't had time to inform them of my change of venue. I was reasonably sure that my claim would be rejected, because after all the forms did have Illinois Central on them-not Soo Line. The first check came without a whimper and was as prompt as you would expect. No questions asked. I was jubilant and probably should have kept it to myself, however it leaked out. Peterson mentioned it and noted that the company found out about the insurance and they were probably miffed because they couldn't exact the vengeance they wanted to. They decided to lower the proverbial boom and can me altogether.

I went back to the Chicago area for Christmas, and told anyone that wanted to listen - that I got fired.

Once the holidays were over, it was time for me to make a serious decision. Was I going back to Chicago or would I stay in Superior and try to get my job back? Years before we would be on our way to Ely or Canada and as we came through the Duluth-Superior area I reflected that one day I would spend at least a week here. I've already done that and then some. At that time I felt that the IC was surely finished with me. Then one day Bruce Hartman called me from Chicago. We talked and he said that the local chairman of our division said that he could and would get me my job back, all I had to do was show up. Right then and there I knew what I wanted to do, and on the telephone no-less. I told Bruce- "thanks, but I'll stay here and take my chances". My decision was made. It was closure.

Winter was setting in. We would have three appeals before our case went to the labor board. The first appeal would go to the regional superintendent, Mr. H.A. Peterson. It would be declined, and now a second denial from Mr. C.C. Leary, General Superintendent.

Another factor that adds to the intensity of this dilemma was a seniority issue. When I established my engineer's seniority, there were two guys going through the Soo Line engineer's training program. These were local boys. The United Transportation Union (UTU) held the fireman's contract. The agreement the UTU had with the Soo, stated that any fireman engaged in the engineers training program would establish his or her engineers seniority the minute they joined the program. I had established my seniority while they were still "cadets", but it mattered not. The repercussions of this agreement would surface later.

In the meantime, the third and final denial of our appeal would come from A.W. Durtsche, Director of Labor Relations. We would now begin the long and arduous arbitration process. By now, I'm beginning to realize that the Soo Line simply doesn't want me! Arbitration is often referred to as the "Labor Board" but its actual name was "Federal Mediation Board". This process could and did take a while as I would later learn.

The entire time the vocational issue was at hand, I was getting to know the Duluth-Superior area, making friends through singles groups and simply having fun with life. I also spent a lot of time around Iron River, Wisconsin, fishing out of my twelve foot jon boat. Life was good.

But again as always we are reminded of the harsh realities of life, mine being that the job insurance was fizzling out and worries of the job were beginning to nag at me. I had been fired six months or so when one day I received a phone call from Jack Peterson. Jack had just talked to Dennis Simmerman the General Chairman for the engineers union. Simmerman had talked to some Soo Line official that had talked to someone at the Illinois Central Gulf. Remember when the Soo Line hired me they had omitted contacting the ICG for any endorsement on my behalf. The reason for the lack of contact was plain and simple - the Soo Line was doing something less than ethical in the industrial world - they were stealing an employee from another company. The Soo had denigrated my case long enough and it was time, for them, to take an in-depth look at it. At least that was the general opinion shared by Msrs. Peterson and Simmerman. I'll never know which ICG official Simmerman talked to and I'll never know exactly what Simmerman said to Peterson. It is my guess that the ICG representative was probably Ed Enzenauer (remember Ed?). Had I a choice in the matter, Enzenauer would have been the person I would have least wanted the Soo Line to talk to. Whatever was said, it couldn't have been good as Enzenauer and George Biscan (Terminal Superintendent) for that matter, both had a belated axe to grind with me. Illinois Central Gulf had vented its calumnious wrath toward me in a way I'll never come to know. There's another flag flown on behalf of the Bud Hoekstra Hate Club.

The rails at the QT Bar were becoming more and more dubious as the time went by. Everyone still agreed that I had a good case but by now some of them weren't so sure that I would get back. One guy said that "if you were coming back, you would be back by now no one stays out of service as long as you have". Another fellow went on to say that he had heard of crews on other parts of the system that were involved in much more serious accidents and were put back to work within six months. Those comments did little for my morale.

It is now the middle of July and my job insurance has expired. Along with that the Railroad Retirement Board was breathing down my neck, more than suggesting that I look for work. Having worked for a railroad all of my working life, there was little I had to offer a prospective employer, and another railroad wouldn't touch me. Each day I would call on some company and walk away with little in the way of encouragement. Once a month or so I would have a meeting with the R.R.T. director over in Duluth. I always had that stack of applications with me and he would always remind me, without fail, that I didn't want my benefits to run out. If you don't tend bar or can't railroad, Duluth-Superior isn't a good place to look for work, at least not in the 80's.

One important milestone had transpired and was one of the most momentous precepts ever legislated. Effective 10-14-80, the Staggers Act or "de-regulation" (partial deregulation) as it was more popularly known. The passing of this act gives the railroads more freedom to lower rates, be more competitive, and eliminate non-profitable branch lines to name a few. Good for the railroads, they finally got out from under the I.C.C. This was truly a momentous time for U.S. railroading.

Later that month a milestone in Bud Hoekstra's life occurred when Jack Peterson called me at my girlfriend's house and told me that the "labor Board" had re-instated me. I was a working man again. The Soo Line had had two great occasions occur in the month of October. Of course de-regulation was one and my re-instatement was the other. It would be another win-win situation for all, although unbeknownst to the Soo Line at the time.

When we were going through the appeals process, we only requested re-in-

175

statement of the job. I didn't want back pay, I wasn't suing the company for any injury, I simply wanted my job back. Of course the company rejected my sincere admonishment, and so when Mr. Simmerman went to the Federal Mediation Board with my case, he asked for re-instatement of all rights, benefits, back pay and full seniority. It was a roll of the dice for both sides. If I came up with half of what we were shooting for - that would be good enough and half was what I was awarded - the right to come back to work without back pay. I felt like the weight of the world had been lifted off my shoulders, I would get another chance - a chance to prove that they were wrong.

I owed Jack Peterson a large debt of gratitude of which Jack said he would settle for a good dinner at his favorite supper club. And so the Petersons, the Bartells and Bud and his girl celebrated at a place called "Dreamland". All in all I owe Jack Peterson, John Graves, Mike Bartell and Dennis Simmerman the world for their dedication to righting the wrong that I was dealt. The Soo Line gave me the impression that they felt that I had crashed that train on purpose.

Chapter 21

Back to Work

It turned out that I was out of service for four days short of a year. The seniority issue was resolved. I would go behind the "cadet's". I would later find out that even one seniority number can make a difference on a terminal the size of the Soo Line at a facility like Superior.

Going back to work would also mean that the rules examiner would be driving up from Minneapolis to go over the rules and give me the rules examination. This guy was always cheerful and because of that, he irritated me as I hated tests and that is what he represented. After the test was taken, and we were shooting the breeze, we got around to the accident. He then sort of giggled and at the same time asked me if I actually did jump on my brake person. I simply answered with "how else can you say that"? That statement told me that the big shots in Minneapolis were not only vindictive they did it with humor and bravado.

I marked up as the fireman on the 7:59 transfer with Ed Markon. Basically the 7:59 would handle an empty train of lumber flats and other lumber related cars. We would take this train of usually ninety plus cars and give it to the "Peg" (Duluth, Winnipeg, and Pacific) at West Duluth. We usually returned to Stinson with a loaded train of a like number of cars. Once this train arrived at Stinson, it would be switched and probably on its way to Chicago before seven o'clock that night. Most of the time it would need a helper. Once the train gained Hillcrest, its two SD40's would handle that train with ease (don't forget that in most places, track speed was 40 MPH). Once we yarded our train we were finished for the day. 418 would then be attacked by the 3:00 Stinson switch engine, worked by seasoned veterans engaged in the quest of getting the work done and going home early. If they weren't done by eight o'clock—they would whine.

I worked the "59" for a couple of weeks, even caught it on the weekend, as the engineer. Business was picking up and I was able to hold a "chain gang", as fireman. Chain gang was a euphemism for pool or "first in first out". When the grain was moving at its peak—there would be as many as five crews in the pool. I worked a couple of trips with J.J. O'Brien and then was set up. I was teetering between being the youngest engineer or the oldest fireman.

My first payday would come and I picked my check up at the roundhouse. There is always plenty of people to be seen at the roundhouse, on this most important day. And so I picked up my first paycheck in a year. Of course like all rails, I kept a time book and had a pretty good idea of what was due me. The check didn't measure up to what I was expecting, it seemed like they might have shorted me a day. One of the guys mentioned that maybe they paid me the 90% they paid guys during their first year. I knew nothing of this. This was the first time I had ever heard of that. I looked at the timesheet that always accompanied the check and yep, each day was about 10% less than I expected. They had found yet another way to screw me. About this time I was ready to air it all out and I did—I was tired of the shit this outfit kept directing at me. About this time I had a propensity to punch someone. First they try to kill me, that didn't work, so then they fired me. Next they screw me out of two seniority numbers and now this. They would stoop this low and continue the perfidy that they were engrained in.

A large company can be very fickle. "Too many cooks spoil the broth" so the adage goes, pretty well fits into the Soo Line scheme of things as it does any railroad or large company.

However it now seemed to me that every cook in the joint was trying to cook my goose, they had declared war on me. What this baneful company can't remember or forget—if I can avoid getting fired again and can stay with the company—I will remember and I won't forget or forgive their actions toward me. The entire year that I was fired, I tried to maintain a clear mind, to go forth with alacrity and acquiescence, to show the company and my friends that I was ready to do the job. Another adage portends that a single straw can break a camel's back. At this time I could not foresee the immediate future nor project the long term effort. I was at the mercy of this corporate menagerie that suffered from the same economic pangs that I did. The old timers used to say that there isn't much you can do to hurt a large company because it is only a piece of paper. They were usually right.

As I proceeded through the Soo Line's maze of setbacks, I could at least look back and count my blessings. Here in Duluth/Superior I had amassed a vast array of friends from more than one or two circles. I was fortunate I had more than one reason to stay in Superior. Several of them were very supportive in my effort to get my job back.

As I look back—I think it would be fun to spend a Saturday night at the Harbor Inn, or better yet—the Beacon. I have some great memories. It would surely be fun to see some of the guy's 'n gal's that I knew in that great place.

During the summer of 1981 I was able to hold 52-53 the way freight to Ladysmith, as the fireman, of course. There were two reasons that I could hold the job. Reason one was that "Big Ed" was the engineer. Ed wasn't the most personable guy that ever ran an engine, but I managed to get along with him. Ed ran his own engine. The other reason was because the job wasn't turning right away, it had dropped a few notches in popularity.

#52 usually took a train directly to Ladysmith, Wis. (it did very little "way work"). When business was good and everything fell into place—then #52 would drop its train, grab another train and become #53. After a short stop at the deli, #53 would be on its way back to Superior.

The daylight trips were quite pleasant if a body enjoyed the many attributes of nature and we went through some isolated country that only nature's children themselves could live in. It was an enjoyable ride as Ed did all of the thinking (as well he should have). I would stay on this job as long as I could and like it. Sooner or later one of the "cadets" would bump me.

On one trip we laid over on one of those beautiful sunlit days. I decided to walk down to the Flambeau River Bridge. I was walking towards the river and as I got closer to the bridge I see a guy coming the other way. My thoughts, as I notice him, are "I'd bet a million dollars that that was Johnny Taksas if I didn't know better". Well........it was.

John had spent his younger days in a CCC camp in the Ladysmith area and now that he was retired and too old to go to Canada, he decided to bring his wife up to Ladysmith, to look back into her husband's youth along with John, himself. Unfortunately for John, yet fortunate for me, John and his wife had hit a deer and their V.W. was being repaired as we talked.

Shortly after I left the IC, I had heard that John was involved in a terrible accident through no fault of his own. At this point I will have to accede to you that of all of the engineers that I have worked with, I probably have worked with John longer than anyone. So John and I talked a good while as John imparts his gruesome experience: We were on 392 and pretty much on time. We knew via the radio that once we had left Harvey, they planned on crossing #51 over from track #3 to track #4 upon our arrival, which would necessitate #51's getting around a southbound drag which was ahead of him on #3 track. As we approached Harvey, I pinched the train down a bit (applied a light brake application). He held onto that brake application until he went under the "clear" (green) signal and also noted that the switch targets were green. Once both he and the fireman called out "lined", John then released the train brakes thinking that his route was clear. John didn't see the switch target change from green to red however his fireman did and immediately sat on the floor while John realizing what had taken place had already put the train into "emergency" and laid on the whistle. John said that his first inkling of what was happening is when he heard Harold Coughlon, 51's engineer yell on the radio to the switch tender "don't throw that switch", which was repeated. Taksas remembers nothing before the impact.

This catastrophe would consume the lives of the engineer and brakeman of #51. The six person crew of 392 would suffer six nonfatal injuries. Passengers would survive 38 individual injuries. Of the four total locomotives involved, three were destroyed. All of the equipment on AMTRAK'S 392 would require extensive shopping. Of course #51 was the hottest southbound train originating out of Chicago. There would be a few disgruntled shippers to add injury to this grotesque debacle.

At the time of the accident, John had nearly 40 years in engine service. His older brother, Frank, had hired out 15 years earlier. I fired for both of them.

Being familiar with the Illinois Central Gulf and especially the Harvey operation, I knew exactly what happened, when I first got word of the accident.

During my career I was privy to two different railroad operations. At both of these facilities the General Yardmaster was overworked to the extreme. Rarely during the course of a conversation with the "general", would the other telephone not ring. These yardmasters were overwhelmed with responsibility. Their ulcer rate was high and their life spans were low. These men would often times have to baby sit someone that was inexperienced and working a new position. What would aggravate the general's daily grind would be a change in the normal daily routine. A change in routine of course affects everyone. I would surmise that the routine in this case was no routine at all

In essence you have an overwhelmed general yardmaster trying to do a job with an archaic system (if you can call it a system at all) with a brand new switch tender that had worked the Harvey job only once before, actually his first day of official employment. I can remember looking at the maze of switches from high up in the cab of an engine and having to look twice to be sure the switches were properly lined. It caused even the older, more experienced guys a certain amount of disparity. When I think back to what this new switchtender was going through. He didn't have the benefit of being able to look down and see the track situation as he was on the ground. Even if he had been able to better see the switches, would he have been able to discern their proper positions? We are missing the experience factor.

All through his incongruous tour of duty the switchtender could only do his best, follow instructions and carry them out in a ponderous manner. The one order that he did follow to the letter was the one where the "general" told him to line the switch for #51 to go south when the passenger train went by. As he saw the passenger train in effect, go by, he lined the switch as instructed. The train that went by was a northbound IC electric train, a suburban train not connected to the mainstream operation because it was electric and had overhead wires. Anyone that worked in train service in any capacity associated with the freight or through passenger operation never gave the electrics any thought, not because they were taught not to - it was simply ignored because it was an entirely different operation, same railroad, same guys. Other than that, it almost didn't exist. It simply wasn't there. Don't get me wrong, we operated under the catenary with certain industry jobs, but otherwise had very little to do with suburban service.

When the switchtender lined the switch, in effect, he lined #392, the passenger train right into the headend of #51. Depending on what radio channel they were on—some guys heard #51's engineer screaming on his radio for the switchtender to not throw the switch. It was too late. The impact speed was probably between 45 and 50 MPH. It was also said that the switchtender was on another radio channel.

An accident occurred for lack of forethought. At least another accident of this multitude shouldn't happen because we learned a good lesson on this one......

...

Getting back to working with Big Ed. We were going east (south) heading for Ladysmith on #52. We were blasting across the Bibon Marsh when I called Ed's attention to a deer that looked like he was about to run into the train. Well....Ed had to see for himself—he didn't believe me. By that time the poor deer is dragging itself up the embankment with only two legs. Now why couldn't this asshole simply blow the whistle? He might have saved that deer. I'll tell you, I felt awful. It was a toss-up for what the poor deer was going through and what and why these old bastards couldn't take our word for whatever was happening. I didn't and couldn't understand this incredulous aspect of the geriatric mind when it applied to running an engine. We killed that same deer on the return trip as it lay between the rails. Praise the Lord!

Chapter 22

Lean Years

My first place in Superior was really a nice place. It was located fairly close to downtown and not very far from work. I had planned to live there until something happened for positive reasons which would enable me to gladly vacate the premises for a life enhancement.

You can move anywhere you want to, but if you can't afford to buy 200 acres or more, you will be at the mercy of your neighbors. The realtors and rental agencies don't know about the idiosyncrasies of a prospective neighbor and if they did, they would keep it to themselves. Intangibles are difficult to measure.

As I settled into my new environment, of course I noticed the comings and goings of the neighbors, especially my next door neighbor. This guy was a man of many toys. I would see a huge boat, ATV's on trailers, and one day I saw him drive a Corvette into his garage. I wondered "what does this guy do for a living", his house didn't quite match his assets if you wanted to throw in his toys. It wasn't long after that when I saw a police car pull up to this guy's house and the man himself walked out of the car in police uniform and then left, still clad in police garb, telling me that he was a police officer, that had to make a brief stop at home.

Wow, I thought, I could've been a damn good cop for the money this guy was making. I was in the wrong racket.

I hadn't given the neighbor much thought until months later I came home and found out that this man's garage was on fire and luckily the fire was eradicated in time to save the Corvette.

A new situation would arise, now the police officer and his family began to show a certain amount of paranoia which is expressed when this family decides to acquire a huge mountain type dog that loves to bark and was not only aggravating to the neighbors but to the officers family as well. The lifestyle of the neighborhood would go down a peg or two because of the endless utterings of this dog. This dog was definitely a watch dog that more than earned his keep.

The police department was also getting heat about the dog and of course that would be passed down to the officer himself. I came home one night and the dog was barking at some kids walking past the house and I had had enough. I called the cops—didn't stay on the line long enough for the call to be traced and figured about all that it would do would be to throw a little more oil on the already well lit fire. The months dragged by and now spring is in the air. One day the cop is running plastic strips or thatch through his chain link fence in order to obscure the dog's vision. A neighbor lady was chatting with him. My window was cracked and so I was all ears. He explained to the lady, the purpose of the thatch and then I heard her ask him "who is calling the police on the dog"? His brief answer was—the guy with the beard. I had the only beard in the building and I now knew that I was a marked man. How did he find out that I had called the cop shop, and for how long had he known this? I knew a cop on the force and I found out through him that the cops had "caller ID" long before it was extended to the public. And so this guy almost knew from the day I called that I (among others) called. That call was placed three, four maybe six months prior to that. If he was really out to get me he either didn't try very hard or I was very, very, lucky. He had to know my car. He had to see it parked around the various establishments around downtown. Not knowing what he knew, caution was thrown to the wind. By watching the guy come and go, I was able to learn much about the man. I knew his days off, I knew what time he went to work, that he was avaricious and possessive, but I didn't know he was after me. Now I knew!

I was lucky. I had heard more than one horror story about this particular police department. I was told by more than one friend—you don't call the cops on the cops. Right or wrong the ball is always in their corner. The deck is stacked in their favor and on and on.

The advantage now goes to the hunted as I now realize I am being hunted. Talk about one covering ones ass. Armed with what I knew, I would go to the bars, sometimes park directly in front and go about my bar side business, with one anomaly—I would not drink, I couldn't and didn't. Tuesday nights were almost always spent at this one place because it had music and the group that I hung around with liked to go there. There just happened to be a parking spot smack in front of the place. Ordinarily I would have avoided that spot like the plague. This night I pulled right in there. I was audaciously baiting the guy while at the same time I had a propensity to avoid him.

On this particular night, one of the ladies asked me if I could drive her home. As we worked our way into the main street, she asked me if I had any beer at home. Of course, I did, and so we headed for my place to get the beer and then head over the bridge. When we were about two blocks from my apartment, sure enough, on come the many lights of a squad car. He had me, in his own insidious way. I left my vehicle and approached the already standing cop. He had planned well as he had a partner with him, an unusual occurrence. I asked him what was the problem?. He replied—you rolled through a couple of stop signs and you were weaving, can I see your license? He looked at the license long enough to memorize it and then asked me if I had been drinking. I don't drink, was my reply. Will you take a sobriety test? Of course, I said. I passed, but I think, although I was cold sober, I had no reason to trust this guy. He may have done something underhanded, which he was known for. After observing the reading on the breathalizer he mumbled something about I didn't do it right and please take another only breath harder into it. I had nothing to lose and did it again. I wasn't the picture of complacency however I had pretty much planned for this moment. Once again—I didn't make the machine do what he wanted it to do. The guys getting frustrated and asks me if I am on any medication. Nope. Are you sure? Yep. This entire scenario turns into a source of embarrassment to this guy, yet in front of a fellow officer. I walked away unscathed wondering what might have happened if I hadn't had that lady with me. I don't think it would've been pretty. We grabbed the beer and my little witness and I went over the bridge. Now that the cat was out of the bag….the heat was on, but at least I knew it.

A few weeks later, I encountered a few "off" duty cops having a few pops. Wouldn't you know it but one of the cops was the guy that was driving the squad the night I was pulled over. He pointed at me and identified me as being the friend of the officer he was driving for that night. The guy that fingered me was shit-faced by the way.

I lived in that place for nearly three years and now it was time to go. The dog was still there, but he quieted down considerably. When Soo line hired me, they volunteered assurance that I wouldn't be laid off. They lied. I was getting laid off as the economy went south. I was working here and there but not enough to afford that apartment and the baggage it carried. I moved to a place on the other side of town where the rent was commensurate with the area. The economy really took a dive. The year 1983 was a very short one for me as I only worked six days. 1984 wasn't much better—I worked 25 days. Earlier in the book when I mentioned the two seniority slots I would lose and what it could mean on a terminal the size of Superior—I was now seeing it. 1985 was a windfall year compared to the two prior years. I worked six months. It was also time to move again. I didn't have much of a rapport with the landlady she was quiet and kept to herself. The only time I would hear from her was when she played her organ or when she would call me on the phone to tell me to turn my stereo down. She didn't play the organ all that often and the last time I heard her play, and it was extensive, they hauled her away in a hearse the next morning. Now it was really time to move and about then a friend of mine told me that his relative had a trailer for sale. I looked at it (it was a dump) but I thought that a change of scenery would be appropriate for the time.

Back in those days of decadent emaciation, the one activity I was able to stay with were my memberships in the YMCA's of either Duluth or Superior. I had a lot of time on my hands and spent a lot of it playing racquet ball, working out in general and of course there was my first love—fishing. If it hadn't been for the YMCA and fishing there is no telling what might have happened. I may have actually looked for a job. In all fairness to the Soo Line (would they know the meaning of fair?), I probably could have worked in some away-from-home-terminal and I may have even developed a liking for it. There were places like Enderlin, Harvey and Terre Hautte that occasionally would require a "borrowed out" engineer, however a move of that proportion would probably give the Soo Line another shot at me, more reasons and chances at knocking me down.

At least in Superior I knew where I stood and if I stayed out of range of their subtle weapons, I would be oblivious to their wrath. There was a breach of trust in there somewhere.

During the time I was laid off, Superior inherited a new trainmaster. I had never met the man but already I hated him because when the company was going to put me back to work, he took it upon himself to proffer to the higher-ups that I take a complete rules examination, alone. The only difference would be was there would be a new rules examiner. They turned on the other guy. One day they surprised a whole bunch of management types and told them that their services were no longer needed. Our once cheerful rules examiner was no longer the man he once was. The Soo Line had gone from everyone's favorite to a hateful place. That goes to show you....there is no honor amongst thieves.

It has been a few years since I began cultivating this odious feeling of recalcitrance and I was languishing in it. The diatribe that this company generated had taken its toll. The hatred had crossed the line—it was now irreversible. I had felt their wrath long before the very same personage that judged me had been bitten by that same snake. It was to be my turn at slaying the dragon. They pissed me off!

On June 9th, 1985 I took some time off of work as most of my family would be up for a long weekend of visiting and sightseeing. In the main crew were sister Kathy and her husband Wayne, along with sister Chris and her boy Todd. On Monday we would link up with brother Chuck and his longtime friend,

Bill Biesen. I can remember when they were kids, two loveable brats. I watched them grow up.

Chuck and Bill were staying at Delta Lodge just south of Iron River, Wisconsin. The rest of the gang wanted to camp and I found them a beautiful campsite on Bass Lake. It was warm, the bugs were kind and there was a full moon. What more could you want? We were all sitting around the campfire enjoying the night, when my one sister asked me where the bathrooms were. Then the party was over as we had to find a campground with at least an outhouse. She didn't do the primitive thing. We had to pick up and go to a more hospitable place. Luckily we found a place, with toilets, that had a vacancy and so we began to have fun again. A little later, Billy said that he had a headache and was going back to their cabin on Everett Lake. As for myself—I had a dentist's appointment the next morning and so it was time for me to make the 55 mile trek back to Superior. My appointment was early and wouldn't take long and so I was back at my trailer when the phone rang. It was brother-in-law, Wayne. He said, "Bud, I'm afraid I have bad news for you". I could tell by the demeanor of his voice, that it was serious, no joking. My inward reaction was one of foreboding. Once Wayne knew I was ready, he then told me that Billy had passed away during the night—they thought that it was due to an aneurism. I told Wayne that I would be out there as soon as I could.

My reaction was one of disbelief, this couldn't have happened. This kid had an awful lot of life ahead of him. He wasn't ready to die. My thoughts then went to my brother who must really be hurting. I couldn't begin to imagine what Bill's wife, Pam, was going through. Bill was only 33 years old. They had three children, the oldest being five. This one couldn't have been any worse than it was. It was highly unexpected, it happened to a healthy person and in the wrong place—away from his family. This kid was like a little brother to me. I was having an abject feeling of remorse and knew that I would have to overcome it in order to safely drive to Delta.

Once I arrived and shared sorrows with everyone, I began to walk around the cabin. I entered one bedroom and there on the wall was a beautiful map of the Iron River area. I looked at it and then all at once I punched the wall as hard as I could. My first thought was "why did I do that?" My next reaction was one of pain. I had broken my little finger on the right hand. I played a lot of sports and did a lot of other bone breaking activities, but never broke a bone. It was a first. For a split second it was a good idea, gone bad.

I later sat down and talked to Chuck. Chuck told me that he got back to the cabin about 1:30. Bill was in bed, but got up and had a beer with Chuck. He still complained of the headache but thought that it might be a little better.

They talked for a little while and then said goodnight. Bill would die in his sleep sometime between then and five o'clock that morning, according to the Bayfield County Coroner.

I couldn't fathom how this fun loving, cantankerous kid could be dead! I could not overcome the poignancy of what happened. This wasn't like Aunt Clara passing away after a long illness it was simply a very heartbreaking anomaly. This kid, this very much alive kid, shouldn't be dead. Words could not have expressed the anguish we shared with each other. He was truly one of our own.

Those of you that remember the standard 40 foot and 50 foot boxcars of the 40's, 50's, and 60's will remember also that they were always painted in various shades of oxide red. Growing up around Chicago, I saw a vast multitude of those cars. If it hadn't been for those cars, I may not have made it out of grammar school. I would read the wording on the cars by sounding them out and then my parents would correct me if I went astray. Monon was probably the first word I ever learned.

Along with the railroads name, advertising, capacities, and car numbers, would often be graffiti. The guys that authored those icons largely remained anonymous.

There was "BOZO TEXINO", "KILROY" (whom I think had more than one father) and of course, "HERBIE".

During this time, the progenitor of "HERBIE" came forward. The guy that was responsible for all of that wonderment was a switchman off the Terminal Railroad Association of St. Louis. After 41 years of railroading, Herbert A. Mayer retired and decided to "fess up". He began his pursuit of boxcar art in 1955 and estimates that his talents have graced the sides of about 70,000 boxcars.

Chapter 23

~~~

North Dakota Beckons

Back in the fall of 1986, I was hanging on the extra board at Superior, Wisconsin. Grain movement through that port was slow because of a poor harvest. Business on other parts of the system was picking up. The sunflower harvest out in the Dakotas was exceptional, along with a shortage of manpower at certain points. Enderlin, North Dakota was one of those places. The Soo Line was more than happy to make my services available to the Enderlin engineer's freight pool. From Enderlin, all train service employees worked in a pool going east 137 miles to Glenwood, Minnesota and west over the Carrington subdivision to Harvey, N.D.-139 miles.

Enderlin means "end of the line" in German and many years ago that was exactly what it was. It has a population of around 1,000 and sits in the southeastern corner of the state. It is hard to say how Enderlin might have fared had it not been a division point on the Soo Line. It has a seed mill that is served by the railroad. Among its other highlights are one bank, a bowling alley and bar, two taverns and a restaurant. I didn't get out there, but I'm pretty sure there was a tractor dealership out on the highway.

Everyone enjoyed the same seniority as manpower came out of one big pool. There were no yard engines and any switching was done by a road crew usually coming on duty and paid for actual time consumed while performing at the seed mill. They usually kept an old run-down geep for that.

You never knew which direction you were going until the caller came pounding on the motel room door telling you what time you were called for and what train it was. If I had my "druthers", I would have rather gone west than east. The only difference between Harvey and Enderlin was that maybe Harvey had one more tractor dealership than Enderlin. I had worked into Glenwood from Superior many times. Besides it seemed like we always had bad trips going in that direction. Luckily I only worked three trips going east. Harvey crews worked 154 miles to the Canadian border (Portal). One road switcher worked around Harvey and it went to work at 2:30 AM. Can you think of a more do-lorous time to go to work? Those guys worked the full twelve hours every day and they had that far off, empty stare like a soldier does after he has been on the line for a few months.

When the caller told me that I was being forced to Enderlin, I moaned and groaned, however inwardly the thought of going somewhere else was appealing. I can't remember if it was due to a union agreement or simply an un-official Soo Line edict but I was also told that I would be there for 30 days. Thirty days anywhere is enough. I took my sweet time getting there, as driving country roads was sort of a hobby of mine. From Superior to Enderlin was a little over 300 miles. It took me two days to get there and I enjoyed every country mile.

Once I arrived I went in to see the boss. His official title was "agent-train-master". He welcomed me with heartfelt sincerity. I told him that I would be here for 30 days and he said that those 30 days would be highly appreciated. I thanked him and then went out to talk to the caller. The caller told me that there was a little motel up the street that was owned by a Soo Line engineer. He also mentioned that the rooms didn't as yet have telephones and so the caller would have to extend to me a personal invite, just like the old days. After b.s.ing with the caller for a while, I told him that I wanted to make a couple of student trips each way before I went on the regular board. These trips would be made preferably during daylight hours. Call me in the morning, I said as I walked out the door.

Normally I would have driven my vehicle over to the motel and then walked over to one of the establishments and had myself a drink or two. However this Enderlin trip just happened to fall into the middle of a self-imposed hiatus that distanced me from alcohol. My goal was a year without a drink and halfway into it, I was true to myself. It wasn't that hard. A side trip to North Dakota wasn't going to upset the applecart and I persevered. Another engineer that was born in Enderlin and had good seniority was also out there. This fellow had a drinking problem and was dry. He had somehow gotten into trouble with the company and had to mind his p's and q's. One night he was bowling with a few of his old cronies and succumbed to the lure of alcohol. It wouldn't have been so bad, but in a terminal like Enderlin you don't get much time off and this guy kept going with the sauce until closing time. By that time he knew he was getting close to being called and so there was no sense in driving way out into the country to his sister's house (where he was staying). He decided to park in front of the yard office and sleep until he was called. When they did call he wasn't to be found. Who did find him? The trainmaster parked behind him that morning and saw him sleeping in the front seat of his car. Knowing what had happened and knowing his history he pulled him out of service. I don't know for sure, but it may have been his last day on the railroad.

I wanted to see if I could quit for an entire year and then determine how much better I would feel both physically and mentally. At the end of that period nothing happened, nothing had changed. I liked to drink but I would always closely monitor it.

Getting back to Enderlin. I had worked with a whole bunch of good guys and had a really great all expenses paid and free trip to Enderlin, N.D. In fact they also paid me.

Operating a locomotive with tonnage behind it isn't quite the same as getting into an automobile and simply driving away. It takes experience. There are no two pieces of railroad alike and it takes many trips to acclimate oneself to the topography of a railroad. One railroad that comes to mind would not examine a fireman for promotion until he had a combined 180 road trips in both freight and passenger service. Other roads had the impression that as long as a guy had that engineer's card he could work anywhere, without much prior experience. The key word to proper train handling is—anticipation. Operating a train takes preparation. Each train is different for a myriad of reasons. The factors that come to mind are the tonnage verses horsepower ratio, placement of loads and empties in the train, rate of speed, lay of the land, and weather. Factor all of that in and throw in a mechanical glitch or two or more. You might have a bad trainline or maybe you have a locomotive that continuously drops its load. You may need that engine on the heavy grade that looms in the very near future or you may want to isolate that unit because of the hill and dale territory and the off and on surges of power that can and will cause an extraction i.e. (knuckle, drawbar).

The Soo mainline west of the Twin Cities is predominately flat to slightly un-dulate. A pair of SD40's can easily accommodate a 9,600 ton train at normal track speed—40 MPH. Had it not been for a couple of hills out on the Portal and Carrington Subs located in North Dakota, two SD40's could handle almost twice that tonnage. Because of these hills the maximum tonnage for a pair of SD40's is 9,600 on the ruling grade which to the top of that precipice is called Siding 280 (MP280). Extending east out of the Sheyenne River Valley is a steep grade that when approached from either direction would resemble a lopsided turned upside down empty ice cream cone on a profile map. This is the 7 ½ mile hill going east out of Valley City. Westbound, the hill is pared down to 3 ½ miles. This is a grade to be reckoned with at almost 1.5 % and the grade that I was concerned with. I had wished that I had had a few more student trips than the two that I was afforded.

Now about our train. #940 this day would have the 757 and 6610, an SD40 and an SD40-2, both similar in horsepower. Loads and empties would be 84 loads and 15 empties—99 cars at 8900 tons, a typical #940 train. What wasn't typical was the fact that the hind 64 cars were huge tank cars loaded with glycol (used to make anti-freeze). When the train was made up in Canada the glycol should have either ran as a separate train or the glycol should have been placed on the head-end of our train. This would be like having a tiger by the tail. We always referred to tank cars as "sloshers" and they could make for problems in train handling, not to mention the fact that those cars couldn't have been in a worse place. You have to remember that tank cars are not and cannot be loaded to the extreme capacity of the car for obvious reasons. For this reason much room in the car allows for "sloshing", which is the movement of liquid reacting to the forces of train and track conditions. More than one engineer has lamented when his train broke in two, something to the effect of "but I had the damned thing stopped". You are stretch braking a train coming to a stop and still have some throttle to unload when suddenly you get a forceful "run-in" of the slack. Sometimes the air goes sometimes it doesn't, but you can almost bet that your popularity went down a notch on the caboose. Now envision what happens when you have 64 large capacity tanks next to the caboose.

We were called for 1100 hours (11 o'clock) and I calculated that if we had the usual trip we would be in Enderlin in time for the "dancing girls".

We were having a good trip and coming into Valley City. I reflected that what with only 30 miles to go the whole works could go out the window as we dragged the train over "280". It would be up to me to guide this train safely into Enderlin. Now the entire train is on the hill and we are down to ten MPH. Sometimes an experienced brakeman will offer welcome advice, but the brakeman I had this day was fairly inexperienced. No help. As we crested the hill, my thoughts went from when to set the air, to how much throttle to unload. The more air you reduced from the trainline (train brakes), the more air it would take to release that trainline, affecting a slower release. Don't forget that the head end of the train will release first in a graduated effect until the last car is released. We have 64 tank cars on the hind end, however, they are fairly new cars and would be equipped with the latest triple valve (individual car brake system). That's a plus. I opted to go with a minimum trainline reduction of 7 pounds. This would translate to 10 pounds of friction against each wheel of each car. Hopefully, I would apply the brakes at the correct place on the hill. If I applied them too early, it would cause the train to stall. If I applied them too late, I would be running a train out of control. Once I knew that we had the hill made, it was time to draw off 7 pounds from the trainline. Remember, the tank cars are still rolling up hill. I was going about 22 MPH when I did this. Now it would be time to think about gradually notching down on the throttle. I never like to shut down below throttle five, (there are 8 throttle positions) especially with the impending reaction of those tank cars. Shutting down power, coupled with the time lapse between notches, should be gradual. I was up close to 40 MPH when those 64 loaded tanks decided to really let me know where they were. When they rolled in, I knew we were over the hill for sure. Looking at the speed recorder, I noticed that we were at 43 MPH without any loss of momentum. Maybe I should go to throttle four. I can feel these tank cars pulling back, rolling in, and just causing havoc back there. I hoped that the conductor was all right. He was no stranger to that hill, but I would have to apologize when we got to Enderlin. We are up to 47 when I shut down to throttle three. My thoughts ran from "I'm sure glad this track is in great shape" to "if there is a derailment, they usually give the engineer a 3 MPH over the limit buffer". After all, they know it is impossible to run a train at the exact speed. Now my heart is in my throat, and my palms are sweating. How many times in my career have I felt this way? If the air goes (trainline severence) that surely will indicate a derailment. If that happens—I might as well grab my grip and start walking because I'll never work here again. All the while, the back end of the train is seemingly moving back and forth. I did have another option. I could have gone deeper into the trainline which could have resulted in an extraction, or simply stopped. But that wouldn't have been so simple. I already was in throttle three, with not much pulling power, and I didn't have the luxury of knowing the lay of the land. Luckily the train began to slow and my nerves gradually began to revert to normal. The brakeman commented "boy that sure was a fun ride"! I said nothing. However, my thoughts went to "accolades to the guys that work the tracks around here". I will live to fight another day!

Later waiting for the hind end to get pulled up to the yard office, I had one more chore. That would be, to apologize to the conductor, and hope that he wouldn't be too irate. As the conductor rolled off the caboose, I motioned to him. I tried to explain my dilemma as an inexperienced hogger on this particular pike. He heard me out and then said that the train was made up backwards and even if he did get a rough ride, it wouldn't have been my fault. I nervously countered with, "you mean you got a good ride back there?" "Never better", he replied. How do you figure? I then grabbed a handful of rolaids and washed them down with a cup of coffee. There were no "dancing girls"!

Now we are at the 30 day mark and I go into the bosses office to tell him that I'm outta here and goodbye, it's time to go and all that. He says—I can't let you go. My reply was—we agreed to 30 days. Everybody involved knew it would be 30 days and now you're telling me that that wasn't how it worked. With that he gave me an exasperated look of desperation. Some pondering ensued and then he said: I'll take a look at it and let you know tomorrow (31 days) if you can go home. Upon hearing that I simply loaded my little car up with everything in the world that mattered to me and headed for Superior.

I didn't stop to smell the roses on the trip home as I wanted to make sure my trailer furnace would run and just to make sure the place hadn't been inundated by thieves.

Once I had arrived in Superior it didn't' take me long to realize that I was still within the doldrums of middle class complacency. I hadn't gained a damn thing. I made a ton of money out there but it didn't matter at all. My furnace wouldn't work and all of that money went into that. That pissed me off but I surmised that I had gotten a million dollars worth of experience about life. Had the Soo Line understood that, would they have sent me there? That was the attitude that was instilled in me by the railroad.

And now it was time to call Enderlin (the phone still worked). The gentleman I wanted to talk to came on the line. I didn't tell him that I was calling from Superior. He gave me the okay and thanked me. He doesn't know to this day that I wasn't going to stay there any longer than we had agreed upon.

In retrospect, and previously in this book, I mentioned the impeccable standards that the Illinois Central enjoyed regarding knowledge of the physical characteristics and the time afforded an individual before it became time to get examined and finally run an engine alone.

And of course, I wrote extensively about the wreck I had at Moose Lake and spoke of its repercussions. This accident is attributed to lack of experience and the company's lack of respect for experience. I had always felt that an engineer should know the railroad he is running over. I had defied my own principles and for that the Soo Line showed me no mercy. I vowed that I would never let them do that to me again.

And now you wonder after reading this chapter why I wasn't more insistent about student trips, especially after they fired me for almost a year.

Instead of forcing me out there for 30 days, that entire 30 days could have been easily consumed making student trips, and justifiably so.

At the same time, I knew that the engineers at Enderlin were at the end of the line in more than one respect. I wasn't out there trying to piss anyone off (they would probably be pissed sooner or later anyway). The snake had already bitten me and already it was coiling up for another chance. I knew that, but at that stage of the game, I elected to play it. I wasn't going to be some kind of martyr. They hadn't broken my spirit—they simply provided me with a nice little vacation that I relished.

194

Of course, I covered my ass as best I could. I had the benefit of knowing this time that: yes this outfit could jeopardize my life, and I knew what I was up against.

The Milwaukee Acquisition

In the year 1960, the Twin Cities had 11 major railroads operating within their boundaries. By 1980, due to mergers, consolidations and a bankruptcy or two, that number would dwindle to six and soon thereafter to five.

The Rock Island had declared bankruptcy and now was being sold piecemeal to the highest bidder, or whomever the sitting federal judge felt was the most deserving of his approval. The Milwaukee Road would be the next railroad to be dissolved in federal court.

More than one railroad wanted the opportunity to grasp that part of the Rock known as the "spine line", which ran between St. Paul and Kansas City and was currently under lease by the Chicago & Northwestern. This route was also coveted by the Soo Line. It would be a prize, making either of the company's president and stockholders more than just a little bit giddy, as it fit like a glove on either railroad. The spine line offered to funnel grain from the northern reaches of the mid- west to the ports of New Orleans, Houston and all other gulf ports. It was a prized plum to be sure.

Partial de-regulation went into effect under the guise of the "Staggers Act" or de-regulation. This would open the door for railroads to get out from under low density branch lines, be more creative in setting rates and be more creative - period. Had the Rock Island been able to hold on a little longer, what might have happened?

What did happen was that the Soo Line would not get the spine line. It wasn't a surprise that the court ruled in the CNW's favor. CNW had been leasing it and already had its foot in the door and so would get the nod. CNW won the first battle, however there was another fight already in the works. 1983 would be the year for the Chicago & Northwestern.

The principal bidders vying for the pared down 3100 mile version of the Milwaukee were Chicago Milwaukee Corp., Grand Trunk Western, Chicago & Northwestern, and Soo Line in that order.

Chicago Milwaukee Corp. wanted to operate the railroad as it already was. The core element of this company had already put Milwaukee Road into bankruptcy and its chances would not be good. The Grand Trunk had designs on the Milwaukee because of its Chicago-Duluth connection with the Duluth, Winnipeg & Pacific (the "Peg" was another Canadian National subsidiary). The GTW channeled enough traffic to the Milwaukee during the winter of 1981-82 to keep the Milwaukee afloat.

The Milwaukee actually made money for a while. The Grand Trunk and Milwaukee Road would have been an end to end merger. The "Trunk" had already proven that it was good for the Milwaukee. The deal was condoned by the trustee and anyone else connected to the Milwaukee was pulling for the GTW.

I myself was rooting for the "Trunk" and I worked for the Soo Line. Had the Soo Line prevailed, I could see myself in the heart of what had to be a nightmare for a newly located employee and being the bottom man at Superior, I could easily see myself on my way to the Twin Cities living out of a suitcase again.

Alas - - the Grand Trunk-Milwaukee Road was not to be. Trunk management grew tired of being a contestant in a game that it couldn't afford (410 vs. 570 million) to be in. Its parent company, the Canadian National didn't think much of it either when they disdained to help GTW financially. Tired of seemingly beating its head against a wall, the Grand Trunk bowed out of the fracas when it signed an agreement with the Burlington Northern for mutual coordination of operations with the BN. The deal was signed on the 9th of September to be effective on the 1st of January 1985.

The final decision would come down to either the CNW or the Soo Line. It was looking like the loser of this battle would at least come away with trackage rights between the Twin Cities and Kansas City.

On the 26th of July, 1984 the I.C.C. voted, with only four of its seven seats present, for the Soo Line 4-0. The recommendation did not have to be filed in Federal Bankruptcy Court until September 10th. Why the short-handed panel voted to begin with, and so far in advance of the deadline, is arcane and should have been dis-allowed.

Knowledgeable people in the railroad field had fully expected the I.C.C. ruling to be in favor of the CNW, were now undecided as to who was going to get the final nod. On February 9th, 1985, Judge Thomas R. McMillen, ruled in favor of the Soo Line, however interestingly told the Soo Line not to do anything for 90 days, lest he change his mind. The judge pointed out that he based his decision toward public interest. He went on to stress competition, employee protection, freight rates and national defense. CNW immediately threw in the towel. It had already wasted much time, money and other resources in an effort to swing this gargantuan deal and offered that it would not appeal.

Judge McMillen's surprising decision would go down in the annals of railroad history as one of perplexity. Someone wondered aloud that perhaps the good judge had unknowingly made a personal concession to the Soo Line in light of the CNW's triumph over the Soo Line when it was awarded the "spine line".

Chapter 24

~~~

Welcome to St. Paul

I recently read a piece out of Trains magazine that told about the Union Pacific recently completing the new Kate Shelley Bridge, replacing the old one. What caused me to chuckle was when it said that trains would be allowed 70 MPH over the bridge.

I remembered a bridge over the Kettle River on the Soo Line Brooten, subdivision, going from Superior to Glenwood. As we crossed it, I would look down, far down, and always have the same comment "I don't think we would drown, but those rocks sure look awful nasty".

The Brooten sub was dark territory (non-signaled). We would approach the bridge on a curve. You couldn't see the bridge until you were right on top of it. Track speed was 40 MPH as was the bridge. For a long while the lead locomotive would hit the bridge at speed and then do a reactive lurch as the bridge and the regular roadbed or track didn't seem to be lined up. This would occur only on the westward trip, but it surely would give one a start. The guys finally started getting their trains down to 25 MPH or so, on their own and shortly after that the company made it official. About that time unbeknownst to me, I was making my last trip on the Brooten line. We hit the bridge at 25 MPH and as soon as the engine cleared the west end of the bridge, my brakeman called his brother, our conductor, 125 car lengths back, and simply murmured……..we made it.

Once I had tied up after making that trip, I was informed that I was transferred to the Twin Cities until further notice. It wasn't a surprise—I knew it was coming. It was just a matter of time. Once again I was expected to put my life on hold. There was no regard whatsoever for my personal life. I had recently gotten involved in the Big Brother program through the Duluth YMCA. I had completed the screening process and was sanctioned for the program. My little brother was from West Duluth. Our relationship had never really gotten off the ground because it didn't have a chance to. The Soo Line did it again! I mentioned that to my boss. He alluded that when he had heard about my being "forced" to the cities he remembered that I was involved in that program as he was sent forms to fill out. He suggested I take my vacation and try to get it all squared away. I would have to do that. I would have to say goodbye to my many friends, and I would have to change all personal plans that I had going on. Of course I would have to explain to Kyle, my little brother, what it was. I didn't see Kyle, but his mother understood and would explain it to him. Our relationship hadn't had a chance to go far enough and so that's the way it happened.

I guess the Soo Line thought that I lived in a car and owned no possessions. This company was like a "stiff prick", it had no conscience. I would have to leave my trailer where it was and hope that it would simply vanish. I could walk away from it without any repercussions. Luckily it happened that way. The last time I looked into that trailer park, it wasn't there!

I showed up in St. Paul on the 26th of May and checked into the Excel Inn, right off #94. I talked to a Mr. Rick Horace of crew management and he told me that I could stay there as long as I wanted (but not forever). This would be my new home, a sort of enlarged jail cell with maid service. The summer of 1987 was very hot in the Twin Cities. One day I was walking through the lobby of the motel wearing nothing more than shorts. The motel clerk asked me where I was going dressed like that. I replied that I was going to go running. She suggested that I might be a little crazy—running in the middle of such a hot day. I agreed with her and out the door I went.

A bunch of the Superior rails had an apartment not far from the motel. These were switchmen that couldn't work in Superior and moved to the cities where there was a lot of work. I called over there to see if I could get one of the guys to show me around. Tom Becker was glad to show me how to get over to "Pigs Eye" and maybe introduce me to a few of the officials. We drove down to the hump and then down to Dunn (east end of the yard), there we turned around and went back west, stopping at the yard office (top end). We went upstairs to the second floor and into the superintendent's office. The "Boss" just happened to be in his office and beckoned for us to come in. Becker introduced me as the newest engineer in the Twin Cities. I was given a warm welcome and told that my talents were fervently needed. I was more than surprised at how young this man seemed to be. I mentioned the guys age to Becker, and we both agreed that in a year or two with a job like that, he'll begin to look more like a super- intendent of a major railroad and less like a recent college graduate. The fol- lowing day Rick Michalski would show me the entire picture. We drove over to the Ford plant, which employs four yard engines around the clock and three more Ford hauler jobs (transfers) that originate at St. Paul Yard (Pigs Eye) bringing a train of automobile products to the Ford plant and returning with a train to St. Paul. Next was Southtown, another Milwaukee facility. Southtown had about twelve jobs starting there. From there we hopped over to Humboldt, which usually had eleven or twelve jobs. Shoreham no longer had any jobs originating.

And now that I was officially on the St. Paul board, it was time to start making student trips. For my first trip, I wanted a daylight trip to Portage. The caller alluded that a trip to Portage was a waste of time. I would never catch one of those jobs, anyway. I would go to Portage on #402 with Whitey Boughton, the #1 engineer on the river. It was a good trip. The brakeman and I decided to stop at the hotel bar for a couple of beers. Whiteys train got called for the early morn. I slept in. Being a student, I didn't have to go back with that particular crew. I caught #203 in the early afternoon instead. This train, at the time, consisted of two blocks, one of which is set out at Dunn (St. Paul) and the head end went up to the Ford plant on the night hauler. The road power went to the barn. There was a catch, however. This train would go like hell and more often than not get into Portage early. The River crew would also run like a banshee until it got to a myopic point out in the middle of nowhere, called "Duke". Duke is out in the middle of a vast backwater, a swamp replete with mosquitos and the ennui of waiting. You have made a textbook run and now you will sit out in the swamp, wasting fuel for 2-3 hours because St. Paul Yard doesn't have room for your train. Essentially you're waiting for the 10:30 PM Ford hauler to come on duty so that the Ford parts will evaporate as he takes them up the hill to Ford.

My next student trip took me out to Ortonville, Mn. on one of the coal empties. I would spend a most relaxing four days waiting for the loads to come back. These trains would go to Montana, get loaded, and return. When the train arrived at Ortonville, we would take it to St. Paul. We'll cover the H & D later.

A student trip to Glenwood, Mn. would be next. We had a good trip and I thought that I would spend a great deal of time on that particular piece of railroad. Ironically, I never made another trip out there. I made other various and sundry rides with instructive engineers, but never there again.

I would always try to make my trips coincide with whatever was going on in my life at the time. In order to line these student runs up, I would have to call crew management in Milwaukee to be sure that they would condone my request. I sort of knew which callers to avoid and which ones to talk to. I would call the caller of my choice and say something like: "it looks like they want me to go on the Bayport job", and it always worked. I was calling my own shots. And then one day I was going through that same spiel when the crew caller blatantly came right out and countered my statement with: "no they don't, they want you on the 3:59 Extra Top End." That was when I ran my first solo as an engineer in the cities.

The River Subdivision itself had six jobs plus the way freights 248 & 249. Hastings had a switcher and a road switcher. Red Wing had a switch engine and Wabasha had a patrol which actually was a road switcher. Winona had a switcher and La Crosse had a road switcher. I liked the river and made it known to the crew callers that I would work those jobs as most guys stayed away from them. I worked the Winona switcher for a couple of days in July and then in August I was forced on the Wabasha patrol for two weeks.

I had been on the Wabasha probably about four days when one day we were switching Lake City. There were still two main tracks and we were using both of them. We were sitting on the westward main and had our train together, air tested and ready to cross over to the eastward main for the trip to Wabasha. We had one train, 202, showing on our track sheet. Our conductor called 202 on his radio with no answer. He then asked me to call him on the more powerful engine radio. I complied and again got no answer. That indicated to our conductor that 202 wasn't in radio range and thus wasn't yet in the picture. About three quarters of a mile north of the depot at Lake City is a curve that could easily obscure the vision of an approaching train and also do likewise to someone looking for an approaching train. It was broad daylight, had it been dark you would easily see his headlight.

Not getting a response from 202 and after throwing both crossover switches for the crossover movement, the conductor told me to back the train across to the eastward main. As I began to nose into the eastward main, I looked across the cab and out the window and I see one of the biggest headlights I have ever seen. This is a manifest freight train that just a couple of seconds ago was going 50 MPH. As the train got closer it was shrouded in dust which will happen as a result of an emergency brake application. Once I stopped my train, I was able to back it into the clear on the westward. Had I put my train into emergency it would have taken me 30 seconds to reset the "PCS" (pneumatic control switch). Thirty seconds would have been about 30 seconds too much. As it turned out 202 got stopped probably 30 to 35 cars west of the crossover and wouldn't have hit us anyway. We shoved the train onto the eastward and lined everything straight up so that 202 could advance with a clear block signal.

I stayed on the engine but I could see my conductor and 202's conductor having an agitated discussion. It looked like 202's conductor was doing most of the talking as one of his fingers was doing a whole lot of pointing.

Our entire three man crew was in the cab for the trip east to Wabasha. It was a quiet cab, not much to say when you consider what almost happened a few minutes ago. The three of us realized that had that other train hit us, it really wouldn't have been anyone's fault. Sure they would have pinned it on us. The other guys had no choice but to ride it out. They were scapegoats. They couldn't very well fire the defective radio or radios, consequently they would have nailed us.

Over the years, I have thought about that particular incident and have always concluded that had we respected one rule, the "five minute rule", it wouldn't have happened. As far as I know this writing is the first time that the incident has been brought out in the open, years later, and no one cares.

In the meantime the cadets (from Superior) also were forced to the cities behind me. The one guy apparently took his lumps and went back to Superior as soon as he could hold a job. The other guy started playing games with the company. He would jump on a job that would be off and when it was time to work that job, he would move over to another job on its days off. I was working the Wabasha patrol when one beautiful day I tied up at Wabasha and there was a message that one of the cadets had bumped me, however after talking to the caller, we both agreed that he would need a pilot, and that pilot would be me. The caller and I had agreed earlier that I would be his "go to guy" for the river jobs, I loved it out there. This guy was one of the two guys that went ahead of me in Superior.

Well—the younger of the two cadets decides to come out there in an environment that he knows nothing about, and now I'm the pilot. We agreed that I would run the engine to Red Wing and that he would run the already backward engine back to Wabasha. That would have been okay except we were running ahead of a hotshot and I couldn't get him to move the train fast enough to clear. When we got to Wabasha, I could see Pat Hepburn, the engineer on 202, just glaring at us as he negotiated the red block we caused him to endure.

I don't think the guy stayed around Wabasha very long. I know that sometime during that summer the company decided to send him to a place that didn't have days off—Harvey, North Dakota. That was like the French Foreign Legion to most people on the railroad. I don't think he stayed there very long. The last I heard he was working for the Burlington Northern.

As I mentioned before, the summer of 1987 was very hot. St. Paul Yard had the stench of rotting grain, permeated by the heat of the sun. Huge piles of dead mayflies were found near the doors of the yard office. The mayflies had an odor of their own. It was also a good year for flies. To the flies "Pigs Eye" must have been Paradise. I had an engine where someone had somehow wedged a portion of their lunch behind the front wall of the engines cab. It had a rotten smell and a plethora of flies to boot. Now that I think about it, I should have gotten another engine.

I was still in the Excel Motel when the phone rang. It was the caller and he advised that he had a notice of investigation. He read the notice to me and said that it was signed by some guy named "Wallstone". I called my union representative and gave him the time and date. Each engine has a daily inspection card that must be signed by an inspector. I had never signed one of those cards before and a FRA (Federal Railroad Admin) inspector took note of it and wrote it up. I was told that the company was fined $500.00 I told the union guy that I had never heard of that before. He said "all they want you to do is take five days on paper". I told him - "I'm not signing anything". He then said that the requirement is stated in the engineers handbook and "would I please take the five days? It really didn't mean anything - you wouldn't actually do the time". "Alright I'll do it, but only as a favor to you"! Good! That's what we ended up doing.

"Wallstone" turned out to be Don Walztoni, road foreman whom I got to know over the years. He was a decent sort. He ended up retiring from the engineers training center.

A few days later I received a call from my good buddy Rich Horace from crew management in Milwaukee. You probably remember him from earlier in the chapter when he told me that I could stay at the motel as long as I wanted, but not forever. Well….that all changed. I was at the Excel about six weeks and apparently that was a bit more than the powers that be bargained for. There was no gray area, no bargaining whatsoever. Get out! Be out of there before check out time or its all yours. Luckily the Michalski brothers had room and that became my new home for almost a year. Welcome to St. Paul!

Chapter 25

‿

The Soo and the Milwaukee

January 1st, 1986 would be the official signal for the Soo Line to embrace the Milwaukee Road along with the Minneapolis Northfield & Southern. It would be quite a day's work for a beaming Dennis Cavanaugh, now President and Chief Executive Officer of the Soo Line. Canadian Pacific would be proud of its parentage.

Soo would be getting a shorter Twin Cities—Chicago route (421 vs. 448 miles) that would be double tracked and could run at 60 MPH in most places (versus Soo's 40 MPH). Other perks would give Soo a southern gateway vis-à-vis Milwaukee's Chicago-Louisville line.

The Soo Line would gain entry into Kansas City from Chicago which would be about 500 miles. On a more circuitous route, a 656 mile route between St. Paul and Kansas City would be decadent at best and the Soo would probably opt to route Twin Cities—Kansas City traffic over the "spineline". Both Chicago and St. Paul routes would share trackage from Savanna, Ill. to Kansas City, 366 miles. Two high capacity hump yards would be included, one at Bensenville, the other at St. Paul.

The Milwaukee enjoyed trackage rights between St. Paul and Duluth. That would also be included in the package. It usually handled one train each way, on a daily basis, from the Duluth, Winnipeg & Pacific. Later, two or more trains while the Grand Trunk was courting it.

On the downside - the Soo Line would have to pay off the Milwaukee Road's outstanding debt, which in the Soo's case amounted to 383 million dollars. The Soo would inherit Milwaukee's suburban service (commuter) which ran on two different routes. The number of protected employees would expand and that would soon be another bridge to be crossed.

Lastly - what to do with the other Chicago-Twin Cities mainline? Use it or sell it? Geographically the Soo Line and the Milwaukee Road were not a good fit. It wasn't an end to end deal.

And now we come to the immediate needs department. Trackage rights between Shoreham and St. Paul Yard (Pigs Eye) over the Burlington Northern have been in the works. July came along and with it came trackage rights over either BN's St. Paul or Midway Sub.

The BN dispatcher had at his disposal the double tracked Midway Subdivision, once Great Northern, which had a westward ruling grade of 1.3% or the more user friendly St. Paul Sub, once Northern Pacific, with a westward ruling grade of 1.0%. The NP route is a half mile longer. Both are double tracked.

Almost always the BN dispatcher would run Soo Line trains over the St. Paul Sub. because most Soo trains lacked dynamic braking and the locomotives that did have dynamics usually were tagged and not in service. The Soo proper, never had dynamic braking. Anytime the dispatcher wanted to run a Soo train over the Midway Sub, he would first determine whether or not that particular engineer was qualified to take a train from Shoreham (University) to St. Paul via Midway. Not many engineers were mettlesome enough or maybe foolhardy would be a better word, to accept that particular invitation. Burlington Northern engineers would not bring a train down either subdivision without functioning dynamic brakes.

The process for learning the Midway Sub hadn't yet been thought of. The Soo Line wasn't going to furnish pilots and the Burlington Northern didn't have the manpower for such a venture. Of course there would be the need for a 12 or 13,000 ton freight train to practice on. Availability would be a major concern. Big freight trains don't grow on trees, at least not for practice purposes.

Because Soo Line crews wouldn't or couldn't use the Midway Sub, BN dispatchers would lose a lot of flexibility and consequently Soo Line freight trains would have to wait in the clear at Shoreham until the BN could handle any eastward trains. Quite often the Soo train in the holding pattern would either "die on the hogs"[1] or once the BN could move the train, there wasn't always enough time to get that particular train over either stretch of track, yard it and get the power to the roundhouse. Of course that was only feasible if nothing unforeseen occurred. The actual running time between University (Shoreham) and Hoffman Ave. (Pigs Eye), was slightly less than 30 minutes. If the train was a mainline crew change somewhere around Pigs Eye i.e. Hoffman Ave, the yard office, Oakland or Dunn, a brave dispatcher might stick his neck out and run a train that was close to exceeding the 12 hour, hours of service mandate. The Soo Line and Burlington Northern were always feuding because of this. No train could leave the Twin Cities on any railroad without the sanction of the BN dispatchers for they held the keys to the kingdom and anyone disputing that would have to choose his words carefully. On occasion nothing would move into or out of Pigs Eye because someone in the Soo Line hierarchy wasn't nice.

The procurement of Daytons Bluff was also looked at as an absolute need.. The "Bluff" became available when its owner Chicago, Burlington & Quincy (the Q) along with Great Northern, Northern Pacific and the distant Spokane, Portland & Seattle merged to become the mighty Burlington Northern. The year was 1970.

Daytons Bluff was always on the mind of Soo officials. It was usually vacant and stood, for all the world to see, across from the general yardmasters tower at Pigs Eye. It surely was coveted by the Soo Line.

The makeup of the "Bluff" entailed six tracks well over a mile long, four lesser tracks in the back unit plus two lengthy stub tracks almost three quarters of a mile in length. These two tracks could easily be converted to regular tracks with the installation of switches on the east end. Track conditions were exceptional.[2]

I'm sure at times when Soo was suffering from acute yard congestion, that usually empty yard sitting across the mainline looked like a great big lollipop. To date it has been nothing more than a mirage. Quite often BN will allow Soo to yard an overflow train, or to keep a train in a holding pattern away from the ebb and flow of more fluid traffic. Also Northern States Power (NSP) coal trains used the bluff for staging purposes. Daytons Bluff has been a carrot dangled in front of the Soo Line management for many years.

Let's take a closer look at what the Milwaukee would bring to the table. St. Paul Yard (Pigs Eye) was opened for business in 1956. For a major yard it could have been even larger. At the time it was built, it was adequate and nobody could foresee the future. I would imagine that once the BN had opened Northtown (1970), thoughts of the Milwaukee buying the "Bluff" had already become a popular pastime. It became apparent that the Soo management would try to make Pigs Eye its exclusive freight yard in the Twin Cities Terminal. The "old" yard was still in place and was being used for building TOFC trains. Its days were numbered as the City of St. Paul wanted to beautify its riverfront. Soo was again pondering the use of Daytons Bluff for that purpose. The BN was non-committal and the Soo Line would have to use a corner of Shoreham instead.

When I arrived in the Twin Cities in the middle part of 1987, St. Paul Yard was glutted. Every available track had a train or portion thereof on it. I remember hearing a BN dispatcher making an open comment on the radio one day: "Don't you guys have any tracks that you can run trains on?" Ultimately Soo would be able to add two more tracks, a long departure track along the mainline and one additional track in the "swamp", which served as a receiving yard. Geography would dictate how trains would enter and leave. They came in all directions and conversely did the same when they departed. Typically, a big train from the west would enter the yard by shoving back into one of the long tracks of Dunn and conversely, a train off the river might have to put itself away by shoving into the swamp.

Leaving Hoffman Ave. with a train for the Hastings & Dakota portion of the Milwaukee, the dispatcher has our train pointed toward the river and the Merriam Park Subdivision. It is a ten mile trek to Southtown Yard on the mostly uphill 1.33% grade. At the top of the hill is Merriam Park and the gateway to the Minnesota Commercial Railway Co., a non-union switching line. AMTRAK uses this route to gain access to Midway Station. Passenger trains will enter Soo's Merriam Park Sub at Hoffman, cross into Midway Station on the Commercial and depart the station and the Commercial at St. Anthony entering BNs Midway Sub and eventually, the high speed at University on its west coast venture. The process going east is reversed. No passenger trains have to make a back-up movement. It is a pull through operation. When we pass the home signal for Merriam Park, we are also at the top of the hill and now our train begins to pick up speed. We round a curve and we are faced with the Mississippi River and the ten MPH "high bridge". Most engineers, for obvious reasons, hold the ten MPH requirement with rigid compliance.

Our destination is Southtown or So. Minneapolis Yard which sits at the south end of the downtown area. Southtown was once a bustling place serving as the coach yard and local marshaling yard for Minneapolis industries. The lion's share of business was generated by the I & M (Iowa & Minnesota) Milling complex, which ran along Hiawatha Ave. for one and half miles or so, and kept three switch jobs working around the clock. By the time I was introduced to Southtown, the coach yard was gone, however, the garden job (yard switcher) and the I & M jobs ran around the clock. There was a four o'clock St. Paul transfer and a midnight transfer to Humboldt Yard. The Shakopee Patrol also originated at Southtown. It was a morning job that got to Shakopee via the CNW (M & STL) at Hopkins. Its sole purpose was to bring cars to the Rahr Malting Co., switch and return with cars to Southtown. That job was eventually given to the CNW.

The Ford yard was strictly intended for the service of Ford Motor Co. and its sole purpose was to build the compact pickup truck called the Ranger. The Ford line begins at Fordson junction and extends for about four miles to the St. Paul neighborhood of Highland and the end of the line. Ford owns and maintains its own hydro-electric dam on the Mississippi River adjacent to the plant, which is unique.

The business of switching the plant requires two day, one afternoon and one night yard engines. When the economy is good and the public is buying Rangers, there will be three transfer or haulers around the clock. Soo Line and Ford operate a train called the "Ford Fast" and is described as a rolling warehouse and is exclusively operated as a solid "Ford train". When I worked the night hauler, we referred to it as #425. The night hauler went to work at 10:30 and if #425 was running normal, we would be changing power at Hoffman Ave. about 11:30. The contents of our train were all pretty much "shutdown" cars. Usually the head end of the train consisted of "frames" and you can't create a truck without first having an under frame. The balance of the train had to be spotted in the "houses" at no later than five o'clock AM.

Not a lot of space was wasted when they built the plant and the yard at Ford. It gave you the impression that along with the truck it built, the yard was also compact. As you cross West 7th St., Davern is passed through. Davern is a four track yard used for storage and is adjacent to Ford Yard.

There were nine jobs directly attributed to the service of Ford and every switch engine at St. Paul Yard would handle Ford cars during the course of a shift. The Ford Plant was and is very important to the City of St. Paul and CP Rail!

Another important stretch of track is the 110 miles of railroad called "The River" and generally skirting the west bank of the Mississippi. Not only was it part of the Milwaukee Road and its Chicago-St. Paul mainline, there is a bountiful largesse of industry to be tapped. Starting at LaCrosse, the last manually operated tower in the state of Wisconsin is encountered at Grand Crossing (BN/MILW). Within easy view of the tower, the sizeable yard required for switching four way freights and for servicing local industry, is west of the tower. The LaCrosse road switcher is assigned to this task and will quite often run to Winona with cars.

About 27 miles up-river from LaCrosse is the city of Winona. There is enough business here to command a five day per week yard engine. The way freights set cars out at the "dump" or Mankato St. and the "yard" engine will bring them down to Franklin St. to be switched off the main into the tiny yard adjacent to the depot. Once the switching is done, the job will tend to its chores along the riverfront. The last move of the day is to switch the Froedtert Plant.

At mile post 341.2 sits the river town of Wabasha. It is here that the "Wabasha Patrol" holds court. This job will do more than its share of work. After switching cars left by the way freights the night before, the patrol will switch the mill down by the river, gather up its cars for Red Wing, and then switch the giant elevator complex at Lake City. Once the work is done at Lake City, the final move is to put the train away and tie up at Wabasha.

Red Wing, Minnesota is our next stop. Nestled between the bluffs and the river, it is a picturesque place as are the other towns along the river. The Red Wing switcher does its work quietly and efficiently. It is one of the better jobs on the railroad.

Our final stop on the river is Hastings. Two long hour engines ply their trade here. The day job switches the setouts that the way freights leave and it services the mill, giving it two switches daily. The night job does whatever is left over from the day shift and switches the automobile complex at Cottage Grove. The night job is described as a "road switcher".

We can't talk about the river without mentioning the way freights. Trains 248 and 249 make the big setouts and pickups at the above locations. Without these trains, the river towns would not get their cars. Number 248 starts out of St. Paul in the late afternoon and 249 begins at LaCrosse around eight o'clock PM. These two jobs can be heavy lifters.

Milwaukee Road's river division is most remarkable inasmuch as it enjoys an excellent source of revenue generated from a major point spaced about every 30 miles. The land between these cities, provide some of the most beautiful country known to American railroading, graced by the Mississippi River.

When two railroads come together, the better facilities are retained while the excess is disposed of in a gainful manner. With acquisition of Milwaukee's "Pigs Eye" - Shoreham became expendable. At the time of my new venue (5-87), about half of the tracks at Shoreham were gone. At that time, the Soo Line was confident that the BN would sell Daytons Bluff to them. The scuttlebutt also had it that the University of Minnesota was taking a long look at the property. That never developed because of the amounts of petrochemical waste that inundated the area due to decades of exposure from the maintenance of heavy machinery i.e., locomotives. As it turned out, the tried and true shop facility would remain on a "wait and see" basis. To look at one of those old flagstone shop buildings, you first think of the word "archaic", however once you enter, it becomes a modern facility. With the demise of Shoreham, Humboldt Yard comes into the picture and becomes more and more important. It always was the "linchpin" for local industry. Now with the addition of the MN & S and the abeyance of existing Shoreham, Humboldt will have to carry the ball on the other side of town. Humboldt is large for a satellite yard and is about five miles west of Shoreham.

Only a mile and a half east of Humboldt is Camden Place, a source of much business. Almost one and a half miles in distance, it is an industrial spur in the truest meaning. Once used by the passenger trains of the Soo Line to gain access to the Milwaukee Road station in Minneapolis, the varnish cars are long gone. The tracks of the "Camden" are now being plied by paper hauling boxcars, gondolas for scrap and covered hoppers filled with a variety of material.

Entering the mainline and going east from Shoreham for a little over eight miles, Cardigan Junction is encountered. "Cardigan" is where the Soo's St. Paul Sub. and the mainline (Paynesville Sub.) come together. Slightly over five miles in distance, it originates off the BN's St. Paul Subdivision at Soo Line Junction. Before the Milwaukee acquisition, the hand throw switch at Soo Line Jct. didn't get much use until Soo began using Milwaukee's St. Paul Yard for its new hub. Before that, any industry on that piece of railroad was switched by a job originating at Shoreham via the Paynesville Sub. Cardigan Jct. has a small yard of four tracks that are largely used for storing rock hoppers destined for Dresser. Of course there is also a "wye".

We have touched upon facilities and trackage that become expendable when a merger or a railroad is flat out sold to another company, in this case, another railroad. The afore mentioned are tangibles and can be readily assessed. Intangibles cannot be measured, although they are valued. The paramount example is - people. People form the very core of any organization and are the heart, soul, and foundation of a company. I have seen the effects of a merger before and the men that formed the labor force of each company were different breeds of cat.

The Soo Line Railroad would give an outside observer the impression that it was methodical, efficient and the work force was proud of their company. Some would indicate that the Soo Line was a laid back railroad, molded by the territory that it served and above all, the people that graced its employment rolls. Soo Liners were given the opportunity to both work and make money. Labor and management were a cohesive force, put together by a seemingly happy people. On the day they hired me a Soo Line official told me that the Soo was good to its people.

It didn't help matters when shortly after the Soo Line takeover, it demanded all Milwaukee Road logo and other memorabilia taken down and banished from the property. This thoughtless action didn't exactly bond the new company to itself and made it more difficult for the Soo Line crews to have a more amiable transition into the now abrasive blend of rank and file. All of this was courtesy of the new Soo Line management.

The Milwaukee Road on the other hand, if its management had a philosophy at all, it was just the opposite of the Soo Line. They, the leadership of a once proud company would form an anathema between labor and management. If a person could find a word for it, that word would be - intimidation. Through that the Milwaukee mentality as we Soo Liners called it, wasn't much of a mentality at all. Although the Milwaukee side had a vast reservoir of good people, these men were beleaguered by a middle management whose only countenance was clouded by asperity.

The Milwaukee "brothers" in the Twin Cities Terminal were first introduced to Milwaukee's moribund future in the middle to late 70's. By 1980 it was clear that the Milwaukee Road had seen better days. Those employees with good seniority (i.e. 20 years or more), had no choice but to ride the storm out and hopefully persevere. The younger guys would be beset with financial worry which led to ulcers, gray hair and being "brow beaten" by a panic stricken management, absorbed by its myopic tendencies. Labor would be forced to make concessions, taking pay cuts and having crews shaved in an attempt to heighten productivity.

It was right about 1980 when the Soo Line began to show differences in its approach to the labor force. The company seemed to be going through a mild transition, a different direction and weren't as receptive to the supplications of labor. When a company changes its policy in an effort to achieve a more favorable end, it isn't necessarily a negative ploy. It might be looked at with disdain, if you are on the labor end and it might even hit the rank and file in the pocket book. Labor will ultimately be the last to know. Soo Lines corporate strategy was on the move. Under the auspices of Dennis Cavanaugh, Soo's conservative image would take a turn. Soo lost out to the CNW in the race to procure Rock Island's "spine line", it now would focus its attention to the downtrodden Milwaukee Road. The Soo Line would prevail as mentioned earlier and would be newly entitled "Soo/Milwaukee". Nineteen eighty-five would propel the Soo Line from a conservative, yet steadfast operation, to a slightly more contemporary look. It must have made Dennis Cavanaugh proud to see his boys trying to unobtrusively be part of the show - Soo Line finally got in the phone book! When any company makes an acquisition, there are parameters. People are moved or moving. Although it is usually a good situation for the company, it almost never is for its employees.

By the way - Canadian Pacific, at the time, owned 56% of Soo Line stock. That would mean that any decision making would always be under the scrutiny of the CP and would be a source of preponderance to Cavanaugh.

Once the labor guidelines are established i.e. protection agreements, dovetailing of seniority rosters, prior rights, etc., etc., the time comes to put these agreements into practice. Usually there is a dominating railroad. In this case, the Soo Line bought the Milwaukee Road which made it the stronger of the two by virtue of its financial condition. Oft times (or so it seems), the labor force of the little guy gets the better end of the deal. It must be easier to write up labor agreements if you favor the underdog. Witness IC-GM & O and Soo-Milwaukee. Of course a lot of it depends on which side of the coin you are on when it lands. Everyone looks at an issue from their own perspective. (When I speak of the conditions set forth vis-à-vis merger or acquisition, it for the most part, will pertain to employees in engine service).Being the victim of more than one of these events, I feel more than qualified to speak of them.

First of all no one in the labor force likes to even think about a corporate change that eventually will affect them. The reasons for this are numerous. Some of the factors are loss of seniority, having to work at a strange facility, even finding that facility. Working for and with different supervisors and having to work with guys that look at you as an intruder, that feel as though you are there to take their jobs. For most of us, meeting new people isn't easy under the best of conditions. Sure there are protective measures installed to prevent financial loss, but don't forget that the bottom line is to eliminate people. Of course no two of us look at a situation the same....trust me on this one....everybody hates a merger.

The final phase of a corporate coalescence is of course the actual implementation. This is a time for it to click as a cohesive unit. This is where new people work for new people and old people work for new people and new people work for old people. It's an awkward time for all concerned. Pretty much the poster child for this would be when Soo went with "Pigs Eye" for its main freight yard. St. Paul Yard[3] was in a more strategic location, was larger than Shoreham and the opportunity for expansion looked promising at the time.

There was no power struggle as the Soo Line stepped aside and allowed the Milwaukee managers to stay in place. This included incumbent yardmasters. The Milwaukee regime would have new blood to kick around and the Soo Line guys were just the ticket.

Remember, the Soo Line treated its employees with respect. Most of the Soo guys used to say...."I looked forward to going to work". The Soo Line exuded complacency whereas the Milwaukee Road approach would be one of acrimony. Blending the Soo Line men into the mentality of the disdained Milwaukee would be like buying new shoes for a person, albeit the wrong size. One Soo Line crew working at St. Paul for the first time asked the yardmaster "what train are we making up?" The yardmaster came back with - I'll worry about that, you just do what you're told! That helped set the tempo and attitudes for this "new company".

Let's try to examine the mindset of the men that attempted to operate the Milwaukee. From what is gathered through the actual way that these men reacted to the three bankruptcies and re-organizations that the Milwaukee underwent, it had to be a trying time for both leadership and labor from the top to the bottom. No one goes through ten years of strife without showing some wear and tear for it.

The men of the Milwaukee Road were no different than anyone else under the threat of losing their jobs. Drinking, always a great pastime when rails get together, became more than just a pastime. The social aspect of alcohol was surpassed to a more personal level through the uncertain threat of upheaval. That pressure was circumvented through the use of alcohol.

Drugs would enter the picture, but not on the same level as alcohol. Once the random urinalysis evolved, we would joke about who should have taken the test, the guy whose number came up, or the official that brought him over there? If you knew the effects of various drugs and most of us did, you could tell who was on what.[4]

Alcohol and drugs were catalysts to the hostility that Milwaukee management would show to its own and to the germane Soo Liners. Hostility has a trickle-down effect and the rank and file Milwaukee men would oft times show resentment to the hapless Soo Liners. Not all of them, but enough to make a difference. It is always interesting to be in a place you don't want to be, and then be verbally chastised for it to boot. The favorite phrase emanating from the voices of both Milwaukee management and labor was: "we wanted the Grand Trunk to get us"! My stock retort to that was: "so did we" or "you don't know how much I wanted the Grand Trunk to get you". I would have thought that the Soo Line would be better than bankruptcy, walking the street etc., etc. Beggars can't be or shouldn't be choosy. It was incredulous.

Now that we all knew that we weren't going to be one big happy family, it was time to accept the dichotomy of it all and get to work. During the course of the "acquisition", you were never let to forget who was running the show on the prior Milwaukee.

The Milwaukee regime held court at St. Paul for about five years until the Soo gradually, through attrition began replacing, with a certain design, certain personnel. Most of the guys that ascended into management levels began on the ground as switchmen, brakemen, or clerks. Some railroads seemed to favor engineers.

The management structure that the Soo Line extended to the present Milwaukee Road, were pretty much the same people that were running the show before the acquisition. The pitfalls of retaining the current management would gradually surface in coming years. The individuals themselves through their own morose lifestyles would leave St. Paul for a variety of reasons, each one - negative.

There were a couple of new yardmasters that thought that because they went to "yardmaster school" - they were smarter than the guys on the ground (crews). One of them was out to cut a "fat hog in the ass" from the get-go. He had aspirations of going up the ladder in record time. This man was a snake and thusly we called him the "Sidewinder". He did manage to elevate himself, but was scorned wherever he went.

On the other end of the totem pole was a man we shall deem the "Sandman". It is unfortunate that we cannot refer to these people by using their true names. Alas, the laws always seem to protect the "bad guys". In my 42 years of railroading and all other years that made up my life there was only one other person that could match the Sandman. That would be "Murphy". "Murph" was spoken of in the early part of the first book. If you looked at Murph from an educated distance, his demeanor could be humorous. When you looked at the "Sandman" and compared the two, the difference is that there was nothing funny about the "Sandman". How many words are there in the dictionary that have a negative definition? Although there were many definitions or words I could have used, the "Sandman" fit nicely and for obvious reasons I elected not to use his or the "Sidewinders" true names.[5]

---

[1] To "die on the hogs" meant to exceed the hours of service rule.

[2] The information provided in this text is pretty much up to date at the time of my retirement in early 2002. Since then changes have and will be made. At the conclusion of this book I will make an effort to bring everything up to date.

[3] Pigs Eye is a euphemism for St. Paul Yard.

[4] Because you knew what the repercussions of drugs were, didn't necessarily mean a person was also taking them.

[5] "Murphy" or "Murph", "Sandman" and the "Sidewinder" are euphemism's and are used for obvious reasons.

Chapter 26

The Gunpow Incident

The story you are about to read happened on AMTRAK's Northeast Corridor near Chase, Maryland. The date was January 4th, 1987. Its main focus is a train accident that took the lives of sixteen people. This accident was caused by sheer carelessness which was attributed" to drugs and alcohol. Once the multitude of tests were performed and the facts were determined, the outcome would serve to point a guilty finger at one of the engineers. What he would say would degrade the proud profession of the locomotive engineer. He would foment the wrath of many a Washington denizen in an effort to save his own hide. This miscreant was responsible in more than one way, for creating a maelstrom that would throw the railroad engineers profession into turmoil as he alluded that railroading was inundated with alcoholics and drug users. A shadow was cast into the eye of the public. The aftermath of these findings would have a perverse effect on every engineer working on the nation's railroads.

Bay View Yard is located almost four miles north of the old Pennsylvania Station, now AMTRAK, in Baltimore. Bay View is Conrails main switching yard for the Baltimore area. In an effort to balance power, Conrail train ENS-121 would be called for 12:15 PM. It would operate out of the window[1] and run as light power, three units Bay View to Harrisburg, about 100 miles. Ricky Gates would be the engineer and Edward Cromwell the conductor. Gates had a total company service of almost 14 years with over ten years as an engineer. Cromwell would also be close to 14 years as a brakeman/conductor. ENS-121 seemed to be in good hands.

Bay View has very little to be offered in maintenance support and so on weekends there is no one available to inspect the power, and so the engineers are required to inspect their units and report any discrepancies.

ENS-121 announced that it was ready to go and received the signal to depart. Almost simultaneously, AMTRAK train 94 the Colonial, departed Baltimore station. The drama is beginning to unfold.

The dispatchers plan was for the Colonial to overtake ENS-121 at Gunpow, which is a remote-controlled interlocking where four tracks diverge into two tracks before the bridge over the Gunpowder River. Gunpow is a little over eight miles north of the station. No. 94 had in its train consist, a car that was restricted to 105 MPH. The conductor had informed 94's engineer at the time the crew went on duty at Washington, D.C. that there would be a 105 MPH speed restriction because of that car, however, he failed to notify the dispatcher of the situation. Had he apprised the dispatcher of that car in the first place, the situation would probably have changed at Baltimore.

Unaware of 94's restriction, the dispatcher ran the train out of Washington ahead of the already late Metroliner no. 112 even though 94 had to make one stop whereas 112 had none.

The Colonial and the Metroliner were both at Baltimore at the same time. Had the dispatcher been aware that #94 had a 105 MPH restriction, he probably would have ran #112 first allowing the slower #94 to follow, and holding Conrail ENS-121 at either Bay View or Gunpow, possibly altering the track situation with different times in different places.

In actuality, the Colonial would lead the way. The engineer on #94 armed with the knowledge of having the 105 MPH train chose to operate at 125 MPH ignoring the restriction. No. 94 would have a "clear indication". ENS-121 would have a "stop" indication. The crew of ENS-121 had ignored the signals displayed for its movement and thusly ran by a positive stop signal indication, running through a power switch and coming to a stop. Now ENS-121 was directly ahead of the Colonial. Train #94 would collide with ENS-121 at an estimated speed of over 120 MPH. The engineer on #94 didn't have a chance. Later tests would indicate that had #94 been operated at the lower speed of 105 MPH, the collision would have still occurred, only the impact would not have been as great and the injury rate would probably have been eased.

ENS-121 suffered no injuries. The head locomotive stayed on the track. The entire consist was shoved some 900 feet. The middle unit was heavily damaged while the hind engine was completely destroyed.

No. 94 would suffer 16 fatalities including the engineer. Among the dead would be the daughter of a prominent Washington politician. 174 injuries were also sustained.

Both AMTRAK units and the head three passenger cars were destroyed. The rear nine cars were later salvaged for future operation. Considerable catenary was torn down. However, other than rolling stock, track repair would demand the lion's share of repair costs. The actual cost of the wreck was $16,561,000 and that was before civil suits and other court litigations would be rendered.

At this juncture, let us take a brief look at the engineer on the Colonial. Jerome Evans was 35 years of age at the time of his death. He too, was and ex-Penn Central engineer. Unlike Gates, Evans had been reprimanded for minor speed violations on two separate occasions.

Gates had already been assessed a thirty day suspension for going by a stop signal. Another time he was given 7 days off after speaking to a crew caller in a "belligerent and threatening manner". He was described by one Conrail official as being "overconfident and surly". A review of his work record indicated nothing out of the ordinary other than persistent absenteeism. Gates averaged a little over three days per week at work in 1986. Although this would indicate that something was wrong—when asked about Gates record, a Conrail road foreman of engines stated the work records were reviewed on a monthly basis and that this engineer's absenteeism wasn't considered to be excessive. Overall, Conrail supervisors were supportive of Gates demeanor however no one denied that Gates didn't have a drinking problem.

Both engineers, Gates and Evans, would share one dubious distinction—they both had poor driving records. You may be thinking—"what's that got to do with anything?" The pitfalls of having an audacious driving record will surface later. For that reason, we will have to address the driving records of both engineers. The driving record of ENS-121's conductor was never mentioned.

Before the accident, Gates had been convicted of twelve traffic offenses, including 9 speeding violations that resulted in two suspensions of his driver's license between 1972 and 1985. Early in the morning of December 5th, 1986, after leaving a tavern, the engineer was arrested for driving through a red traffic signal, driving through a stop sign, and driving while intoxicated. After failing police sobriety tests and submitting to a "breathalizer" examination that revealed a 0.12 percent blood alcohol concentration. This occurred exactly thirty days before the accident at Gunpow.

Examination of the driving record of Jerome Evans showed that he had a penchant for speed as he was cited 11 times for speeding between 1969 and 1984. His disdain to the speed restriction in his train would not completely exonerate him as being a factor.

The official cause of the accident determined by the National Transportation Safety Board (hereafter:NTSB). The NTSB determines that the probable cause of this accident was the failure, as a result of impairment from marijuana, of the engineer of Conrail train ENS-121 to stop his train in compliance with home signal 1-N before it fouled track 2 at Gunpow. Contributing to the accident was the failure of the conductor/brakeman of ENS-121 to observe the signal aspects and to alert the engineer when they became more restrictive.

However these events occurred, it is clear that the crew of ENS-121 left Bay View yard without having performed a complete and proper test of the "automatic cab signal" system, they left without the required working console radio, without having performed the required brake test, with the alertor whistle muted with tape, with the deadman pedal inoperative and possibly with a bulb missing from the signal indicator of the ACS system. The crew of ENS-121 may or may not have circumvented these afore mentioned safety devices, but because they left Bay View without these safety features being operable, contributed to their guilt.

In an effort to support their conclusions, a multitude of tests, covering every aspect of the accident were performed. The signal system at and around Gunpow was found to be in perfect functioning order. Sight distance tests were made between 1 PM and 1:20 PM with both overcast and later bright sunlight. It was established that the signal aspects could be seen in dull light at distances of 300 to 500 feet greater than they could be seen in bright sunlight. The crew of ENS-121 attested that the sun was shining brightly while trackside witnesses recalled that the sunlight was from "shining brightly" to "overcast"

The speed recorder on the 5044 was tested and found to be ½ MPH off under speed.

Sight and stopping tests performed with the same locomotive consist ENS-121 would use that day showed that had the crew of ENS-121 taken normal measures to stop their locomotives, could have easily done so.

The results of the toxicological tests indicate that the crew of ENS-121 were inattentive or distracted from their duties prior to the accident, because they were impaired from the effects of marijuana and possibly the after effects of alcohol the night prior to the accident. However there was some mild consternation due to the delay in taking toxicological tests after the accident. There were several other tests given or performed, I chose to focus on the most important of them. Overall the testing was thorough and conclusive.

A trickle-down effect would take place among the various agencies connected to the accident. The National Transportation Safety Board would find fault with the Federal Railroad Administration and the FRA would subsequently take issue with AMTRAK. At the very bottom of the pecking order would be Conrail. Conrail had trackage rights over the Northeast Corridor. Conrail would consequently bear the lion's share of liability and absorb most of the heat. Congressional hearings would become the order of the day and there would be, and justifiably so, hell to pay.

The federal government would step in and prescribe stringent safety standards for the eligibility and certification of each and every locomotive engineer on America's railroads. Of course if an individual railroad wanted to take training

218

and testing beyond the realm of federal standards that would be fine with the Federal Railroad Administration. The FRA regulations would pretty much resemble a federal document as it was not without bureaucracy, red tape, and redundancy.

It would take the FRA a little over 4 ½ years to produce this directive, and was 61 pages long. It also must have necessitated a job opening or more. The FRA would dictate to the railroads, what they already knew and for the most part, had in place—an effective training program along with stringent test standards.

The training and testing would encompass and create new engineers and for a period of less than every three years, experienced engineers would have to again pass the same test. Also experienced engineers hired from another railroad would be subject to this procedure. After 12-31-91 every engineer would have to be certified. Railroads that didn't already have a simulator were seen shopping for these "educational aids". Any and all engineers already working as such would suddenly have to produce a stellar driving record. A "DUI" would be subject to the scrutiny of the FRA and you may not be given a chance at certification until one year after the infraction. If a DUI is incurred after certification, the employee would have to undergo a screening by a review board and would be forced to be evaluated by an "EAP" (Employee Assistance Program) counselor. I would imagine the producing of individual drivers' records was brought on by the audacious records of the engineers involved at Gunpow as mentioned earlier.

In an effort to avoid being verbose, I will briefly touch on "Qualification and Certification of Locomotive Engineers" regulations as established by the FRA.

All engineers will have practiced good personal safety i.e. driving record and will be conversant in the obedience to operating rules. They will be knowledgeable in locomotive machinery and the workings of air brake systems on locomotives and freight cars. Will be afforded on the job training for the purpose of train handling and will be well versed on the physical characteristics of the railroad that he or she will be operating on. It will be insured that each employee have a knowledge of federal regulations. Lastly, visual and hearing acuity will be evaluated.

There is also a long listing of FRA infractions, such as running by a signal, tampering with safety equipment, etc. The list of penalties for these failures is extensive. Fines for company violations are embodied in six pages alone.

Engineers, without warning, will be rode with by a company supervisor no less than once a year.

On most railroads the aforementioned requirements were already being implemented, however, there were a couple of areas that the FRA brought out. First of all the why's and wherefore of piloting. Everyone had their own interpretation of who needed a pilot, when, and where. The FRA attempted to put their cards on the table with this. One drawback to this would be that these rules would not be necessarily available to the rank and file.

The other factor—"physical characteristics of a railroad", are given little importance on some railroads. Much time is wasted on learning about nomenclature that probably will never be encountered during the course of a career. To my way of thinking, physical characteristics is the single most important aspect to be commensurate with safe and efficient train handling. To this the FRA more than stresses the knowledge of the lay of the land and signal location. Having the ability to anticipate goes a long way in an engineer's ability to safely operate a heavy freight train. Certain railroads give little credence to this very important factor. A key word in train handling is "anticipation". Accolades to the FRA on this one. Because an attempt to more accurately define "piloting", and physical characteristics are professed to be important, this whole "Qualification and Certification" process is not an entire waste of time.

Also to be mentioned was the FRA's attempt to hold the hand of each railroad involved. The railroads turned around and convinced the FRA that they should have more discretion in formulating their own programs. The FRA, with certain acumen, agreed.

Another key word that is never mentioned by the regulating agencies or by the railroads themselves is the word "experience".

When the U. S. portion of the Canadian Pacific put their "Certification" package together, it appeared that the fellow in charge of putting it in place had carte blanche with the checkbook. The more senior engineers felt that this man was creating a nice little playpen for himself. He went out and bought the most sophisticated simulator available, occupied an extensive suite and surrounded himself with a large, yet capable staff. They were gonna make new engineers and create havoc on the older, experienced engineers.

While I felt that this FRA sponsored and CP approved package was a good way to measure the ability of a new engineer, it was an awful way to spend money on engineers that have been running engines and trains, and in some cases, all of their adult lives, not to mention the time and inconvenience that the individual and his family would suffer because they were being forced to learn how to do jobs that they already had been doing over a period of years. They would learn about the terminology, i.e. buffer forces, tensile strength of a type "E" coupler, and dynamic brakes that he or she has never used and never will. What the company did not realize is that if the majority of guys wanted to and could sit in a classroom for five days they wouldn't be working for the railroad to begin with.

Let me give you a hypothetical example: Bob Schultz is an engineer working a yard engine at Terre Hautte, Indiana. Bob dropped out of school in the 9th grade. He has 44 years of service on the Milwaukee Road and has just a hair over 6 months to work at which time he will turn 65 and will retire. He has never had to run anything more than a switch engine and now, at the very end of his career, is forced to learn technology that he has never used and never will have the opportunity to use. And all of this happens inside of a week. He has been on the same job for 15 years and has always done his job in a credible and professional manner. Bob has never been away from Terre Haute, has never been on an airplane (what if he was afraid to fly?) and has a sick wife in need of attention.

Another example and a true story I might add, happened to an older engineer that still had a sick child at home. This man lived in the Twin Cities and had been working a switch engine for a considerable length of time. He was easily within five years of retiring. It was his turn for A.E.T. (Advanced Engineers Training). He would pass the written tests but he couldn't pass the "simulator" test. For this he was given 30 days off without pay. He was coerced into passing the second time by threat of dismissal. These are only two examples of how a man's life can be turned upside down.

It is not my intention to aggrandize the simulator nor do I attempt to vilify it. The simulator is a good innovation and should be used to measure the ability of a prospective engineer (in training). It belongs in the classroom to be used as a teaching aid. To force an already experienced engineer to simulate his abilities on a machine is a poor measure of an experienced engineers train handling capabilities. The students were getting higher scores on the simulator than the regular engineers! To a man that has been running an engine any length of time, the simulator is nothing more than an expensive video game.

In retrospect, I look back at the horrible event that took place at Gunpow on that day. In essence the powers that be took an already sad situation and made it worse, albeit some good came of it but the imbalance is strongly in favor of antipathy. Good men suffered because of the lack of true justice, when a drunkard and drug user spills his guts to tell his captors anything they want to hear so that he can save his own ass. The wrath of a politician and the ego of a railroad official are also brought to light.

As I conclude this chapter, I am reminded that alcohol consumption is prevalent on U.S. railroads and always has been. I cannot condemn the crew of ENS-121 for having had a "few beers the night before the accident. I don't know of anyone that hasn't had a few beers at least once or twice on the night before a workday. Twenty-three % of operating department employees are admittedly "problem drinkers". (That is not to say that that entire number drink on the job).

I would guess that the number of marijuana users within that 23% range is probably less than 1%.

What took place at Gunpow that day, was simply "the straw that broke the camel's back".

---

[1]A window is an expression used on the Northeast Corridor. This window was established between Washington and Philadelphia. The hours range from just after midnight until around six in the morning. It will vary at each location and is intended to keep freight traffic from interfering with AMTRAK trains.

Chapter 27

Twin Cities Terminal

One day in the fall of 1987, I was called to pilot a rock train that was sitting at Cleveland Avenue on the "Short Line". The engineer was experienced, but had never been on the 1.3 % grade of "Short Line Hill", or the Merriam Park Sub. This engineer was actually older in seniority and had only recently arrived in St. Paul. He was another one of the guys that relocated due to the sale of Lake States. He was working the 3:30 PM Top End Job, when the yardmaster told this crew to get into a taxicab and "dogcatch" a 95 car solid rock train at Cleveland Avenue, which is pretty much the top of the hill on the "Short Line". Even though this guy was new to the Twin Cities Terminal, he knew his geography and wasn't going anywhere without a pilot.

When the engineer asked for a pilot, the yardmaster told him that he would get back to him and then moments later after a brief consultation with a supervisor, tried to talk the engineer out of it, telling him that he didn't need a pilot because he had an experienced crew, and they would show him the way. The truth of the matter was that he didn't have an experienced crew, at least not on the "Short Line Hill". In fact the yardmaster was new himself as a yardmaster and didn't know his ass from a hole in the ground. His boss told the kid to try to talk the engineer into going it alone. These were people in trusted and responsible positions that were quite frankly, laying someone else's life on the line and at least their jobs. This was done under the pretext of safety, and surely a travesty to each and all rules of safety.

They were admonishing this man to bring a 95 car train of rock, one of the heaviest commodities known to railroading down a 1.3% grade, which for the final mile descends into a 1.8% grade between Fordson Junction and Chestnut Street.

The caller didn't know the particulars and he told me to talk to the trainmaster on duty and he would fill me in. I found the trainmaster in the tower, apparently keeping an eye on the new yardmaster. He was apprising me of the situation, and then up the spiral staircase came our superintendent, the same guy I met a few months ago. This time he wasn't as friendly as he was back then as he barely acknowledged me, if at all. Was it because I was called to pilot a train that he felt didn't need a pilot? Did I represent some kind of a challenge to his authority or was he simply having a bad day. After meeting this guy the first time, I began to hear stories. It seems that his day could easily be ruined by the slightest transgression. He seemed to lighten up as he approached the yardmasters desk. Our new yardmaster was making up a train in reverse. He had tacked 25 cars of rock onto the hind end of a road train and the superintendent casually mentioned that "not too many engineers would be happy with all of that weight on the rear end, especially next to empties". It wasn't conducive to good train handling and so the adjustment was made.

I had now met the young superintendent on two occasions and had witnessed personality extremes both times. I always try to see for myself rather than believe "hearsay". The guy proved to me that he was a jerk. Our young yardmaster also had a bit of a reputation and was already looked at by crews with disdain. Watching the doting superintendent show his young minion a trick or two, I could tell that the ingratiating yardmaster and his mentor were already good buddies. Over the years I would find that these two would fit "hand and glove", as they were both insidious characters.

The yardmaster had already had a nickname. He was referred to as the "Sidewinder". I needed a reference term for the superintendent and came up with the "Sandman".

Railroading in and around the Twin Cities is a mid-westerners version of doing it in the mountains and is to be taken seriously. I'm not trying to be a geologist, but I've often wondered—did the bluffs make the river or did the river carve the bluffs? Some folks, to be safe, would say that it all happened in a symphony of natural events and probably wouldn't be wrong. Hoffman Avenue Interlocking sits at the bottom of these collective hills and acts as a funnel for the routes leading to it. The major railroads have to come through Hoffman in order to cross the Twin Cities Terminal. The Burlington Northern does the dispatching and owns the lion's share of trackage in that vicinity. Nothing goes through Hoffman without first talking to the BN dispatcher. On a normal day, over 100 train movements are made through Hoffman interlocking.

Of course the railroads that operated in the T.C.T. to form the BN were the Great Northern, Northern Pacific and the Chicago, Burlington & Quincy. The "Q" fed Chicago traffic to the GN and NP and terminated at Daytons Bluff which was its only yard facility in the T.C.T.

The Great Northern held sway at Union Yard, Minneapolis. Westbound traffic leaving Union would go either via Willmar or St. Cloud but would subsequently end up at a junction in Nolan, N.D. Nolan is 40 miles west of Fargo. The Badger and the Gopher (same train) would run to Duluth via GN's 160 mile Skally line.

Eastbound traffic would ply the 11 mile Midway Sub and terminate near Hoffman Avenue. The grade percentile on the Midway at 1.3% is steep and is definitely dynamic brake territory.

The Northern Pacific went up today's St. Paul Sub. from Hoffman Avenue and had an easier climb at 1%. Northtown Yard was its gateway to the Northwest. Staples was the first division point west of the "Cities". NP also ran to Duluth over its "Duluth Short Line" from St. Paul.

The Chicago & Northwestern in an effort to connect itself from South St. Paul yard to the eastside yard and its 400 route or Chicago mainline would have to cross everybody else's mainline within that network of tracks that ranged from Westminster Street to Hoffman Avenue, about two and one half miles. The movement of any CNW trains of significant length through this maze of trackage could and did tie up the three interlockings that made up the miles of the puzzle for quite a while. The CNW had to negotiate a grade percentile of 1.5-1.65 on tortuous curves in an effort to gain the confines of E. St. Paul and the eastward mainline.

All railroads operating into and through the Twin Cities would be challenged by the grades that formed the operating patterns of the T.C.T. No railroad was immune to the hills that had to be encountered in the daily exchange of cars between railroads.

Now I'll get back to where this chapter began. The "powers that be" tried to talk my engineer out of wanting a pilot to bring a 95 car rock train down the very steep and dangerous hill. He had never been there before. The entire crew rode up to the train in a taxicab. I mentioned to our crew that we would need an air test which would be time consuming. Determining whether or not we had functioning brakes was a definite priority. The train had been there long enough to have possibly been tampered with by kids and had to be inspected before we endeavored to come down the "hill".

While we were waiting for the air test, both the engineer and I wondered aloud about the lack of respect that the company showed for this very serious piece of railroad, casting experience to the wind. In one breath they preach safety and in that same breath they tell you to circumvent it. I went on to relate my experience at Moose Lake where I was called for a job that I was totally unfamiliar with and asked for a pilot. The caller stated that if he had a pilot, he wouldn't need me and that the crew would show me the way As I was beginning a new job for a different company, I decided to do the Soo Line a favor and accept the call.

Someone said that they had a sixty day rule, like a trial period and after all—I wasn't trying to piss anyone off, it was a fresh start and I honestly felt that the Soo Line was a cut above jeopardizing anyone's life or job. I was naïve to say the least. It wouldn't take long during the course of the trip to realize that I was all by myself in the cab of that engine. The person with me was simply taking up space and knew less than I did about running to Bemidji and back. (I did make one student trip).

The long and the short of it was that we were nearly killed, although physically unscathed, it very easily could have resulted in serious injury or even death. This story has been told earlier in this book and I want to finish by simply stating that when the "smoke cleared", the Soo Line showed me no mercy. I walked the streets for nearly a year before the Railway Labor Board re-instated me.

Given the mountainous periphery of the T.C.T., all trains should have been equipped with dynamic braking. The Milwaukee Road ordered all of its GP and SD40's with dynamic braking, however due to its financial status could not find the cash to maintain or repair them, ergo they were soon out of service. Once in a blue moon you might find a unit with a functioning dynamic, but not often. The Soo Line never opted for dynamics. Its Twin Cities operation avoided those steep grades for the most part. It was not without its share of steep grades when you consider the likes of Byron, Valley City and the 19 mile grade that ran from Superior up to Hillcrest and usually commanded a helper. CNW was another road that ran up and down the 1.5 to 1.65 % grade from Westminster to their East side yard sans dynamics. Northwestern would not see dynamics until the Chicago Great Western came into the picture.

As mentioned earlier, BN crews do not come down either hill without dynamic braking. I'm sure it is of mutual accord i.e. BN management is equally happy to provide dynamic equipped locomotives as it is for the crews to have it. I'm sure BN management would be more than poignant if the foreign roads using BN trackage all were as dynamically endowed as the BN is, especially the dispatchers. As it is and has been the BN looks the other way on that issue. The Federal Railway Administration, the government's regulatory watchdog on railroad safety, also seems to be non-committal in that area.

Sometime in early 1994 the Soo Line and the Burlington Northern had a trackage equality issue settled out of court. BN dispatchers were showing favoritism to Canadian National trains between the Twin Cities and Duluth. Soo parent Canadian Pacific is a direct competitor of the Canadian National.

Railroad map of the Twin Cities.

Chapter 28

The Extra Board

Working The Soo Line extra board around the Twin Cities was a lot easier than working the ICG extra board with its numerous starting points and having to buck all of that Chicago traffic. The Soo Line extra board also protected the road jobs and there was no commuter service. The ICG Chicago terminal had 19 starting points (counting outlying jobs) versus the 11 starting points of the combined Soo and Milwaukee.

As I was new to the Twin Cities it meant that I had a lot to learn. The hills around St. Paul would be a new experience to a flatland railroader and train handling techniques would definitely have to be changed. Learning the lay of the land, yard tracks and names of guys you work with are all part of coming to a new terminal. Counting both Soo and Milwaukee facilities, there were close to 60 jobs including outlying jobs, on the river. Unlike most guys on the board, I enjoyed working the jobs on the river and the crew callers knew that. We had an un-official agreement to that effect.

Just about anyone can learn to run a locomotive by itself. It starts to get more complicated when that engine becomes a big train. Now factor in the physical characteristics of the particular railroad that that train will operate over. Unlike an automobile which can be driven for the first time by just about any driver in any place, a train needs preparation and planning just to make a safe and effective stop. One of the key words associated with train handling is the word "anticipation". You cannot anticipate if you do not understand the physical characteristics of the railroad.

When an engineer comes to a new railroad or a portion of a railroad that he isn't familiar with, he will ask for a pilot. The definition of a pilot in the rule book is: "An employee assigned to a train when the engineer or conductor is not acquainted with the rules or portion of the railroad over which the train is to be moved".

With the Soo acquisition of the Milwaukee Road, came an increase in freight traffic. Any excess engineers on a certain terminal would be moved or forced to work at a terminal in need of manpower, this can be temporary and in my case, permanent. The company paid me an incentive of $5,000 to re-locate.

There were a lot of new people trying to adjust and get acclimated. There were Soo guys from both Shoreham and other points, a very few boys from the Minneapolis, Northfield & Southern. Lake States came upon us and then later, the engineers from Dubuque would begin running all the way to St. Paul, - 249 miles. These people would need pilots. Incidentally, very few, if any, Milwaukee engineers wanted to "break in" or learn the Soo mainline from St. Paul to Glenwood.

With the emergence of Lake States came a bevy of transplanted people that elected not to stay with the new company. Although these guys were more than familiar with their original territory, they couldn't know their way around the T.C.T. or the river. Nineteen eighty-eight would be the year of the pilot. The first guy I would pilot was a fellow from Fond du Lac. We worked the day hump together and I never saw or heard of him after that. The next fellow was another engineer from Fond du Lac. We worked the afternoon Ford hauler. He seemed to be a lost soul, pouring out his personal life. Apparently about the time Lake States was conceived, his wife asked him for a divorce. Not a good time in this man's life. I heard later that the guy had suffered from a nervous breakdown. About ten days later I would pilot another engineer from Fond du Lac. This fellow didn't seem to mind the transition and would ultimately end his career in St. Paul. An engineer from Gladstone (Escanaba) came next. Gladstone was a major terminal for the Soo Line on the Upper Peninsula. That part of the railroad was once known as the Duluth, South Shore and Atlantic. It wasn't but a few days later and this guy suffered an accident and received a disability. A few months later I piloted an engineer from Stevens Point on #402 down the river. We had a good trip and this guy was good to work with. Almost two years later I was called to pilot an engineer to Portage. It was the same man that I had worked with in 1988. He explained that shortly after we worked together the first time, he became very ill and now that he had overcome his sickness he was ready to try again. The last guy I would pilot from the former Soo Line or Lake States was another engineer from Stevens Point on a trip to Portage. The particulars of this trip will be covered in the River chapter.

The guys that I piloted for the most part didn't have a very good transition rate. Out of five guys that I piloted from the old Soo or Lake States, only one seemed to make the adjustment in stride. The other four became pawns or rather scapegoats in upper managements quest for notoriety. It was tough on a family.

The best day I ever had on the railroad was a pilot's job. One day #7, the westbound Empire Builder was caught in a derailment east of Portage. The engineer and assistant engineer or fireman exceeded their hours of service and a Portage freight crew was used to bring the train into St. Paul. The Portage freight engineer had never worked on the Merriam Park subdivision and requested a pilot upon their arrival at St. Paul. I boarded the train at Hoffman Avenue and guided the train up the third shortline and into AMTRAK's depot atop the hill. I got off immediately and hailed a taxi cab back to my vehicle at Pigs Eye. I was on duty less than an hour including the taxi ride.[1]

One beautiful Saturday morning I am working a day top end job and we are shoving cars into the swamp. The head man climbs up on the engine and points to an economy type pickup truck that for some unknown reason was parked under the sanding tower at the adjacent roundhouse complex. He comments that our superintendent must have gotten lost because that was a strange place for his truck to be. As I looked more intently at this person, it looked like he was watching us with binoculars. I always carried binoculars with me for birds. I hesitated briefly as I asked myself…."wouldn't it be fun if the guy watching us with binoculars became cognizant of the fact that he himself is being watched with binoculars"? This guy was known to be vengeful and it wasn't a good idea to get on his bad side. I couldn't resist. When it dawned on this guy that he too, was being watched—down came the binoculars and then up again briefly and then down again as if in disbelief. The audacity! Suddenly sand was flying everywhere as this man put his vehicle into gear and reacted in a most predictable manner. My head was nearing the chopping block. He shall be known as the "Sandman" from this day on.

The Sandman and I bumped heads earlier when I was called to pilot a rock train (Chapter 27, The Twin Cities). Although we didn't have words, it was clear that we weren't going to be pals.

Of course the hostler incident can't go without being mentioned. A hostler is a man that runs locomotives within the confines of the roundhouse. The hostlers had their own little extra board. However, on great occasion it would get exhausted and the hostlers would have to borrow an engineer from the engineers extra board. I stood for a 11:30 PM road job when the caller called and told me that someone had laid off at the last minute in the roundhouse and I would have to "hostle" that night. It really pissed me off because I got screwed out of the the road job plus I knew the guy that laid off. He was probably drunk somewhere.

When you work as a hostler the preferred dress code called for the wearing of a helmet. I didn't wear a helmet when I worked my normal job and I wasn't going to wear one in and around the roundhouse. I was in and out of the foreman's office all night and he never said a word. About 6:15 AM I was in the office and both the foreman and the general foreman were there. The general foreman immediately noticed that I didn't have a hard hat on. He touched on that very subject when the night foreman chimed in that "yeah—you'd better wear a hard hat around here"! I mentioned that helmets of any kind gave me a headache—I couldn't wear one in the army. The general foreman at that time admonished me to go home. "Maybe you'd better go home! At which time I did a bit of a "shuffle off to Buffalo" and out the door I went.

Somehow I knew that that wasn't going to be the end of it. And sure enough here came the letter inviting me to a formal investigation in order to explain my role, "if any", blah, blah, blah. That always cracked me up "if any". You were always dead before you went in there. It was a kangaroo court no doubt about it.

The day came and the company or the roundhouse produced three witnesses, the general foreman, the night foreman and a Mexican that couldn't speak English, so how could he hear English? Not a good witness. I think the good folks at Pigs Eye, the ones making the presentation, felt that what the roundhouse people were trying to do was a waste of time. We were in there about ten minutes when the general foreman volunteered that he would like to waive the investigation, but only if I promised never to work in the roundhouse again. Everyone voted…yea! It was win-win, for all of us. As it turned out, we were all unwitting liars. Almost three years later the caller called me and begged me to take an open hostler's vacancy that he forgot about. We were always playing the favors game and he was a good man to do business with. I acquiesced and very quietly worked the four o'clock hostler's job.

You didn't command a whole lot of respect working the extra board either. The Milwaukee side of the railroad always had engine transfers or better known as change-offs. The change-off would swap power for power that needed repair or servicing. Whenever and wherever an engine was needed the change-off would deliver it and either bring another unit or units back to St. Paul or return via taxi cab. The change-off scheme of things called for their own little extra board. When that board was exhausted they would usually call an engineer off the engineers extra board. This day I would provide the body they wanted to work this change-off. The change-off only has an engineer and foreman.

Our first job was to take three MPI5AC's from St. Paul over to Humboldt. By the time we got to Humboldt it was time to go to lunch (beans). The yardmaster tells us where to leave the power and I decide to leave my grip, my home away from home, on the lead engine. My foreman knew one of the guys working the "west lead" job and borrowed his car so that we could drive over to

Denny's for a quick bite. When we got back, the power was gone along with my grip. I went into the yardmasters office and told him that my grip was on the units that were moved and that I wanted it. Of all the Soo yardmasters this guy was probably the worst of the bunch. In fact he was the only bad one. Again I enjoined this guy that my grip was gone and I wanted it. The only important items were a pair of decent binoculars. What was really important was that I wasn't gonna let him lose my grip. This jerk began talking and I couldn't understand him as he talked fast. Finally I figured out that he wasn't happy about our going off company property. I told him that I really didn't give a shit what he was mad about, if I didn't get my grip back it was going to get uglier than it already was. He walked away from me then turned around and said that the engine with my grip on it would soon be up to the "west end" and I could then retrieve it. What an asshole! I did learn a good lesson however always keep your personal property within arm's reach.

Another adventure in the saga of Bud Hoekstra took place on a part of the Minneapolis, Northfield & Southern, now called Soo Line. One of the big cable networks was in the process of laying cable along the MN & S. In order to lay cable you had to have a ditch. The only way to have a ditch was to make one. The cable company had a special car with a huge blade on it that cut vertically about two and one half feet down, thus creating a narrow trench. Of course it was an extra job and the crew was also pretty extra. The trick was to pull the blade through the ground at 1 ½ or 2 MPH. If we went much over 2 MPH the kid foreman they had would get nervous. He must have had three or four guys working for him. I remember that it was a very hot day and it seemed to me that we were being overworked because of this kid's ego. We worked all day in the heat. When we began to slow down because resistance increased and in order to return the balance, I had to increase power and gave it another notch and yet another notch and when that happened our young foreman more than admonished me to stop. That was when I found out that the blade cost about $5,000. The kid acted like it was the end of the world. We had apparently hit a huge boulder that after laying there for a million years or so, it wasn't too eager to move or be broken up. I asked the guy if it was going to affect his bonus, he said nothing and walked away. I guess we pulled the blade off its mounting when we hit that rock. For a minute I thought the kid wanted me to pay for the blade. The good part of it was that those guys got a break from the heat.

A sad event took place on the 21st of February 1989. Gregory Carpenter, a non-railroader, was crushed by a load of lumber that shifted in the boxcar he was riding as it slammed into a cut of cars in the bowl after it came off the hump. He was 26 years old and aspired to writing a book on the romance of railroading and hopping trains. I mention this only because I may have been around there somewhere. The death of this young man came when the proponents of railroading were in short supply.

I worked the extra board for almost three years. One day I decided that I needed a regular direction in life and working a regular job with days off would be a step toward attaining that goal. I couldn't hold a decent job and would have to take a job that no one else wanted as I suffered from a serious lack of seniority. I worked the extra boards of two different railroads for a long while and now it was time to settle down. Nineteen ninety had come along and for the most part I was able to hold the midnight top end. It had Sunday and Monday off.

---

[1] A day's pay is constituted by a start. A start is any assignment called for regardless of its quitting time or total time consumed.

A Dad and His Son

Ironically, I write this story on Father's Day.

A dad and his son went fishing in a creek just south of the city of Winona, Minnesota. The creek emptied into the Mississippi River at that point. The railroad also was very much there and straddled the creek. The boy decided to go to the other side, using the railroad bridge for conveyance. The father paid no attention, pre-occupied with his fishing. The boy, too, wasn't focused on much more than fishing and didn't heed the pulsations of the train that was about to overtake him. Suddenly the boy was trapped on a bridge that offered no mercy. There was nowhere to go but down. The father watched the entire scene with disbelief. He watched the train run over his son. His son was gone! The engineer engaged the emergency brakes of his train, but it was too late, the kid went down. Anyone that had witnessed this debacle would have bet that this kid was dead. He had been run over by a speeding AMTRAK train. In fact the train and all of its cars had gone over him, leaving his lifeless body almost connected to the ties. The father said that he never realized how much he loved that kid until he saw that happen. When the kid stood up, he had tears in his eyes. His boy was unscathed! He literally had been hit by a train, at speed, and walked away from it. It was an amazing event. Father and son would fish for years to come.

Chapter 29

The River

The Mississippi River Valley is one of the most spectacular geologic formations in North America. To me it is without a doubt the prettiest in the midwest.

Although I couldn't work any of the River jobs on a regular basis, when I did catch a trip I would always reflect on how fortunate I was to be there and was getting paid. In a way it was good that I couldn't hold a regular job in the freight pool because I didn't want the novelty of the River to go away. Of all the places off the Twin Cities extra board, the best one was the River. When the phone rang, I always hoped it was for the River.

Installing Centralized Traffic Control, along with single tracking, had the River Subdivision in full swing when I was called to "deadhead" to Winona for a work train until further notice. It was July 1988 and it was hot down on the river. The work train was put on in an effort to support the track department while they were in the throes of single tracking. We would haul any materials needed for this project to the job site. The job started out of Winona at 0500. It would have Saturday and Sunday off.

Because we started work at 5AM, we were never in sync with the section crew. The section guys started at 6 AM (early to minimize working in the heat). These guys always brought their lunch whereas we were living out of suitcases and always ate in restaurants. The road agreement for eating was unlike the yard agreement. The yard agreement called for twenty minutes, the road agreement specified "sufficient time".

One fine day we stopped at a tavern that had food. Twin Bluffs happened to be within eyesight of the company property. The brakeman and I were both prior rights Soo Liners, the conductor was a Milwaukee man. He stayed on the caboose, eating his lunch while we planted our feet under a table. About the time we put our order in, who should walk into the restaurant but the project supervisor, another Milwaukee man. This guy was quiet, yet overbearing. Sure the agreement called for sufficient time, after sitting with this fellow as we watched him sip his glass of water and he watched us eat our lunch, sufficient time became too much time. This man had suffered from hard work and oppression. Throw in a bankruptcy or two and you have the perfect recipe for a Milwaukee official. There was no sufficient time. I've seen a few section foreman in my time. They all had a particular brand of tyranny.

As mentioned before, the crew callers and I had an un-official agreement. If a River job came open, they would call me first. No one complained. Everyone was happy - they didn't have to leave home and I didn't have one.

Whenever I would be summoned for this work, I would find the ritziest motel in the area. My first question to the innkeeper would be "do you have a Soo Line account?" The answer was always yes. Nothing was said when I checked into the Holiday Inn at Winona until that motel sent the company the bill. By then I was back working at St. Paul. The company was pissed and wanted to make me pay the bill out of my own pocket. I was looking at about $2,000. My local chairman performed some kind of miracle and got me out of it. I was reminded by him to stay out of the Holiday Inn. We peons weren't entitled to be flamboyant with the company's money. Whew!

The actual single tracking of the River Subdivision would be comprised of nine sidings, averaging almost 11 miles between the switches. The shortest distance being between Duke and the double track at Blackbird, 8.5 miles. The longest segment would exist at three locations, 13 miles between Homer and Minnesota City and another 13 miles between Weaver and Midland and again another 13 miles between Midland and Lakeview.[1]

By going from double track "automatic block signal" territory to single track "centralized traffic control" the 103 miles of single track has lost 25% of its efficiency, however, has gained a savings of about 20% in maintenance costs.

The Milwaukee Road would always enjoy the benefits of its water level route between LaCrosse and St. Paul. With the exception of the steep hill coming into or out of St. Croix, it would be free of grades of any consequence. There is some undulating territory between Lake City and Frontenac however the rest is pretty flat. Of course, when you traverse a river such as the Mississippi, there is always the risk of flooding.

The state of Wisconsin would subsidize the rehabilitation of the River, Tomah and Watertown subdivisions of the former Milwaukee Road. That would be almost 322 miles. The track project was completed on the River in early to mid-

1989. The Tomah segment had yet to get started. I don't have any information on the Watertown Sub. because that was out of my seniority district, hence, I never worked over there.

I often wondered if the state had a thorough understanding of what the Soo Line meant when they discussed track rehabilitation.

The best days on the River are in the fall. An engineer not only gets paid, he gets to take in the beautiful scenery afforded by the trees that grace the Mississippi, along with it's great bluffs.

One fine fall day our crew was called for a test train at 11 AM. It was a Saturday and the test train was on its way to St. Paul for the weekend. The train itself had come off the Dubuque Subdivision. They wanted me to run the train at 25 MPH until otherwise advised. Roger!

I was sitting there enjoying the ride. We were probably around Kellogg or Weaver when the door opens behind me. It is Don Walztoni, our traveling engineer on the River. I didn't know he was on the train. Don suggested that I get a cup of coffee when I was ready. He of course would run the engine. I said "okay, but don't get me fired"! We had three cars and the coffee pot was on the rear car. The hind car had one of those picture windows with auditorium seats. In front of the seats were a commanding series of gauges, meters and monitors. Railroading was on its way into the next century.

As I walked into the car I happened to pass my conductor, Phil Steber. Phil didn't know Walztoni was on the train either. When he noticed me, all at once he jumped up and wanted to know what I was doing back there while the train was moving. I busted out laughing because Phil had overreacted. I said relax, I know you think I'm crazy, but I never wanted a cup of coffee all that much. We all had a good laugh including Walztoni, once I got back on the engine and told him.

I never was good at math and always squeaked by when it came to tests. I just wasn't a classroom guy. Although I shied away from organized education, I liked my job well enough to try to analyze the most effective way to handle a freight train over a specific piece of railroad. My brain functioned much better when it was allowed to keep its own schedule and I could determine the best approach.

One morning I was called out of LaCrosse for some freight train with a general tonnage of around ten thousand tons, a normal train. What wasn't normal was that I had a student engineer and a traveling engineer whom I'd never met before. We had another train ahead of us but we wouldn't find that out until River Junction. By this time it was too late, I had foolishly put the "trainee" in the engineer's seat and as we were snaking through River Junction we encountered a huge bank of fog. We're going along at about 25 MPH and I yelled at the trainee to "get some air". Right away it was clear to me that the kid didn't know what I was talking about, and I wasn't sure where the ass end of that other train was. The traveler kept his composure through this temporary dilemma. The smoke along with the fog cleared and we never saw the previous train again.

I wasn't sure what this kid was used to as far as vernacular was concerned. I know that different railroads use different terminology and that I wasn't sure what level of training this guy was at. Maybe I should have asked him before I let him run the engine. I know he didn't respond when I told him to get some air. The traveler never said a word. It was at River Junction in the fog that I decided to relieve the trainee.

Once we got going the fog cleared. It was to be another beautiful day on the river. We were moving along at track speed (50MPH). We were approaching Red Wing which has a permanent restriction of 30 MPH through town. As you leave Lake City, going north, you lose the river for 15 miles or so. As you near Red Wing, the train drops downhill before the river is again rejoined. It isn't a steep hill, but a hill nonetheless.

A new and interesting innovation that was now included in our train paperwork was a profile of the train - -loads and empties indicated in a graph type motif. I never was much for newfangled ideas, however I liked this one. The graph would come in handy. What I had in mind as a braking technique would work nicely provided I didn't have a concentration of loads on the hind end. The graph indicated that loads and empties were pretty much interspersed throughout the train. I had used this technique a time or two before and it worked well.

When I began to brake for the slowdown, the train was rolling at 50 MPH in throttle eight. I drew seven pounds of air off the trainline at a selective location and would now monitor the reaction of the train. As was almost always my method was to then draw off two-three more pounds, wait for the air to quit blowing (or equalize), then release the train air and notching down to throttle seven and then in three second increments come down another notch until throttle three is reached (you may have to go to throttle two, depending on the speed of the train). As the air releases the rear end rolls gently against the main body of the train in a cushion effect. Every train is different and you're not always going to get the same results. This day it worked perfectly. The traveler asked me if I always came through Red Wing that way and I answered: "lately I have". He went on to say that my train handling habits were textbook, accolades from the boss. That was another reason to have a good day. Any day is a good day when the sun is shining and you are on the river!

Another trip I had was just the opposite of the aforementioned run. We were called for some train that came out of Dubuque at 11:30AM. The makeup of the train was 120 empty auto racks. This train was almost two miles long. A train like this would have to be handled with kid gloves. In fact any train that long, made up of solid cushion draw bars was impractical to operate. I wondered if there was some rule of thumb conducive to handling big trains of auto racks that I didn't know about. This train should not have been allowed on the railroad. However, I would do my best.

The head 20 cars were to be set out at Hastings. I managed to get through the 30MPH slowdowns at Winona and Red Wing without touching the air (train brakes). Because this train had the flexibility of a giant rubber band, I would bunch or gently gather the slack by shutting down the throttle in one mile increments. I would begin at a place called Blackbird, about eight miles from Hastings. From Blackbird to Hastings the grade is very subtle and downhill. I didn't take this into consideration and the train didn't slow as I anticipated. Now I'm between a rock and a hard place as I have to slow to at least 15MPH to enable the brakeman to get off in order to make the 20 car cut. I had no choice but to use the air, making a minimum reduction. If I kept the brakes applied, the train would stop prematurely and so I crossed my fingers, kept the engine brake applied, and released the train air. I got away with it. Somehow, I got away with it. The train kept on rolling. We had just passed a yellow signal meaning the home signal at the bridge would be red, a definite stop. Coming around the curve, I now can see the signal. I would let the air blow until the train stopped. It wasn't stopping and I had to put the brake valve into emergency. I got by the absolute stop signal by about three feet. Luckily we had good radios and I mumbled to the brakeman not to make the cut, as I would shove back a bit. Once I captured the air, I shoved back the few feet that I needed. Shoving back a few feet with a train like this wasn't easy. Don't forget that I had a conductor on the caboose which was almost two miles away. The gentle slope would help me to stop while shoving back in throttle four.

It was eerily quiet, as if the whole world was watching, but apparently the only ones in the world that really knew were me and the dispatcher. Once we made the set-out and of course got the signal to proceed, I told the brakeman what had happened.

We were able to yard the train in no time at all by first pulling into one of the long tracks at Dunn. Someone made a cut and we pulled the balance into the swamp and took the power to the roundhouse. I registered and then got the hell out of there. I figured that the dispatcher must have turned me in and I wanted to be away from there. It was very quiet. The last thing the brakeman said to me was "we lived to fight another day". I didn't live very far from St. Paul yard and I called the dispatcher on my home phone. I explained what had happened and apologized. The dispatcher came back with "I knew you had your hands full with that train, just try to be more careful in the future"....I kept it quiet. I thanked him, he was a real gentleman.

I would later ask a seasoned veteran on the River if there was a correct way to handle a train like that. He assented that the way I did it was about the only way you could do it. He also added that keeping ones fingers crossed wouldn't hurt either.

I seemed to remember the bad trips more so than the good ones. Another trip that comes to mind happened right before Christmas of '89. I was called to pilot the engineer on #950. The train originated at St. Paul. The engineer was originally from Stevens Point and I remembered him from my Superior days. Our power consist was an ugly one. We had an SD60 in the lead, a dead Soo SW9, and a Soo SD40. It was an ungainly sight. By the time we received our okay on the air test, and our departure was sanctioned by the yardmaster, it was getting late.

As we left LaCrosse, climbing out of the river bottom, I didn't feel that our train was running as fast as it should have. We were losing ground. The weight of that deadhead engine certainly wasn't helping. As you went east you were steadily going up hill. The heaviest pull eastbound was at Raymore, before Tunnel City and the tunnel itself. Coming up to Raymore we began to smell the smoke of sticking brakes. Sure enough, our deadhead switch engine was the culprit. I told the engineer that the one thing I didn't want to do was stall in the tunnel. We would have to stop on the steepest grade eastbound on either the River or Tomah subdivision or risk stalling in the tunnel. I wasn't about to gamble and we stopped at the end of double track, clear of the signal (the tunnel is single tracked).

We were lucky enough to rectify the problem, notified the dispatcher that we were ready to go, and received the signal. By then the dispatcher wanted to know if we thought we could make it into Portage before our 12 hours was up. All I could say at that time was that we would try. It was a toss-up. I would later apprise him of our situation. As it turned out we had enough time to make Wisconsin Dells which was always a safe haven for crews dying on the hours of service.

A taxi cab would provide the final transportation into Portage and a relief crew would bring the train the rest of the way. As we entered the yard office, I was informed that the trainmaster wanted to see me. Entering his office, he queried, what happened? I told him pretty much what is written here and he admonished me to get some sleep. I didn't need to be reminded. I was definitely exhausted.

When a crew exceeds the 12 hour rule, they have to have 10 hours rest. We were called exactly on our ten hours rest.

On a final note, there was a BNSF dispatcher that had a monotone voice that was tailor made for nights. A train heading for Chicago would complete its air test and get a "highball" from the car department commensurate with a highball from the yardmaster. All that was left was to inform the BNSF dispatcher. If the dispatcher was ready to take the train he would say "come on down and take a ride on the river". Words cannot convey the true effect it had on a crew. You had to be there…..at night, on the river.

---

[1] Midland and Lakeview are newly designated time-table points necessitated by single tracking.

Chapter 30

New Guys

My brother went braking on the Grand Trunk at Blue Island, Illinois. He was a new guy. On his first pay trip, his crew was switching out "bad orders" (defective cars). The bad orders were to be "kicked" into an empty stub track. Brother Chuck was instructed to ride the first car earmarked for the stub, slowing it while tying down the hand brake. As the car rolled toward the stub, he noticed that the car wasn't slowing down and that the hand brake was not taking effect as the wheel was simply spinning. The car went out the other end of the stub track coming to rest in a pile of dirt mixed with other miscellany. What was defective on the car was its hand brake.

His conductor alluded that he knew that Chuck would be a good man when he saw him bail off of the errant car. "That showed me you had good sense", quoted the conductor. Welcome to the railroad, Chuck!

In the early part of 1990, I began looking for a regular job to hang my hat on. A job with regular days off and going to work at the same place and time was beginning to appeal to me. Hell, I was 47 years old and had worked the St. Paul extra board for nearly three years. I had recently bought a home close to Pigs Eye and was hankering for some kind of a routine. Of course, it couldn't be a very good job, as I had little seniority and was vulnerable to be "bumped" at any time. Most guys looked at the "midnight top end" as the literal meaning of "whip me, beat me, kick me". There was no doubt about it, the midnight commanded little respect. The good aspect of taking the midnight was that no-body else wanted it but it had days off - Sunday and Monday. I rationalized that "you had to crawl before you could walk" and the midnight would be a start.

One factor that I overlooked when I took the job was….who worked the job on a more or less regular basis? Status symbols are everywhere and the railroad is no different. I found out that not working the midnight was a status symbol in itself, nobody worked the midnight on a regular basis.

After working the job for a couple of weeks, I took solace in the fact that I wouldn't be on it forever - it simply seemed that way.

If you took a general consensus as to what job was the worst, it would probably be a toss- up between the midnight and the 11:59 hump. Some guys preferred the hump. One thing you knew when you took the midnight - -if there were any new guys, you would be working with them. I don't remember if the economy got better or maybe a few retirements caused the company to get caught short, they hired an endless stream of new guys. There were people from all walks of life.

What with the burgeoning influx of new switchmen and ladies, the company decided to establish a training program. It was headed by a fellow named John Ode. John was a most affable man and would be the right man for the job. Toward the end of each class, John would select an engineer to run an engine back and forth in an effort to teach the recruits the proper way to get on and off moving equipment. The engineer would have to take two days off his regular job in order to be available. The two days were short and easy with a thirty minute pep talk at the end given of course, by the engineer. The engineer was afforded two day's pay.

Two of the guys in this class were friends of the director of personnel. They went to his church. I didn't know it at the time but as I was giving my concluding speech, looking and talking to twelve new hires, one guy stuck out. He had a smirk on his face that told me immediately that I did not want to work with this guy, but I knew I would sooner or later because I worked the midnight top end which was a magnet for "newbies". I had a feeling that this guy would be a "newbie" for a long time if he lasted that long. I would later find out that this guy had friends in high places however he would prove my assessment to be correct.

All in all it was a fine tribute to be selected and I was happy to do it.

One of the first subjects to be touched upon when teaching new hires is to give an explanation as to the meaning of the letter "F".

Did you ever notice the letter "F" displayed on the end of a diesel locomotive? Ever wonder what it meant? In my many years of running an engine, I had always knew what it meant, but never thought I would have to give a dissertation on it until I started working the midnight "top end".

Most nights at least for a while, I would have brand spanking new guys and

I would have to explain which end of the engine went in reverse (back up) and which end of the engine came ahead (forward) which is where the "F" (front) came in. The "F" signified the front of the engine and with a little deductive reasoning it usually wasn't too difficult to establish where the rear of the engine was. What would confuse a new guy would be that the "F" on a switch engine was always on the long hood end opposite the cab. On a geep the "F" or front was always on the cab end. A few railroads ran their geeps long hood first, offering better crew protection and the "F" would be displayed on the long hood end and the cab end would be the rear. Thank goodness those engines were a long way away from St. Paul, as it would have only threw more fuel to the flame. Most of these guys had all they could handle and didn't need any more distractions. It took me awhile to understand how contradicting the direction of an engine could be, after all these were new guys. I had been on the railroad over thirty years and I tried to remember what it was like to be a new guy. I did this quite often.

A major safety issue on railroads operating in the T.C.T. is the lack of training "new" or inexperienced men get on the physical characteristics of the T.C.T.[1] This makes an already dangerous situation - volatile. A case in point is the signal at Division Street. It is on the left or wrong side, but is not for the track on the left. The signal is for the right track or track 2, as you move west. Obviously it was put there for utilitarian reasons. Railroads don't always practice what they preach and a new employee has yet to learn that, especially when he or she is in unfamiliar territory.

One night I was working with one man, a guy that had recently received his conductors card and was forced from Harvey, North Dakota to temporarily work at St. Paul. We were told to take an eight unit consist - not your everyday package of power, and shove a stalled train going west. This conglomeration of units consisted of four bad order units, four running and four not. Ordinarily I would run this power from the west end, however that unit was dead, hence, no heat. It was cold and the end of the night and I foolishly elected to run this power, with a new man, eight units away from the point, from the other end.

Of course the signal at Division Street was red because there was a train occupying the track beyond. You couldn't go by the signal unless you talked to the dispatcher. My recently transferred or should I say "forced" switchman from Harvey, insisted that I could go beyond the point that I stopped at because there was no reason not to. I knew that the signal at Division Street was for us and this kid had been placed in a predicament not of his choosing. In fact the more I thought about it, the madder I got. I got off the engine and walked back to the other end, where my fellow crewman was located. When I got back there

247

he told me that the signal was for the other track and to look at the rule book. I came back with "these outfits don't always play by the rules and that conductor's card you have in your wallet gives you a false sense of security and will get you killed. If they can't kill you, they'll fire you!" As I walked back to the controlling east unit, I tripped over some heavy wire that somehow got deposited onto the right of way. Now I was really pissed what with my knee all scraped up and the thought that if I really got hurt, the company would have come back and said that I shouldn't have been off the engine. Once I gained the east unit, I called St. Paul Yard and told them that we were not going to shove this train with this anomaly of units, and please advise the east hump dispatcher that we wanted to go back into the yard. It didn't take long and we were tied up and my brand new conductor from Harvey, N.D. and I were walking upstairs to see the trainmaster. I told the kid that I wasn't turning him in I simply wanted to establish the fact that the company was using him for a scapegoat and I wanted him to be there.

I explained to this lad that he was a new man in his own more familiar bailiwick which was the 152 mile Portal Subdivision which encompassed the area Harvey, N.D. to Portal, N.D. and had hardly had enough time to learn that pike. After looking at the timetable my guess was that there may have been three, maybe four absolute signals each way. They treated this kid and many others like him as if they were inter-changeable parts. It jeopardizes everyone's safety and the situation translates to very unsafe.

The trainmaster on duty listened to my spiel and said "okay". I said, "No it's not okay". I did what I could, I voiced my opinion, but alas, it fell on deaf ears. The company encourages these labor/management discussions, but rarely do they act on anything.

Before I left, I asked the kid what time he put off duty and he said, "7:59". I looked at my watch and it was twenty minutes after eight. I said, "It's after eight o'clock and I'm still here because of company business". The kid said, "I've already turned the time slip in and the box is locked". "We'll get someone with a key to retrieve it and then you can fill out another time slip, this time reflecting the ever accruing overtime that we were on". Welcome to the world, kid!

One night our last move was to yard some train and bring the power through a clear track, to the top end. Not much to it, I had a new "head man" that had been on the railroad about three months, however I seriously didn't think he was any smarter today than he was on day one. Once he cut the power off, he climbed back on the engine and fell asleep as I approached the next switch. Now I had to wake this guy up in order to gain access to the ladder track or lead. The switch is now thrown and instead of staying outside and throwing the other three switches, here he comes, back on the engine and fast asleep. I move the engine about 15 feet and then stop for the next switch. Again I have to extend to this guy a special invitation and was beginning to get agitated. He finally throws the switch and sure enough he climbs back on the engine and before I can move 15 feet he is asleep again. This time we had words, again I had to yell at him to wake up. As soon as he closed the door, I reached over and locked it. He threw the switch but could not get into the engine cab. He stood outside as we trundled down the clear alley that we at last had gained. Once the engine finally stopped, this kid made a beeline for the trainmasters office and told the guy that I wasn't very nice to him. The Sidewinder called over the bitchbox that the trainmaster wanted to see me. I entered the office and there stood this kid and the trainmaster. The kid looked like he was crying. The trainmaster queried with "what happened"? I answered with, "the kid couldn't stay awake and I thought that maybe a little fresh air (it wasn't that cold) would do him good". About that time the Sidewinder (yardmaster) comes into the office, apparently ready to offer a helping hand should his talents be needed. He was a disgusting person. He was disgusting by design. This new guy that snitched on me was also disgusting however he was disgusting by accident. It was a disgusting place. Now that the boss was satisfied, we were free to go. As I approached the door he motioned to me to stick around. Now we were one on one. He confided that we no longer can call people names that we had to be careful etc., etc. There was no point in arguing about an already acrimonious workplace that just got worse. Bring on the clowns.

And then there was the tale of the "hand brake express". A heavy eastbound train had left Glenwood with a new crew. The engineer had recently gotten his license and the conductor was also a green horn. Managing and operating a train of this dimension was a new experience. Anyone embarking on a new career or a positive change in the job situation will usually approach it with a fresh attitude. They were gonna do their best, and they had cards to prove it.

I had worked with the engineer numerous times on the midnight when he was a switchman. He seemed like a decent sort until he received his engineer's card. Suddenly he was a cut above everyone else as he no longer talked to anyone. I didn't know the other fellow, but I wouldn't have been surprised if he had been a transferee from another land.

As luck would have it, they encountered a "kicker" or "dynamiter"[2] in the train. Some "kickers" occur only once or twice and others cause the train to go into emergency every time the engineer goes to apply the brakes. That will ruin a trip in a hurry. This train had a set out to make at Humboldt and the crew of #940 was hoping that its problem would be eliminated with the set out. It wasn't to be. When the car department gave #940 their air test - the air dumped again. That would mean that the "dynamiter" was still in their train.

An experienced crew would have done one of two things....either sat at Humboldt until the car was eliminated through isolation or gone ahead with the thought that if they set the air and it went into emergency—so what. Remember that's what it's there for, the train goes into emergency and may or may not cause a serious accident, the crew won't get fired or even scrutinized for it—their ass is covered.

These guys didn't know that. All they knew was what they had heard around the railroad or maybe were taught at the engineers training center. An emergency application to a moving train might cause an accident. Covering your ass comes from years of enduring the trials and tribulations of working for the company and or knowing the ropes. Some guys never quite figure that out, others it only takes longer.

The only way to pinpoint the whereabouts of a hypersensitive triple valve is to find out where it isn't. The car department will start isolating cars by turning the angle cocks[3] in increments of ten cars at a time working from the rear end of the train toward the engine, until the car is finally found. This can be a long and tedious process depending on how lucky you are.

These guys had devised their own plan and left Humboldt with the "kicker" still in the train. Somewhere between Humboldt Yard and Bandana Square (the top of the 1% grade into St. Paul, ending at Hoffman Avenue) they would set approximately 35 hand brakes and would circumvent the use of the train air. They had no functioning dynamic brake. The neophyte engineer would use the engine brakes along with the help of the 35 hand brakes to maintain track speed down the mountain type grade. The 50 or so loads behind the hand brakes would simply push the train down the 1% grade. This was not a good plan.

Had they tied the hand brakes while waiting (the conductor ties the brakes down or does all the work) at University for the signal to gain access to BNSF'S mainline, it would have been quite a spectacle to watch man and machine horse that train out of there and keep it together. Where they tied the hand brakes is unknown as that information is unavailable. Maybe it was done in increments— here and there. It was a most bizarre stratagem. When these boys would finally get off this train for the last time—they would have defied just about every rule in the book, in some way shape or form.

While this story is developing, I was on the 2:30 PM Ford hauler. We were coming off the Ford line approaching West Hoffman with a signal to enter St. Paul Yard. I noticed that the signal on the mainline was "high green" or clear. This track is adjacent to the track we were running on. A voice comes over the radio calling "Ford hauler"? If you could truly whisper over the radio, this guy was trying to do just that. Again I heard—"940 to the Ford hauler". "Go ahead #940," I answer. Again there was a muffled whispered transmission. "We're on track one...do we have the signal at Hoffman"? I asked—"is this an emergency"? I receive a garbled reply that sounded like he said "sort of". I went ahead and relayed the information to him after we established that it sort of was an emergency.

When #940 came by us, we smelled lots of brake shoes that were in the process of turning red. We could see sparks almost fire spewing from the trucks of the locomotives. The train was destined to be yarded at Dunn. It must have been a real spectacle when it passed the tower at St. Paul Yard. When he came by us, he was going about 45 MPH on 25 MPH track.

To make a long story short, I think both the union and the company shared the same opinion. The crew of #940 was never seen again.

As always, there was a seniority dispute due to the acquisition. I never did completely understand the machinations of it. However, what I did understand, worked like this: there were four Milwaukee engineers that had at the time of the acquisition, gotten their engineers qualification. For some unknown reason, these guys had almost no seniority but for a good period of time these guys would enjoy better seniority than those of us that did it the hard way. It wasn't fair to the men that held prior Soo Line seniority. Once again the company and the union unite to kick me in the ass. The good news was that sometime in 1994 (I think it was effective 1-1-94) these guys would lose that illusion of grandeur. As long as I could work the midnight, I didn't pay much attention to what went on with seniority.

One day in February of that year, another engineer reminded me that the seniority issue had reverted back to the way it always should have been. On that note I began to look around and found out that I not only had gained those four numbers, I had gained a few other numbers through normal attrition. It was time for me to leave the midnight.

How many times did I say to myself...if I can get through this...I can get through anything? If I was short on patience when I took the midnight, I had acquired enough through perseverance to last me the rest of my life. Working that job was a challenge I could not ignore and I went the distance! In the almost three years that I worked the midnight, no one was injured and I only attended one investigation due to negligence on the behalf of my crew.

One night our switch foreman forgot to take the skate out from under a loaded covered hopper and when we pulled it out of the track, the skate jammed into the frog on the lead and literally caused the west truck to disintegrate. This guy had also run a car over the derail at North Star Steel. The lead track going into the North Star complex which was down-hill had for some unknown reason, a derail. About the only thing this device was good for was derailing cars for which it was intended. It was good at it, I might add. Cars don't roll up hill, yet the derail persevered to add the occasional anomaly to those affected. Early one morning we did the inevitable, we de-railed the only car we were handling. A definite mistake was made, however, this guy wanted to tell the boys upstairs that the wind caused the car to go over the derail. When he apprised me of his plan, I laughed and suggested that management wasn't that naïve and if he wrote that on his accident report, they wouldn't fire him for the miscue, they would however, fire him for trying to make fools of them. I didn't see the report that he submitted, however he must have heeded my advice because later down the road, he managed to get into the engineers training program which led to his ultimate demise on the Canadian Pacific. The last I heard, he was working for another railroad as an engineer.

Earlier in this chapter, I mentioned a fellow that gave me the impression that he looked upon his being hired on the railroad as a sort of joke. I didn't want to work with this guy, his demeanor told me that, but I knew sooner or later I would have to. Ultimately that day would come and it did. The first shot out of the bag—the guy is 25 minutes late. Almost every time I worked with this guy, he was late. All in all, I may have worked with him no more than ten times (more than enough.) He usually worked the night hump when he could. I remember the last time I worked with him, however. We had to shove the Minneapolis transfer up the hill in its quest to attain Southtown. The "hill" is about five miles in distance. It was probably about 20 degrees, cold if you're standing out there wondering when to pull the pin thus separating our power from the train that we are shoving. Our friend wasn't embracing the concept as he kept looking back at me for the sign to pull the pin. We were going between 5-8 miles per hour, and every time he looked at me with that "now?" expression, I would simply shake my head and utter - "not yet!" This guy had been on the railroad well over a year and actually thought that we were trying to "kick" this train up the hill. This fellow probably had a high intellect but was one of those individuals that had difficulty with the "basics". Had it been anyone else, I would have told him to come into the cab where it was warm. I would tell him when to pull the pin. He wouldn't need to pull the pin for a good 25 minutes or so. Had he shown an interest in his job, he would have known that. Most predictably this fellow was injured while working the hump and I never saw him after that.

Another fellow, named Eric, that I had occasion to work with, although he was fairly new, was good to work with. We had a good rapport and would have some good conversations through the course of the night. He worked about a year and a half, then disappeared.

Nine or ten years later my wife and I are trying to sell our house. The prospective buyer had an issue with asbestos, which had to be removed. Our real estate man found a guy that specialized in asbestos removal. It turned out to be my old buddy Eric from the railroad. He quit the railroad and started his own business. Eric quoted the cost for removal to be $1300. Later, as I was making out the check, he quietly said "make it out for $800."

We're all pretty much familiar with the phrase: "the names have been changed or omitted to protect the innocent". I don't exactly throw names around in this book. Most characters names are simply omitted as a matter of preference, and in a few cases, have been changed for good reason. I have further comments to make on a few individuals and they will remain anonymous.

Another fellow I worked with both on the hump and the top end asked me if I stopped at any of the "clubs" before work. Of course I didn't, however he went on to say that he had consumed two or three beers every night before coming to work. One night we went to beans on the midnight and he stayed on the engine. This idiot forgets to turn his radio down and I get blasted out of an almost sound sleep. I yelled to the guy to turn his fucking radio down. He took umbrage to that and threatened to kick my ass. I invited him to do just that and then advised him not to show up for work drunk. The last I heard this guy was injured on another job and received a large settlement. I would think that by now he's probably dead.

Another new guy was actually an older guy that was on loan from Enderlin, N.D. He was a long way from home and wasn't real happy which was understandable.

One night some cars came off the hump a bit faster than they should have and caused the track to roll into the side of another track that was being "rolled".[4] The skate[5] man climbed up on the engine. He said that he had heard that boxcars and such could and would fly through the air but alluded that for the most part, he thought it was exaggeration, but now he was a believer. When I first looked at the guy...my first thought was - Ned Flanders! This guy was Ned Flanders both in looks and mannerisms. He tested the waters on the railroad and went on to greener pastures.

Then there were two guys from Iowa that had worked on the section gang for the track department. If you had to describe the one guy in a word it would be—unlikeable. This fellow was quite presumptuous and must have thought that because he worked on the section that there was nothing else to learn. He had all of the answers he just didn't know the questions. That can be dangerous. One night we were sent to the BN-Northtown with a train. It had been quite a while since I had been there and wasn't completely cognizant of the track layout. This punk had the audacity to berate me for it. I lit into him pretty good and it wouldn't be the last time. The other guy was a complete opposite. He was friendly, easy to work with and openly conceded that he had a lot to learn. This kid had already gotten himself into the yardmasters program and had already worked as one. I would have gladly defined him to be a valuable asset to the company, however it wasn't to be. He failed a random drug test for the last time and was out and out fired. I think the company dropped the ball on this one, they could have worked with this kid and the company would have benefited. It fell on deaf ears. I wish him luck.

About the year 1993 we began to hire a few women. Guys looked at that with mixed emotions. I told myself not to draw any pre-ordained conclusions and that it might be just what the doctor ordered to overcome the doldrums of the night shift. I had never before worked with a woman and now that I look back, I can't complain. If you remove the strength factor, the women are just as good as the men no better no worse. One of the ladies that I worked with has advanced to a fancy job title at St. Paul. We also had a couple of lady engineers and they also did a fine job.

I worked the midnight top end for almost three years and some weeks I would work with as many as seven or eight different guys, all new. Some nights I would have to tell myself that if I can get through this, I can get through anything. More than half of the new guys left. Some left because after trying it, they realized it wasn't for them. Others quit because they simply couldn't get it and a few were asked to leave. The majority of the guys that left did so because of personal injury. It all boiled down to the metaphoric phrase: "some guys stay new guys longer than others" or everyone is different.

[1] T.C.T. is an abbreviation for Twin Cities Terminal. [2] A dynamiter or kicker is a car that has a defective triple valve inasmuch as they are hyper-sensitive to a normal trainline reduction and will cause the trainbrakes to immediately go into emergency. [3] Every type of rail car has its own air brake system. The system must be charged up and air from the engine is admitted to each car through an angle cock located at each end of the car. [4] A track that is being "rolled" is a track that has been coupled and is being placed into its ultimate train for a later departure. [5] A skate is a heavy piece of metal equipment used to prevent a track of cars from rolling out onto another track or lead.

Chapter 31

Ford Hauler

Prior to the Soo Line's acquisition of the Milwaukee Road, the mainstay of Milwaukee's St. Paul business was the Ford Plant, which generated exclusively the Ranger pickup truck.

The Milwaukee, the Soo Line and now the Canadian Pacific have shared a great partnership with the Ford establishment. It was a most lucrative and fine business concept for both companies. From the beginning the Milwaukee would interchange with the Wabash at Chicago. The Wabash would amass cars from the automobile companies around the Detroit-Toledo area and forward them to the Milwaukee for the St. Paul destination.

Today - the railroads have changed in name only. The service is still a good one. We went from Milwaukee Road and Wabash to Canadian Pacific and Norfolk Southern.

As before, I've mentioned #425 the "Ford Fast" (the Fast Ford would have sounded better, however Ford wanted "Ford Fast", and so it was). Ford also favored the term "Fordson", hence Fordson Junction and other Ford places.

There were times when I could work the 10:30 PM night hauler which handled #425's loading. #425 was the hottest westbound train out of Chicago. It was often described as a rolling warehouse. Other trains handled Ford cars but #425 is exclusively operated for the Ford Motor Company. On occasion the train would be filled out with miscellaneous tonnage that just happened to be going in the same direction the Ford cars were going. Officials would comment that it always worked as long as the plant was spotted before 5 AM. Interestingly, prior to my being able to take the job, it was held by two different yet very senior engineers. I had little seniority compared to them but it must have been a better job than I thought it was, or these guys wouldn't have been on it and of course it was nights.

As mentioned earlier, the night Ford Hauler was a rolling warehouse. When Rangers were in hot demand and business was good, there would be three haulers around the clock. However, the night hauler was the train that the plant radiated from, everything spun off of that.

For some reason the Ford line seemed to be a carefully kept secret. The Ford line was not listed in the timetable. The timetable did mention Otto Street on the Ford line and did specify that track speed "on all other tracks not indicated was to be held to 10 MPH". Other than that, nothing was said. For instance there was the creaky wooden trestle just beyond Fordson Junction. The entire time I was at St. Paul, the rule was—"no six axle engines will be operated over the trestle". Yet, that particular precept could not be found anywhere in print. That rule was strictly obeyed for more than one reason. Nobody wanted to get caught running those engines by accident across that trestle and nobody wanted to capsize while putting all of that extra weight on an already questionable structure. Some guys were plain scared while crossing it. If you looked down and then realized what you were riding upon, you had no problem understanding their dilemma.

CP Rail began buying these big, long and powerful six axle engines. After a while they began running #425 with a single unit, and of course it had to be one of those newfangled computer type engines and the situation steadily gets more complicated and frustrating.

The first night I ran one of these units was an omen of things to come. The train was a light one, maybe 25 cars and had a new unit with six axles. I called the yard, and told them that it was forbidden to take six axle engines over the Ford trestle and was told that it was now permissible. Six axle engines could now operate on the trestle. Here was an unwritten rule that was unwritten. Suddenly six axle engines were sanctioned. Just like that! The next morning I called the engineering department and was told that the trestle had no restrictions on it and never did. I learned something, I'm not sure what, but I learned.

The other point of contention was running these single units backwards from the Ford Plant. I've got over sixty feet of locomotive and it is difficult if not impossible to see the opposite side of the crossings. There is no place to turn an engine at the Ford Plant. One trainmaster suggested that I station the "head man" on the point. Of course it just happened to be −15 degrees outside and wouldn't it be easier to either provide two MP15AC's (like we used to?), or maybe the CP could do something totally bizarre like place two GP40's into captive Ford fast service, even paint "Ford Fast" on the sides of the units? But of course I also suggested that that was probably too easy.

On two different nights I approached the CP subalterns, delivering the outside line telephone number of the Bensenville roundhouse and then would remind them that Bensenville and Pigs Eye were owned by the same company and wouldn't it be great if you guys talked to one another?

Another source of irritation was the fact that they were equipping these new units with the new control stands - a desk console with tiny little knobs to turn and pull and push. Awkward to someone used to the "other" method of control (if the old timers could have seen this they would not only be spinning in their graves, they'd be throwing up). Another example of "if it works—fix it!

Now CP Rail couldn't be trying to keep up with the Joneses could it? One night, while I was trying to change ends vis-à-vis a computer arrangement it dawned on me that all this modern shit they didn't need and paid for would be kicked back into the faces of the ensuing labor negotiators.

One night we were on the night hauler and were rounding the curve approaching the trestle on our way up to the Ford plant. Suddenly my head man screams at the top of his lungs - "there's a body on the track!" I immediately put the train into emergency but still managed to pass the point where this man was located. The curve was on my blind side and was sharp enough that the head man didn't see it until it was too late even at 10 MPH, we still went by him.

What the switchman actually saw was a Native American male who had decided to snuggle his head up to the outside of the rail. If it hadn't been for the massive amount of hair that he had, we would have missed him completely because his body wasn't touching any portion of the rail, just his hair. We literally scalped this guy. The wheel of the engine began pulling at the large crop of hair it was running over and crimped it off the top of his head. By now we are off the engine and our trespasser is beginning to come to his senses and is now on his feet. Suddenly he bolts and the headman wants to chase him. Now we're chasing this fellow down West 7th Street, our conductor called the yard and apprised them of the situation. After a while the cops grabbed the guy and we never heard one more thing about it. Another time we were approaching Otto Street, two days before Christmas, A car neared the crossing with the intention of beating the train. It was clear to us that it wasn't going to make it. When the occupant of the car realized that she didn't have a chance, she applied her brakes and due to the slightly icy pavement, she slid sideways and stopped about ½ of an inch from the middle of my lead unit, and parallel to the train. I approached the car and there was a cowering, very afraid young lady. I then admonished her of the fact that she probably was a lot smarter now than she was a minute ago. I also mentioned that she received a Christmas gift two days early and wished her a "Merry Christmas". It's all in a day's work.

CP had a device they would use to measure slack action and rough handling. Quite often they would have this device on the rear of the Ford trains, never apprising the engineer. Apparently they were satisfied with my train handling skill, as I never heard a word of dissent.

Belatedly, I extend to you the following addendum: The Ford Motor Company, after many years of contemplation, had finally decided to close the doors of it's St. Paul Ranger facility. This plant had generated jobs for the St. Paul community and was the focal point of the Canadian Pacific Railway which employed many people in that direction.

Sadly we say goodbye to our Ford friends, hoping that one day it will again be accessible and prosperous to St. Paul in every way.

The Ford Motor Company was our best friend in St. Paul and we will miss it.

On December 16th 2011, the Canadian Pacific ceased serving the Ford facility.

Chapter 32

H & D

The Hastings & Dakota portion of the Milwaukee Road was often thought of as being built for the purpose of bypassing the Twin Cities in an attempt to expedite freight traffic to the west. Those beliefs were unfounded. The H & D was the brainchild of the city of Hastings, Mn. Given its geographic location, Hastings would be a natural transportation center. As of yet, no railroad existed between Hastings and St. Paul and the good fathers of Hastings looked to the west with inspired prescience when a valuable land grant was bestowed to them. The official land grant would include only parameters within the state of Minnesota i.e. Hastings to Ortonville which was finished in late 1879. The early H & D. would juncture with the present day mainline at a place called Benton Junction. Benton Jct. is no longer there, but was located near Cologne at about mile post 451.6.

When the bridge over the Mississippi linking Hastings to St. Paul was completed on 12-7-1871 and the Short Line and Benton Cutoff were finished in 1880, traffic over the H & D would begin to dwindle as the new route into St. Paul and then west from St. Paul would signal the end as a through route for the present H & D. Passenger trains, and along with time freights, would use the route well into the 1920's, but not with the same magnitude that it once did. The H & D between Hastings and Farmington had seen its last train come the mid-thirties.

In later years the H & D still in use would run from Benton Junction to Ortonville. Crews running trains over the H & D would report for work at St. Paul Union Station for passenger service, Pigs Eye, or Southtown, for freight service. Trains would operate over three districts to complete their journey west. First would be the Short Line (St. Paul-Southtown), then the Benton Cutoff (Southtown-Benton Jct.) and the Hastings & Dakota (Benton Jct. –Ortonville). Crews originating in the Twin Cities would work to Montevideo (143 miles). Montevideo is both the county seat of Chippewa County and the largest town west of St.

259

Paul on the H & D. The next crew would work from Montevideo to Aberdeen, S. D. (153 miles).

The natural charm of western Minnesota, along with its bucolic setting - is by itself. Once the suburbs of the "Cities" are left behind, the topography becomes inundated with rolling hills. Passing Glencoe, the hills yield to farmland, with an occasional lake interspersed here and there. We will traverse this flatland of corn and soybeans for about sixty miles and then the farmland will yield to the Minnesota River Valley. The towns of Minnesota Falls and Granite Falls are left behind and for a seemingly long while we pass through a wooded area. The woods and the river go hand in hand. We are quite near the river but we won't see it. Montevideo comes and goes and now we encounter wetlands mostly encompassed by Lac Qui Parle State Park and Wildlife Area. Here we see a wealth of aquatic wildlife. The flora and fauna always adds a nice touch to any trip. Passing Appleton we return to flat farmland as we near the end of our trip to western Minnesota at Ortonville and the state line.

The H & D had two jobs that took care of the heavy hauling. They were trains 605 & 604 the tri-weekly way freight that ran out of St. Paul, tying up in Montevideo every other night. These trains ran heavy during the grain season.

The Glencoe patrol based out of the latter was a daily job except Sunday, that switched the Green Giant plant and other industries at and around its namesake. Usually the last move would be to take cars out to Chanhassen for Lyman Lumber. That was and is almost always a daily move.

We can't forget the "Monte" patrol, which switched both 605 and 604 on the days when they ran. Once a week they would trundle out to Milbank, S.D. and interchange cars with the BN. Milbank is the first town west of Ortonville. It was a sweet job. The engineer owned his home in Montevideo and was set. He enjoyed his enviable situation for quite a while until they sold the railroad out from under him. His next job would be the afternoon hump at Pigs Eye.

Besides the BN 54's, another occasional train that would be sighted on the H & D was what the railroad referred to as the Reubel Turn. This job would usually be called to start at St. Paul and proceed to the sugar beet plant at Reubel, pick up its train, bring it to St. Paul, and tie up. Hence, the name, "Reubel Turn". Of course this job was an extra job and was called only when the sugar beets were moving. The plant at Reubel, because of excessive steam escaping everywhere, hampered visibility and was not a favorite place for train crews. It almost had a sci-fi effect. BN 54's are mentioned on the following page.

And now it is time for me to pick a nice summer day and to make a second student trip over that portion of the railroad that runs from St. Paul to Ortonville.

We change crews with the Portage boys at Hoffman Ave. The Mississippi River is only a highway away from us. Once we notify the dispatcher that we are ready to leave Hoffman, we get the signal to proceed. The engineer invites me to run the train and I accept. There isn't much trouble to get into with 105 empties on an almost 1.33% grade, uphill. We have the signal at Robert St. and I note the old Chicago Great Western Bridge spanning the river. CGW, the Minneapolis & St. Louis and the Omaha Route (CMSTP & O) all became part of the Chicago & Northwestern System. Each of these railroads had a bridge over the Mississippi River. Interestingly, all three bridges were within five miles of each other. The signal at Chestnut St. tells us that we are lined for the "Short Line" and the route is clear. For the next five miles or so we will be going away from the river and straight up a 1.33 % grade. This day we have three Burlington Northern units, all six axle and all 3000 horsepower. Our engineer advises me that the road foreman wants the third unit isolated (not used), but as long as he's not around, we'll use it. With all three units "on the line", we walked up the hill at track speed (25 MPH) in throttle four. Topping the hill, we have a "high green" at Merriam Park, gateway to the Minnesota Commercial. We are now beginning to drop downhill as we approach the Mississippi River bridge just around the bend. We want to be down to 10 MPH for that. Our hind end is still on the bridge as we skirt around Southtown Yard, all signals green, we pass Cedar Ave. and we are now on the Benton Cutoff. Another landmark is encountered whose name is euphemistically referred to as the depression. The Lake St. depression is a series of thirty-five highway bridges that allowed traffic to go over the railroad and still remain on level ground. It was built shortly after the turn of the century.

The depression as we know it today has become a vast receptacle for any refuse a person may want to make disappear. Here and there lay a collection of shopping carts taken from the local businesses. On great occasion, a dead body will surface.

We have a clear signal at Tower E-14 which serves to protect the once Minneapolis & St. Louis diamond. I ask what became of the tower. "The tower's long gone" replies the brakeman. We begin to hear a garbled radio transmission. The brakeman volunteers that what we are hearing is probably #282, a loaded coal train that the dispatcher earlier mentioned we would be meeting somewhere on the H & D. We go a little further and our engineer makes a clear contact with #282. We are in single track Centralized Traffic Control territory and that means proceed on signal indication, however it always helps to have a "heads up" on the situation before it happens, which makes the radios an asset. Through the radio we now know that Cologne will be our place to meet #282

261

and he is already there. Nearing Cologne, we have a yellow distant signal that either means we'll be stopping or the switch is lined for our train to enter the siding, or both. We opt for the latter and sure enough we have a favorable signal to enter the siding. The dispatcher probably wanted our train of empties to arrive first in an effort to keep us out of the way of the loaded #282. It didn't work out that way however little time was lost. Our next operational adjustment would be a 10 MPH coming into Glencoe, about two miles of it. Leaving Glencoe we won't have another slow order until Appleton, but that will be a major one, 10 miles per hour for the final 22 miles. All in all it's a beautiful day for a train ride. We arrive in Ortonville and I talk to the dispatcher. He tells me that another loaded eastbound train will be leaving Ortonville in about two hours. Because I am a student, I am not subject to the hours of service rule. I lucked out as I didn't relish the possibility of waiting three to four days as my westbound crew would.

The coal trains originate in Montana and are destined for the Columbia power plant at Portage, Wis. The H & D handles four loaded trains per week. Usually when a crew brings an empty train to pass on to the BN at Ortonville, that crew will wait about four days for that same train to return from the mine - loaded. There are variations, however (when wasn't there?). For instance: A train set may be temporarily laid up for maintenance and a crew or two may be deadheaded home. Another example are the BN 54's. The Burlington Northern and the Milwaukee Road along with local shippers have cooked up a deal where the BN would furnish the power, the Soo Line would provide a train crew, a shipper and of course a grain elevator for which 54 cars would be loaded and shipped to the west coast. Why 54 cars you ask? The 54 cars was a cost effective marketing stratagem. Fifty-four cars was and is the optimum tonnage that three SD40's can handle across the Rockies without a helper. Because of that and similar examples, a crew couldn't exactly count on the normal ebb and flow of the coal trains because of the variables.

You are probably wondering about the pay arrangement. If a crew waits the entire four days for the loaded train to return, it would work like this: Our crew brings the empties into Ortonville and puts off duty at 7 PM. After waiting sixteen hours they would then be under their normal pay for the next eight hours. Once the eight hours has been consumed, the crew goes off pay for another sixteen hours. When the loaded train finally shows up and if the crew is still under pay that will end when the crew goes on duty. On the time slip it reads "held away from home terminal in excess of sixteen hours" (more than one time slip is filled out). The crews refer to it simply as "alimony". It isn't easy to make money that way. Some guys pass the time away goose hunting or fishing, others golf and I'm sure there is one or two of them that sit in their rooms reading scriptures. Every crew that works in that pool on a regular basis has access to an automobile. The motel is paid for by the company.

Regulating crews is not only tough on the crews themselves, it is difficult for the railroad to be accurate when calling crews. It is an age old problem for which a solution has not yet been found. I always welcomed a trip in the "coal pool" because it gave me a respite from the rigors of the St. Paul extra board.

Let me share with you an experience I had with a loaded coal train. A foregone conclusion to basic train handling 101 is that no two trains are alike. Over the course of the trip, the brakeman had mentioned more than once that we would probably get the train that had the blue ends painted on the cars. This train was a notoriously bad braking train and that I had better hope that the lead unit had a functioning dynamic brake.[1] As luck would have it, our train was the "blue ender" and the master switch for the dynamic brake on the lead unit had a tag on it explaining that the "DB" was defective and why. The brakeman suggested that "maybe the car department out west did something with the train brakes (car brakes) and maybe they were corrected". Nevertheless, when he told me that the train with the blue ends was a lousy braker - I believed him. Going east past Granite Falls is a heavy grade that goes for about five miles. When you top the hill at the overpass just west of Sacred Heart, that speed is the same speed you will crest the hill at Snelling Ave. the brakemen never fail to mention that and today was no different. The trip went well until we crested the hill at Snelling and started down the 1.33% grade. Armed with the knowledge that my train may not brake normally, I made the usual minimum reduction off the trainline sooner than I normally would. When the train (108 cars) was three quarters of the way over the "hump" at Snelling, we were already over the 25 MPH speed limit. I drew off more air and before I knew it we were at 35 MPH. We were nearing Fordson Junction[2] and our route would take a sharp curve to the left at the Ford power switch. The track speed for freight trains from Merriam Park to Robert St. (to include Fordson Jct.) was 25 MPH. I remembered from somewhere seeing Santa Claus with his sleigh and eight reindeers gleefully prancing across the smoke stacked skyline of the Northern States Power Plant that lay about 100 feet below us and just beyond the CNW's Western Ave. yard. We were now at 40 MPH, I then envisioned a 14,000 ton coal train flying out over the same panorama I had imagined Santa doing, except it would have been me - for real! It was at that same exact time that I put the automatic brake valve into the "emergency" position. The power had already been completely shut off and with the brakes set at "full service", there was nothing more I could do. To give you an idea of how bad the brakes were and taking into

263

account that we were rolling downhill, the train did not stop until we crossed Eagle St. about 1.3 miles after I plugged it (emergency). When we stopped, I looked over at the brakeman and said something to the effect of: I believed you before when you told me that these cars didn't brake worth a damn, and now I believe you twice as much as I did before. "These cars don't belong in service" retorted the brakeman. We were both thankful that we had clear signals. Had the dispatcher elected to hold us for a Ford Hauler at Fordson, we would probably both be dead if not dead or seriously maimed, for sure no longer working for the Soo Line. I was beginning to get that warm and fuzzy glad I'm alive feeling when I was jolted back to reality by the honking of morning rush hour traffic, their drivers already late for work because we had two crossings blocked. Once we got going we were relieved at Hoffman Ave. by a Portage crew. I shared our experience with them and they took it in stride and left town anyway. I never, ever, again heard a word about the "blue end" coal train.

Another trip I'll never forget happened on the 25th of September 1989. I caught another trip off the extra board in the "coal pool". We had only laid in Ortonville a shade over 12 hours when we were called for 1:10 AM on #282, a loaded coal train. "We're having a good trip" said the brakeman to the engineer as we passed over the diamond at Tower E-14. It was slightly past eight o'clock in the morning and we would soon be going through Hopkins. I had the air set as we were on a mild downhill tangent and the speed limit would soon change from 40 to 30 MPH at MP 432. From E-14 to the 5th Avenue crossing is a long straight piece of track that curves ever so gently before 5th Avenue is reached. From a train, on a clear day, you can see traffic crossing in front of you for a long way. Once the gates start doing their flashing and the noise from the electrically activated bells along with the gates noticeably going down, the traffic always heeds the warnings and the train and the motor public can safely co-exist.

On this day it was not to be. From the stoplight at Excelsior Blvd. to the stop sign at 3rd Street to include the railroad tracks was a distance of about 105 yards and every one of those yards seemingly had some portion of a motor vehicle on it, including the railroad tracks. Of course I could only see for the most part, the westbound traffic negotiating the stop sign. When I finally came to the conclusion that my only choice would be to put the train into the "emergency" brake position - I was looking at a semi-trailer with "Super Value" on it. It might as well have been a rolling billboard. The brakeman and I both hit the floor, hoping and praying that the semi-trailer was empty and that we had not killed anyone.

The wheels of the engine gave me the impression that we were riding the ties (de-railed). The train came to a stop just short of the depot, about 1/5th of a mile from the crossing. I walked back to the crossing. It was strewn with semi-trailer parts, sugar and dish washing detergent. The truck driver was sitting in the cab of the truck, staring straight ahead. I'm sure he was in shock. It was a miracle that no one was injured physically and there were no signs of any other vehicular damage. As for myself.....I was tickled to death to be alive and walking. The engines suffered some minor front end damage and some humongous flat spots on at least the lead engine. Those ties that we thought we were riding on were instead, flat spots that were inflicted to the wheels of the engine when the emergency brake application caused the wheels to lock up. When the wheels entered the rails on the crossing, they probably picked up some of the oil or fluids that typically accumulate on busy railroad crossings and slid, giving the wheels a grinder effect. The entire train stayed on the track.

Everyone involved had much to be thankful for. Of course Super Value would experience an acute delay in receiving its shipment of sugar etc. and would be short one brand new semi-trailer. The tractor was unscathed. Once the police department gave us the okay, we would move the train off the crossing and proceed east. The sounds of the flat spots were unnerving. Kerplunk, kerplunk, kerplunk. As we climbed the hill at Signal Tower, I knew that we would not get the train to Cleveland Ave. because the flat spots were sapping the efficiency of the locomotives. We had plenty of time to get to St. Paul but time or no time this train wasn't going any further than about milepost 417. It was an unusually hot day for late September, if not at 90 degrees, pretty close to it. The sun was shining brightly, acting as a magnifying glass. We sat there, cooking from about eleven o'clock to close to two in the afternoon, waiting for a taxicab to find us and take us to St. Paul. Almost three hours baking in this most uncomfortable chamber of acrimony. During our wait we concluded that it would have been a class gesture on the part of the company to send an official out to get us. Maybe they did send an official out for us and he like the cab driver couldn't find us either! Fourteen-thousand ton 105 car coal trains aren't always easy to find, and then of course, maybe they didn't want to find it, given the mentality of the superintendent. I have yet another reason to censure the Soo Line Railroad.

As I write this, looking back almost 21 years, I think as I have often thought, that that accident at 5th Avenue was waiting a long, long time to happen, but inevitably it would happen and it did happen and it happened to me. How many times do you suppose that the good citizens of Hopkins reflected to themselves as they sat hopelessly on this railroad crossing unable to move because he or she was unlucky enough to be bracketed between vehicles that could not go anywhere because of a light or a stop sign. How many times has a victim of that circumstance said to themselves "what happens if a train comes" or "what should I do if a train comes" or even "is this particular traffic network set up to

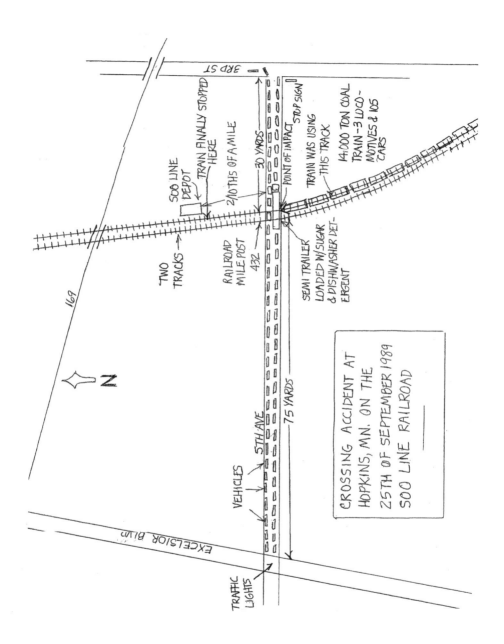

3RD ST

TRAIN FINALLY STOPPED HERE

SOO LINE DEPOT

POINT OF IMPACT

STOP SIGN

TRAIN WAS USING THIS TRACK

14,000 TON COAL TRAIN - 3 LOCO-MOTIVES & 105 CARS

2/10THS OF A MILE

30 YARDS

TWO TRACKS

RAILROAD MILE POST 432

SEMI TRAILER LOADED W/SUGAR & DISHWASHER DET-ERGENT

169

N

5TH AVE

75 YARDS

VEHICLES

CROSSING ACCIDENT AT HOPKINS, MN. ON THE 25TH OF SEPTEMBER 1989 SOO LINE RAILROAD

EXCELSIOR BLVD

TRAFFIC LIGHTS

266

Locomotive Damage

Free Samples

267

More Locomotive Damage

Help Yourself

Unscathed semi tractor attached to remnants of trailer.

Loaded trailer embedded into side of loaded coal hopper.

Now emply semi trailer.

The other half of the semi trailer.

accommodate trains"? "Are the traffic engineers aware of this impending situation"? As I see the situation 21 years later, something was done as the street was altered to form a curve and the stop sign was eliminated at 3rd Street. Apparently this change was engendered by the folks from Super Value according to the Hopkins engineering department.

Later I was called for #248 the river way freight. This would be exactly 45 hours after we put off duty at St. Paul, I would encounter this same train, on the river, only empty, tucked into the siding at Donehower. The Portage boys took that train to Portage, it was unloaded, and now was on its way west for another trainload of coal. That lead unit definitely should have been taken out of service. I would imagine that all three of those units were inflicted with flat spots to some degree. I wasn't able to see whether or not our lead engine in the accident was a part of that consist or not. If it was, I would hope that somewhere on that headend crew there was a big bottle of aspirin because they would need them. The Portage boys always tried a little harder.

When the Milwaukee Road severed its west coast ties in 1980, it kept that part of the mainline from Miles City, Montana to Aberdeen and Mobridge, S. Dakota. This line was retained because of the lucrative coal business. Located across the Minnesota River from Ortonville is the Ottertail Power Co.'s Big Stone City plant. The BN would also feed the Milwaukee Montana generated coal trains at Miles City. These trains would be destined for the Columbia Generating Station outside of Portage, Wi.

During the early part of 1982, the Milwaukee Road divested itself of its South Dakota assets and sold 820 miles of track to the state of S. Dakota, which turned around and leased the coal hauling portion to the BN. The Milwaukee retained trackage rights from Milbank, S.D. to Ortonville.

In 1985 it looked for all intents and purposes that the Milwaukee was going to be an integral part of the Soo Line. Soo operated the H & D for over six years and then on 4-26-91, sold that portion of the H & D between Tower E-14 (Hopkins) to Appleton, Mn., 147 miles. This railroad would become the "Twin Cities & Western" and would enjoy trackage rights from Appleton to Milbank and E-14 to St. Paul Yard. At the time of the sale Soo Line would retain the 22 miles from Appleton to Ortonville. This track was in bad shape and trains were restricted to 10 MPH. Nobody wanted it. During the latter part of 1992 the BN would buy that final link and run the coal trains Ortonville-Appleton-Benson-Twin Cities where they would return to Soo rails for the final 233 mile run to the Columbia facility. The last coal train to run over the Hasting & Dakota portion of the Milwaukee Road, now Soo Line, would be sometime in October of 1991. Farewell to the H & D.

STATION LISTINGS	MP
ST PAUL UNION STA.	410.0
MERRIAM PARK	416.0
SIGNAL TOWER	417.3
SO MINNEAPOLIS	418.9
ST LOUIS PARK	429.4
HOPKINS	431.8
TOWER E-14	435.0
CHANHASSEN	439.5
BENTON JCT.	451.6
COLOGNE	453.3
BONGARDS	457.0
NORWOOD	460.0
PLATO	466.2
GLENCOE	471.9
BROWNTON	482.2
STEWART	488.8
HECTOR	500.1
BIRD ISLAND	509.1
OLIVIA	513.8
DANUBE	519.3
RUEBEL	523.0
RENVILLE	525.0
SACRED HEART	531.8
GRANITE FALLS	541.1
WEGDAHL	549.1
MONTEVIDEO	554.4
WATSON	560.8
MILAN	570.0
APPLETON	578.2
CORRELL	585.2
ODESSA	593.8
ORTONVILLE	600.0

[1] For optimum dynamic braking, all units should have functional dynamics, if the lead unit is not equipped with a dynamic brake or is equipped with one that is defective, it makes no difference how many functional dynamics you have behind, you have no way to control them from the head end.

[2] Fordson is where the 4 mile branch to the Ford plant begins. There is a sharp curve along with a sharp cliff there.

Chapter 33

The Midnight

I was on the midnight for about a year when I got "bumped".[1] Someone must have thought that I knew something they didn't and had to find out for themselves. My only recourse was to jump on the midnight hump which was actually worse than the midnight top end. It had the same days off however, and I knew that it wouldn't be long and the guy that bumped me would be crying "uncle", and I could go back to the "midnight top end" or better known to the accounting department as the 4713. You're never safe under the seniority system. I once had a guy bump me from a hospital bed.

The midnight got no respect. It was the very epitome of "whip me, beat me, kick me". There were three jobs working on the top end at night. There was the 11 o'clock, the 11:30 and the midnight or 11:59. The two earlier jobs always tied up early. The midnight would always have to stay until at least 7 o'clock when the first day job would show up. There were times when the day yardmaster would take a shot at us, utilizing our young and naive talents. For myself, I wasn't so young, definitely wasn't naive, however my crew was and most yardmasters couldn't resist taking advantage of that.

Another consideration you may want to make when pondering whether or not you want to jump on the 4713 is that on Saturday night, the getaway day, around five or six o'clock the yardmaster would send us out to switch North Star Steel. That would pretty much kill tying up early and you would always end up working overtime. This was particularly lousy during football season. I would get home, turn the TV on, open a beer and before the 1st quarter was over, I would be sound asleep.

North Star Steel was an awful place, at least the yard where the scrap was. You needed a tetanus shot just to breathe the air in that place. North Star had its own engine and at times it would be working while we were also making our moves. One morning the North Star engine was shoving three or four gondolas around a curve and into our track and was not slowing down. One of my guys was between the engine and the first car making the air hose connection. I quickly opened the door of the cab and screamed ""get out of there"! At that time the gondolas slammed into us, moving our engine brakes and all. The kid got out safely, however we both were shaken up. Now totally awake on this bright Sunday morning, I was mad. I can't remember if North Star had an engineer that morning or if it was being operated by remote control by a guy on the ground. You don't have to pay a remote controlled engine—benefits. Once we tied up, I went upstairs and related the experience to our fearless leaders. I think it fell on deaf ears.

The Sidewinder was the top end yardmaster one night when about 3 AM he does something out of character. He announces that there really wasn't much to do and that if we got the work done, we could all go home. We watched the 11 o'clock tie up at about 4 AM, the 11:30 shortly thereafter and now the Sidewinder gives us our last move, which we made short work of. Somewhere in the back of my mind a flag was going up. Something told me that the Sidewinder was up to something. I had a bad feeling. The Sidewinder may have gotten a lobotomy while on vacation, because it sure wasn't his style to give the midnight a break. At 5:15 we finished our move and the Sidewinder comes over the radio and says: "tie the engine up on track 27". I trundled into #27, put the cab light on in order to gather my grip and just as I went to open the door, the Sidewinder comes over the radio and says; "midnight don't go anywhere, I forgot that there was 63 cars of coal in the "bluff" (Dayton's Bluff) that has to go to NSP". I knew it, damn it, I knew it! Now this was the Sidewinder we knew!

I continued to get off the engine with my grip in hand and walked into the crew room and hit the talk button on the bitchbox. He answered: "yeah?" Now it was my turn. "I just remembered that I am sick and I'm going home." Usually they want to take you to the hospital when that happens. Whoever the boss was that night must have backed off because he knew the situation. That sort of made him a rat, too.

I don't think I ever went home sick when I was sick. There was a time in my career when I was dedicated to the cause, but not on this railroad.

One night I was experiencing a depressing night, for whatever reason, and decided that going home about 3 AM might just be the change I needed. They had just come up with a new policy. If you wanted to go home sick you would first be driven to a local hospital to be looked at by a doctor. I was feeling nauseous and if they wanted to take me to the hospital, I had no objection. I did add that I wasn't going to pay for it. We went to the hospital, the doctor prescribed some pills and I went home after the exam. Almost a month later I received that hospital bill for the amount of $125.00 I took it upstairs and gave it to the boss. He assured me that the company would take care of it. A month went by and I got another bill for $125.00. I dropped it off at the trainmasters office and he said: "okay". Six months go by and each time I received a monthly bill I would drop it off and the guy I gave the bill to says, "okay". Finally the last time I dropped a bill off the trainmaster says okay and I came back with, no...it's not okay, I'm gonna end up with a bad credit rating because of this, please fix it!

They fixed it alright. A month later, I got a letter from the hospital with a check for $125.00 included and an explanation that the company had paid them twice and they were returning the one payment to me. I knew it was a mistake, but I very graciously accepted the check, cashed it, and you know the rest.

The Milwaukee Road leased 64 MP15AC type switch engines. The lease expired on 1-1-91 and the Soo Line decided to renew the lease for only half of those locomotives, 32 to be exact. The MP15AC was tailor made for the top end. It did its job and did it well. Although the top end wasn't the most glamorous job on the railroad, its engineers enjoyed good power. The keynote issue for the MP15AC on the top end was its visibility.

Soo management decided to go the "if it works, let's fix it" route and replaced the 32 MP's with power that until then I thought was scrapped. So then we began using GP7"s, GP9's and four Caterpillar engine's that they somehow acquired in 1991.

These replacement engines were quite inferior to the MP15AC. In losing the MP15AC, we lost an ideal engine. The "new units" were of the GP car body type and lacked the visibility that the MP's afforded. These geeps were unsafe to work the top end with. To put it in a word—they were "cumbersome". To put it into two words, they were horse shit!

One very cold winter night, the midnight was sent over to Dayton's Bluff to get an NSP coal train. We would take 60 or 65 cars over there once we got our air tested. This night with the wind howling, we had two very drafty MP15AC's and they were cold! It was probably -10 degrees outside and 20 inside. I always tried to take a nap while my foreman would walk the air test, checking each car to be sure the brakes were set. It usually took about 20 minutes. On the adjacent track sat another coal train with two brand new BN closed cab units with those very comfortable bucket seats. I thought to hell with sitting in this drafty dinosaur when we could be reclining in grandiose splendor. It was nice and warm, very comfortable and it didn't take long for the two of us to fall asleep.

The night shift at St. Paul yard almost always had a pusher type yardmaster on the top end and normally would stay in radio contact to the point of being obnoxious. This night would be different as he forgot about us and we had the radios shut off. We had been fast asleep for at least one and a half hours when I woke up and prodded the headman to find our foreman. He too, was asleep on the rear unit of these fine BN locomotives.

Once we were all awake, I called the BN East Hump dispatcher and told him we were ready to go. Nothing was said and no one was the wiser.

We always looked at the BN guys as the rich kids. Everything was seemingly new, it worked, and we were envious if not outright jealous of them.

One night we were all dutifully assembled, ready for work. We wondered what took the yardmaster so long to start barking orders over the bitchbox. This night we were requested to go upstairs for a chat with the trainmaster. Anytime a crew gets delayed with a safety meeting, etc., etc., it usually means that the night isn't going to be a good one, as you are being deprived of getting the work done.

Tonight's subject happens to be: FELA. FELA stands for "Federal Employees Liability Act". The trainmaster tried to explain to us what FELA meant to the company. It wasn't in the company's best interest. Because the majority of guys were new guys, they took the bait and thought that the term FELA was an evil abeyance, and may God bless the company.

Of course they didn't completely understand why they were invited upstairs. As it turns out—FELA is labors best friend and what our supervisors are trying to prove is difficult to comprehend. I was the only one in the room that actually did recognize that the trainmaster (with a straight face) was trying to tell us that because FELA wasn't in the railroads best interest and because FELA was pro-labor it wasn't good for us either.

There were more than a few law firms that exclusively handled FELA or personal injury cases. They made lots of money for both their clients and themselves. FELA was our friend.

After being on the midnight for a few years, for the most part, I got into the habit of first stopping in the clerk's office because their coffee was cheaper. Walking into the large room, I noticed one of the clerks, a longtime fixture in the clerical scheme of things. He appeared to be in dire straits as he was leaning against the desk in an effort to stabilize himself. Someone said that he was having a heart attack. He was already being attended to and I asked myself...what can I contribute to this situation? The answer came in a hurry. Grab a radio and go down to the Belt crossing and stop all trains from occupying the crossing in order to get an ambulance down to the yard office and back on its way to the hospital.

Almost fifteen years later, the guy looks the same as he always did. He no longer works his days off because he is retired. He always says that I saved his life, but I wasn't the only person that helped to get him safely to the hospital that early April morning.

As I mentioned earlier, the midnight got no respect and was used as the "whipping boy". The midnight, because it was the last job to go to work, had to stay around in case an unseen chore should arise. There might be a "bad order" having to be thrown out of a train or maybe a road train would have to be yarded because its crew had died on the "hours of service". If you worked the midnight for any length of time, you came to accept the fact that you would be there until the first day job showed up. On occasion the midnight would end up working into the day shift. I remember one particular night (or day) when a road train had died on the "hours of service"[2] at Humboldt and they sent the 7:00 up there to relieve that crew. That was referred to as a "mission" and as a rule the midnight would taxi cab up to Humboldt and bring that train to St. Paul. I'll discuss the "missions" in a bit.

We wondered why they did it that way. It was unwritten that the midnight always got the "missions". I suggested that maybe it was because the "Sidewinder" was the night yardmaster or the fact that the foreman and I were both Soo Liners. The other guy was new. New guys didn't count for much of anything.

Now we are doing the work that the 7:00 usually does. I am more than a little disenchanted. We are told to bring a car back from the "rip" track as it was "hot".[3] The track that had the car in it was "blue flagged". When a track is "blue flagged", an engine cannot enter it until a denizen of the rip track removes it. As we waited I disappeared into the washroom. About 15 or 20 minutes later, my foreman locates me and advises me that the "blue flag" is off and the rip track foreman is patiently awaiting my presence. We dug the car out and the track was again "blue flagged"[4] so that the rip track gang could go to work.

We then called the yard and the day yardmaster told us where to put the car and the engine. I also wanted to tell him where to put the car and the engine, but thought better of it. He also stated that the trainmaster wanted to see the entire crew.

The trainmaster wanted to know why it took so long to dig one car out of the rip track. Our foreman answered with "the track was blue flagged" and I echoed that I had to use the washroom. I then queried with "how come you sent the 7:00 up to Humboldt to dog catch 484?" You had the 7:00 doing the midnight's job and the midnight doing the 7:00 work. The trainmaster came back with "since when are you running the show"? I retorted that we all were paid the same wages why couldn't we all be dealt with the same level of fairness and decency. I was on a roll and went on to say that "I didn't just hire out on the railroad yesterday and was getting tired of the shit that these punk yard-masters were putting out. I didn't deserve that kind of treatment. Again the trainmaster countered with "so that's what this is all about". "Yeah, it's called parity", I said. At that time I had over 30 years and I was damn well incensed. I was tired of being a pissing post because of some little bastard's whimsical ploy.

At that point the boss announced that our little confrontation was over. I then asked the foreman what time he wanted to put off duty. The trainmaster jumped in with "you haven't put off duty yet"? The foreman said that we were upstairs on company business and would not put off duty until we were finished with our little talk. He wasn't used to that. The Milwaukee crews always put off duty before they got their asses chewed. That was the difference between Soo and Milwaukee rails.

The only "perk" the midnight ever had was its accessibility to the "missions". Missions were extra-curricular work that entailed the shoving of stalled road trains, "dog catching," and anything else that was unplanned for. These chores were always easy and the overtime was there. The drawback to it was that it could be more than difficult to stay awake. That time of the morning, after working all night was not conducive to safety.

Of course everyone had to attend safety meetings, rules examinations, and whatever else management wanted to talk about. The rules tests were bi-annual. The CP had worked out a deal with the Red Wing Shoe Co. to furnish each employee with a new pair of shoes every two years. You had your choice of any style as long as they came with steel toes. Of course wing tips were out of the question. I had at least two pair of shoes that I hadn't even worn. Engineers are user friendly when it comes to shoes. At the end of one of these sessions, when the examiner was answering questions, I raised my hand and asked if we could get tape measures in place of shoes. After all, there were 11 rules in the General Code of Operating Rules that commanded the use of footage or distance. The examiner didn't receive the question very well, but the guys thought it was funny. There was nothing funny about that rule book, though.

In preparation for engineer licensing, the "powers that be" decided to have a trial session for their "Advanced Engineer Training Program". The first one was held for a week in May of 1990. They asked for ten volunteers. If you failed the test - there were no consequences. The official AET, at least for me, was still over three years away. I volunteered for the first one in order to gain a brief respite from the midnight. I would endure three more sessions of the official version, complete with simulator and the rest. I hated them with a passion. I was scheduled for another week of it to begin the day after I would finally walk away, forever.

In the spring of 1992, I was called for jury duty. It only lasted a week. It would both satisfy my curiosity and give me a break from the midnight.

Off and on during my tenure on the midnight, the company would get caught in a manpower shortage. It is difficult to keep the work force balanced, especially when you don't want a work force to begin with. Being on the third or last job to go to work on the night shift had one advantage, if they were short of men, my job would be the last one to get filled. Quite often there would be nobody left and I would show up and would be told to go home. Not a bad way to earn a day's pay. This happened about 25 times. We called them "freebies".

Sometime toward the end of my sojourn on the midnight, a good situation began to develop when we started hearing rumors that the Sandman was being promoted laterally and would be kicked upstairs. During the course of his reign as the boss of the St. Paul terminal, this imperious and volatile individual had succeeded in alienating just about everyone on his railroad and wasn't too well liked on neighboring railroads either.

The unions had had their fill of this guy and recognized that something had to be done. It seemed that the brotherhoods had put their collective heads together and marched upstairs, over the Sandman's head, and issued an ultimatum to the hierarchy. For once the unions and management were on the same page. The company agreed with the unions and quietly announced that they would replace him once they found a comparable position for him and of course a suitable replacement.

One fine spring morning I went upstairs to get some forms and as I ascended the second floor, I could hear someone whistling "the witch is dead" (1965). It was one of the trainmasters. I asked him, "What's the occasion"? We have a new boss, came the prompt reply!

Our new boss was kind of quiet and reserved. Although I hadn't yet met him, I would quite often see him having a cigarette on the fire escape. Although I am close to exaggeration when I say that he gave me the impression that he was bewildered by all that he surveyed. If I could have read his mind, it appeared that he would be thinking something like "how did I get into this mess", or "help"! Of course he was good at what he did and my unwitting thoughts weren't important. Welcome aboard, sir!

The Sandman was given a position of equal substance somewhere within the machinations of the Soo Line building located in downtown Minneapolis. Eventually that would also fizzle out. I last heard that he was doing well, but for another company. The same guy that bragged he was going to fire me was no longer in a position to do so. I was still there however......

One early morning while on the midnight, we were called upon for one of those coveted missions. It was to bring a coal train down from Humboldt with further instructions to follow.

Apparently this was a train that would have come off the H&D. This business was now re-routed because the H&D for the most part was sold. Normally the typical H&D coal train had 105 cars and three SD40's. This day and probably due to the re-routing and possibly a reduction in grades, we were given two SD60's. Instead of the usual 9,000 horsepower, we had 7,600 horsepower. This may or may not have worked, as there was a ten MPH temporary speed restriction, instead of the usual 25 MPH at Park Junction and now it was a fair hill to climb to the top at Bandana Square. We didn't make it. I never purposely stalled out a train but I was so tired that I didn't mind and we were on overtime anyway.

After a nice nap I was awakened by a member of the day BN transfer job. That crew was brought up by a carload of trainmasters. For some reason three trainmasters came along. It was almost as if they were escaping from Pigs Eye.

No one ever asked me, but if I ever own a railroad, I'll always have enough power to move a particular train over any part of the territory it is required to move start to stop and vice versa.

1 "Bumped" meant that someone was exercising their seniority.
2 "Hours of Service". A crew could not exceed 12 hours on duty.
3 "Hot". The car had to be expedited.
4 "Blue Flag". When a blue flag is displayed, it forewarns anyone attempting to move that car, engine or throw that switch, that men are working. The flag can only be removed by a workman of the same class.

Chapter 34

The Hump

This particular chapter will be a short one as there isn't much to say about the hump other than it is boring, especially from an engineer's standpoint. It was the one job that I positively hated. The IC had two humps, one for northbound loading and a southbound counterpart. Pigs Eye had a single hump. When business was good, each shift would have two jobs, only one when it was slow. Most guys hated the dangerous and rat infested place, however there were a few guys that never worked anywhere else. They were a minority, though. The retarder operators always worked there of course.

When I jumped on the midnight top end as bad a job as it was, I always knew that there was one job out there that had the top end beat, it was the midnight hump and I had prepared myself for that day, should I get bumped off the top end and either have to go on the extra board or take the hump. The night hump had at least the same days off as the top end. I really didn't know what I would do it was a bridge to be crossed.

Sure enough, it happened. I was bumped and ended up taking the midnight hump in an attempt to preserve some semblance of regularity. I would put a grand total of twenty one days on that job, about twenty days too much.

As bland as the hump was, it was not without its possible career changing episodes. The Sidewinder was the yardmaster every night that I worked the job. One night he had us go into the bowl (classification yard) to couple up the scale track, then pull it back over the hump and re-hump it. These cars are all weighers and are heavy. The yardmaster is supposed to tell the engineer whether or not he has a clear track to use for head room. Nothing was said and I didn't ask. I have never considered myself an overly careful engineer, and I didn't worry about being unsafe, it always simply fell into place. This night, something told me to watch out as there may be cars on the other end of this track that we were using. Sure enough the little bastard was setting a trap for me. About 15 car lengths down the track we were using, sat a cut of cars waiting for me to run into. Luckily, I was aware of the situation and even though I made a calculated effort to stop short of those cars, the weight of the loads that shoved me, caused me to actually make a smooth joint. Once I was told to bring the cars the other way, at hump speed, I told the yardmaster that I had to pee when in effect I actually had to pull the pin on the car that I inadvertently tied onto. I was laughing all the way, both happy to be unhurt and glad that I out foxed this little rat. The Sidewinder had no scruples it didn't matter what came up he was a full service asshole and would screw you somehow. One night he put us into beans. I always automatically look at my watch to mark the time. We are only entitled to 20 minutes and the rule calls for it to be uninterrupted. Seventeen minutes later, the Sidewinder comes over the bitchbox and gives us a move. I called him on it and he alluded that I was nitpicking. Draw your own conclusions.

Later, more repercussions would develop. One morning after tying up on the night hump, I was driving down the back road and met the Sandman coming the other way. The Sandman didn't know who I was and waved. I responded with both a concentrated and accentuated lip pronunciation of fuck you (we weren't friends). The next morning we tied up at the same exact time and I met him at the same exact location. He remembered from the day before and I learned that his lip reading skills were keen. He went to wave like the morning before. Right away he put his hand down and I reiterated with…..fuck you - again!

As luck would have it, only four days later I was invited to be the focal point of a random urinalysis. What a coincidence. Although I realize that we don't like one another, I also realize that he's got the advantage and will use it when he gets the chance. I later had a conversation with a deposed trainmaster and he confided that those urinalysis tests weren't necessarily random.

There isn't much else to write about the hump. I concluded that the hump was a good place to stay away from. The hump also seemed to be a magnet for injuries.

Weather

The one factor that affects everyone and everything is the weather. There is no getting around it. Railroads are no different, they operate in the elements and are at the mercy of wind, ice, snow, and both cold and hot along with drastic combinations of each. And of course we can't forget rain.

Weather is one of the factors that a good engineer takes into consideration when evaluating his train and its operation. One of the conditions that prevail on railroads running across North Dakota is an accumulation of what is called "snirt". Actually snirt is a mixture of topsoil blown across the flatlands. It eventually will mix with snow and ice and become impacted in cuts and on curves. Usually this condition can only be remedied by the use of dynamite. It will derail a snow plow.

Just plain below zero cold weather can play havoc to the air brake system of a train. Cold weather causes air to lose density making it prone to escape a less than perfect air coupling between cars. Multiply this by 100 and you have problems.

An example of this once occurred when the Illinois Central tried to move a 105 car unit coal train from Champaign to Chicago in bitter cold weather. It took a road crew ten hours to move the train 45 miles with normal power (2 SD40's). The crew could no longer go any further and would have to cut the first twenty cars and leave the ensuing 85 cars to sit on the northbound main waiting for another crew to come and get it.

As a train sits in the cold for any amount of time, the metal on metal tends to temporarily weld the wheels to the rail creating an even more difficult struggle. The IC wanted that northbound main cleared as it created a bottleneck with which a switch tender had to be employed to move the northbound trains through Gilman and onto the Centralized Traffic Control. The weather stayed bitterly cold. That part of Illinois can be very unforgiving when it gets below zero coupled with the wind across the flats an extreme condition to be avoided.

85 cars sat on the northbound main between crossings waiting to be moved. Later the same day another crew dispatched from Markham ironically with the same power came out yet couldn't move the 85 car train. The IC powers that be elected to leave the train there in one piece. As they had no place to put it in the first place, there was no sense in hauling it to Chicago piece-meal. IC was praying for warmer weather and that would be the solution. Later another crew showed up this time with three big units. It was still below zero and the train wouldn't budge. The fourth day brought with it warmer weather and another crew would finally move it to its destination. The joke on the north end would always be that the hillbilly officials didn't quite understand how it worked on the north end in extreme cold.

Wind can readily determine your progress across the railroad. An empty coal train bucking the wind can easily be brought to a stop simply by manipulating the throttle down to zero. Wind has more than once turned over train loads of automobiles, each car stacked three high.

Extreme cold can cause rail joints to snap which railroaders refer to as "pull aparts". This is also called contraction. Crews laying quarter mile sections of ribbon rail in the heat would experience the effects of "expansion". The rail would literally buckle like a big snake. I saw this happen on the Central of Georgia Railway shortly after the Seminole left Columbus, Ga. A gang was working with ribbon rail and the heat caused the rail to buckle. Had that train gotten by the signal, the situation would have been disastrous.

I have seen snow deep enough in the Chicago Terminal where section crews would work round the clock shoveling and clearing switches. Train crews would be called to work and then released after a few hours and for a day's pay.

Working a late afternoon switch engine at Kankakee one winter the snow was so deep that the brakemen were totally exhausted from the impediments of the snow. My engineer allowed that back in the steam days when the snow was deep and the weather was cold was the only time that the switchmen would have rather gone firing. The cab was always warm winter or summer.

Of course when the diesels came (before my time) everybody wanted to go firing according to the old timers.

The coming of the diesels changed not only motive power rosters but the lives of the men affected by them. One engineer alluded to me that as a relatively young engineer with borderline seniority he was able to hold a freight turn out on the road. He went on to say that as soon as the diesels showed up the older heads came out of the yard. Steam enabled him to work the road. His days were numbered when the diesels came.

Chapter 35

Southtown Transfer

Once I discovered seniority, I began to look around. What were my options? One of the jobs available to me was the 11:59 Southtown Transfer. The "Southtown" went to work at south Minneapolis and had Friday and Saturdays off.

Shortly after midnight the "Southtown" would gather up cars destined for Humboldt yard and points west. This usually amounted to 15-40 cars depending on business. It was a good job and almost always tied up in five to six hours. Depending on the days I had off I mostly worked with the same crew. The main drawback was that it was - nights. Nights worked for me as it enabled me to work fairly good jobs. If it hadn't been for nights, the jobs I worked would have been mediocre at best.

Eventually the company changed the starting point to Humboldt instead of South Minneapolis and somehow they were able to bring the job down to just one man. After a while, it reverted back to a "Southtown" start, but still with one man.

What usually determined what kind of night we would have pretty much was up to the BN West Hump dispatcher. The "West Hump" dispatcher was located in the west hump tower and controlled the Midway Sub in its entirety from Hoffman Avenue to University Avenue. It had nothing to do with the west hump operation.

The normal routine for the "Southtown" would be to shove our train out of the yard to clear the power switch at Cedar Avenue. Once the "river" or River dispatcher gave us the signal we would proceed past Cedar Avenue and head for the Minnesota Commercial. Half the time you had to come to a stop in order to throw the switch to enter the wye that permits entry into the "Commercial" along with authority extended from the clerk-operator. The Minnesota Commercial takes pride in being "non-union". While you occupy their trackage, you are always cognizant of this. You think of a guy or two that for one reason or another left the Soo/Milwaukee and ended up working for the Commercial. Anyone trying to unionize the Commercial was fired.

Once we were accorded authority to run our train through their yard usually on the running track, the next stumbling block would be to contact the BN West Hump dispatcher. The dispatcher then acknowledges your radio request for authority to run from St. Anthony to University and then into the Soo Line trackage. The trick was to get the dispatcher on the line, which wasn't always easy. Once you were able to connect with the dispatcher, you had the railroad. I can't remember ever being denied "track and time" because of a conflicting train. One dispatcher in particular never seemed to be at her desk when the Southtown called. One night we exchanged barbs. My tone of voice must have triggered sarcasm. I answered her with the words "look lady". She quickly admonished me with "don't address me as a lady", for which I answered with "okay you're not a lady", at which time she advised me to stop my train and not to move until she got back to me. I simply answered with - roger. We didn't have to stop we were at University for a good 15 minutes before she initially answered. We sat there another half hour and she then told me to bring my train into Humboldt. Now having the signal I called the Humboldt yardmaster and he gave me authority to occupy Soo trackage for running purposes and also a yarding track. He also mentioned that a trainmaster from Pigs Eye was on his way over to talk to me. The shit had hit the fan.

When we were having a good night I have to mention the method of yarding used by the Humboldt yardmaster. We would pull our cars into a track that had our Southtown cars on the other end. Once someone on the east end told me that our train was in the clear, I would stop and we would cut off. After cutting off and looking down the track there would be our Southtown cars, sometimes really close. This move could only work when both trains were short. Tying on to the outbound meant that we would shove out of that track and proceed east on a different track. This was railroading at its best. We were ready to leave but I still had to talk to the trainmaster. He wasn't happy. I related to him our problems with her and he related our company's problems with the BN and its dispatching. We decided that I would call her and try to smooth it all out, which I did after tying up at Southtown. I didn't apologize, I simply stressed that we were all trying to make a living and that we could work it out and that there was no reason that we couldn't get along. What I said was the truth, she agreed, and so we buried it.

If everybody played the game, i.e. did their job, the other guy would have it a little easier. Sunday nights on the Southtown were good nights, but not always.

Once in a while there would be more cars than we should have had because someone else didn't move the cars they were supposed to. Usually when this happened, adding insult to injury, I would get an inexperienced crew. Forget any thought of a quit. One Sunday night I showed up for work and had a young lady for my crew. I had worked with this girl before and knew her to be inexperienced. However she wanted to learn and was a good worker. I found out that she was also courageous. Southtown at night was a haven for drunks and any other member of that society of miscreants. The first thing the person on the ground (switchmen) has to do is to couple up the air hoses between the cars. This night there was three times as many cars as we usually have. These hoses can be difficult for most men not to mention a woman. Nonetheless, she went out there amongst the boogeymen and conquered whatever obstacles the Soo Line presented her through its own struggle to mask efficiency. We were very late getting out of Southtown. I couldn't ever remember seeing the sun rising in Southtown. The BN was most charitable and moved us across its railroad as it should have. We got into Humboldt, got onto our train, got our air test and left. We shouldn't have.

Now that I think back to that night, which turned into day, we should have gone to lunch (lunch at 6:00 AM?).

Our crews were trimmed from three switchman to two and then ultimately to one. At times the one switchman would be very short on experience and I would be alone. Being alone and working nights can be dangerous no matter who you are or how long you've been on nights. When I say alone, I mean that I'm the only one that can make a viable decision or make a conclusive judgment. The one person I have with me doesn't know enough to adequately contribute an opinion.

This particular night or should I say morning - I was very tired. There was no definitive reason for it. Every now and then for some unexplainable reason, I would be more tired than usual and struggle through the night. This would be one of those nights. Nights were for sleeping, not working.

Getting the highball from the car department, we began to roll. The signal at Humboldt Avenue was favorable. We had a short train, maybe ten cars. We had the signal at Camden Place and now I am staring at a "red flag" in advance of the Mississippi Bridge. It was at this point that my mind wasn't functioning clearly. I saw the red flag as did she. I briefly reflected that that flag was always there and was superseded by one of the orders that we had in our possession. It was right at seven AM when the B & B (Bridges & Building) guys were just going to work and the gang foreman had just put the flag up. I should have stopped, could have stopped, however we trundled right on by it just as pretty

287

as you please. Suddenly the radio comes alive with the excited voice of the fore-man "Southtown, you just ran my red flag, stop immediately"! I stopped and was now wide awake. It wouldn't be very long and my engine would be crawling with people from various departments.

They had a new federally mandated set of disciplinary rules in place and the phone was buzzing with the cacophony of discord.

It wasn't long and John Stouffer, our road foreman of engines showed up. Of course he asked that age old question, "What happened"? I wanted to make it easy for everyone involved and simply answered "I ran the red flag". "Was that all?" was Stouffers reply. I countered with "how else can you say that"? I fucked up!

We were now in the car on the way to the clinic for a urinalysis, their latest precept in employee management. All the while we were driving Stouffer seemed to be constantly on the cell phone. He then said to me; "I just talked to the guy running the show over at the engineers training center and he was surprised that your answer wasn't a bit more elaborate". I didn't say anything. Later at the clinic, Stouffer asserted that he had just gotten off the telephone with our new superintendent, as the Sandman had recently been elevated lat-erally. He also expressed surprise, as he also thought that I would concoct some nebulous excuse.

That was the story I was going with. Sometimes the truth can be complicating and outright disappointing. I learned many years ago in another place at an-other time from a good man "that to fess up" would be a lot easier than to fab-ricate a lie. After all - "a lie is a short cut to the long way around".

For my miscue, I was given thirty days, without pay. I can't remember what my crew person ended up with, but I don't think she missed a day of work. It didn't matter to me I needed the time off and used it wisely as I readied my home to put up for sale. When a person suffers a setback in life if he or she looks hard enough, a glimmer of sunshine can and will offset the bad.

Chapter 36

Prelude to an Unsung Hero

The story you are about to read is about a train accident that occurred on joint trackage of the Burlington Northern Santa Fe (BNSF) and Canadian Pacific (CP) railroads. The accident also extended into CP's St. Paul Yard (Pig's Eye).

The geography of the Twin Cities' terminal is composed of steep grades caused more or less by the Mississippi River. The bulk of the Twin Cities traffic has to descend to water level and is funneled from three different subdivisions; they all come together at Hoffman Avenue interlocking.

The train involved was BNSF #144 destined for Galesburg, Illinois with 74 loads and 15 empties in tow; the tonnage was 8,528. At BNSF's Northtown Yard, an air hose between the seventh and eighth cars was changed and replaced by another hose of excess length. The locomotives were dynamic-brake equipped, tailor-made for holding back a heavy freight train on the heavy grades around St. Paul. Soon after leaving Northtown Yard, the train began to nose down the hill toward St. Paul. The engineer began to use his dynamic braking with little or no effect. When dynamics are employed, it causes the train to come against the locomotive. Instead of the locomotives pulling the train, the train is actually pushing the locomotives due to both the retarding force and the descending hill. The entire train is "bunched" against the engine. The bunched train caused the lengthy air hose to crimp, thus preventing the air brake system behind the seventh car to respond to the demands of the automatic brake valve. The engineer had roughly 8,000 tons shoving him on that steep hill with nothing but the dynamic brakes of two units and functioning brakes on the seven cars directly behind the engines.

As they came around the curve at Division Street, they could see the home signal at West Hoffman was red, indicating they must come to an "absolute stop". The engineer had repeatedly tried to alert the dispatcher via radio of the urgent situation, this being an emergency if there ever was one! Now it was too late. Even if the dis-

patcher had been able to respond to their calls, the die had been cast. There was no recourse but to wait ..... and pray.

Because of a prior movement, the dispatcher had lined the route at Hoffman Avenue into CP's St. Paul yard. A set of locomotives was supposed to cross from, BNSF's Dayton's Bluff Yard to the CP St. Paul Yard via Hoffman Avenue interlocking. The crew on that power had overheard the engineer on #144 desperately trying to contact the dispatcher and apprise him of the situation and ensuing tragedy. Knowing that #144 was out of control, they refused to take the signal intended for them as they would have most definitely been run into by the runaway freight.

By this time, #144 had already run by the "absolute stop" signal at West Hoffman and was nosing into the 10MPH crossovers at 50+ MPH. The yardmaster at St. Paul still wasn't quite sure of the situation, although he knew there was a runaway train somewhere close. Little was he to know that in a few seconds he would be eye-to-eye with the engineer of #144 for a split second. The lead unit stood straight up, vertically in the air, aligning the cab with the tower and third floor of the yard office.

The train miraculously snaked its way for over a mile through the yard on tracks that weren't much good for traffic over 10 MPH. After running head-on into some parked locomotives and shoving them into another train, the runaway train finally stopped behind the yard office. This caused the trainline air hose to sever at last, triggering the brakes on the other 82 cars to finally go into "emergency". The engines and the head 32 cars derailed, wreaking havoc on the CP facility. Speed at impact was estimated at 47 MPH.

Here is my story.

An Unsung Hero

It was Valentine's Day, the year 1996. I'm Engineer Bud Hoekstra and I decided to show for work early which would allow me to fit in an extra cup of coffee before my shift started. I rarely came early and little did I know at the time .... it could have cost me my life.

The time was about 11:40 on a cold, ten degree night, however, very calm and eerily quiet. Entering the yard office I noticed a small group of fellow employees at the far end of the hallway. They were in a state of exuberance as they thought they were gonna watch a train wreck at someone else's expense. They had no idea that they would be the focal point to this developing drama. Wondering what the excitement was about, I turned the corner going into the crew room. I first noticed Switchman Larry Bastien sitting at the table with his 2-

Looking at heavily damaged yard office.

Another view. Author had to climb out of the window.

Remains of footbridge and the debris that moved it.

The brick office building with the tower withstood the impact.

Razed locomotives.

Employee parking lot unscathed.

way radio turned on. Larry casually commented that "the BN has a runaway train on their hands". At that time Road Foreman John Stouffer came into the room. We exchanged the usual small talk and then all hell broke loose. We could hear the rumble of steel, materials and structure moving toward us. When the lights went out we knew we were in trouble. As soon as that happened, John Stouffer tried to get out of the room and into the hallway. I'll never know to this day why I stood in his way and would not let him pass. I remember saying over and over "don't panic, don't panic"!

It didn't take long and we realized that had Stouffer reached the hallway, he would have been about as thick as a dime. Crushed.

The three of us had to climb out the window. We looked around and saw the debacle that we stood amidst. The overhead walking bridge was gone. It was now draped across the boxcars that were helter-skelter. Locomotives were scattered and in disarray. There was a thickness of diesel fumes that the calm night enhanced. Our thought was that we should shut down any engines that were still running. That accomplished, I noticed that the St. Paul Fire Department could not get its men or equipment across the tracks to where there may have been people buried in the wreckage. I had an idea of who might have been missing and their approximate location within this gigantic assemblage of steel. I realized that even in normal circumstances, St. Paul Yard is not easy to get around in and especially if you haven't been there before. Looking south I could see lights from emergency vehicles that came up the back road from Newport and may have been looking for some direction. I knew that the St. Paul emergency crews couldn't get their equipment across what we railroaders referred to as the "swamp". The swamp sat west of where the rescue equipment was needed. After what I'd seen, I felt that if anyone was buried within the rubble, it was at the north end of the yard office and accessed only from the east side.

I decided to drive my car down to the hump at the south end, and try to bring the emergency vehicles back north, crossing to the other side, at the hump and almost immediate access. They followed my lead.

Trainman Rick Vitek was found to be trapped under a loaded covered hopper of corn. It was a desperate situation and for a while it didn't look as if the rescue workers were going to get air to Vitek as diesel fuel was trickling in and mixing with the corn, thus stifling his breathing. Perseverance won out and Rick Vitek is alive today.

In retrospect, this story has already been written. I didn't write this story about the event or the people. I wrote it about me and the role I was to play that night.

Afterward a company official took attendance and accounted for everyone. We were given the choice of staying or going home. About twenty of those men chose to go home, not knowing at the time that that would be their last day on the railroad as they were afforded a disability pension. My foreman and I elected to stay and we ended up working twelve hours.

I did get a brief thank you from Stouffer. I haven't seen Vitek since I watched them carry him away. Given the multitude of possibilities, it was miraculous that no one was killed. I walked away with a sigh of relief, genuinely glad to be alive.

Chapter 37

Stoppages

Torrential rains upstream would cause the Minnesota River to join the already overflowing Mississippi River to shut down rail operations at St. Paul. On 6-28-93 the flood crested at 19.65 feet. Looking down from my vantage point atop Dayton's Bluff, I could see all of Soo's St. Paul Yard and BN's Dayton's Bluff Yard. The flood hadn't met earlier predictions and was still a foot short of expectations. BN and Soo Line would keep their mainline's open while engaging the Wisconsin Central and the Chicago & Northwestern for detour routing. The flood would cost CP Rail two to three weeks of normal operation, to say nothing of the inconvenience it bore shippers. The estimated damages and all other costs would come to somewhere around $100 million. Fortunately, the railroads around Hoffman interlocking had invested their efforts toward the eventuality of such a disaster and weren't totally unprepared.

In the year 1969, four railroad unions came together to form the United Transportation Union (UTU). These organizations consisted of the Brotherhood of Railway Trainmen, Order of Conductors & Brakeman, the Switchmen's Union of North America, and the Brotherhood of Locomotive Firemen and Enginemen. A fifth union, the Brotherhood of Locomotive Engineers (BLE), declined to be included, preferring to go it alone.

When the idea of the UTU first surfaced, a large number of men in engine service were hoping that the two enginemen's unions would come together. Likewise, the other three unions made up of conductors, brakemen and switchmen would become one. The end result would have been two strong unions, one representing the enginemen and the other for the men in train service. As an enginemen, I had watched the BLF & E and the BLE bicker back and forth over some issue, never getting anything resolved. The company must have loved it. My sincere feeling was that if the two unions would unify, we would be a lot stronger. It wasn't to be. Later, because the two unions didn't come together, it would bring repercussions to enginemen. I can attest to this.

The Soo Line over recent years had elected to avoid national bargaining preferring to negotiate with the brotherhoods on its own. The UTU membership hadn't had a new contract since 1988, well over six years and talks were going nowhere. Finally after a 30 day cooling off period, both parties were released from mediation.

At 12:01 AM on the 14th of July 1994, in the heat of the summer, the UTU called a strike for which other unions would honor. The issues at hand were, crew size and pay. Benefits would also be discussed at length. The crew size issue would boil down to giving the company the option of staffing its crews as it saw fit. Road crews for the most part would be two, an engineer and a conductor. This would also apply to yard crews. A typical shift at St. Paul would have an engineer and foreman on each of the three top end jobs, and a utility or swing man would be available and used by the discretion of the yardmaster.

Early in 1988, the Soo would withdraw from the American Association of Railroads, only to re-join that organization one year later. While the unions sought solidarity - the Soo Line went with the advice of its northern ownership and stayed independent. And now the lines are drawn. The UTU would finally take these same Canadians to task, the ones that stood in the background while the Americans did their bidding. After all those non-contract (six) years, shit was finally going to happen. I was glad for the UTU, sad for the seemingly spineless BLE, of which I was a member.

Because it was a big terminal, the strike itself would be a big operation. The UTU had its command post set up near Shoreham. Other visible points were highway 61, the Belt Crossing, Southtown, the Ford Plant, and Humboldt. Hastings had its denizens. When you consider the Soo guys and the Milwaukee guys, it was a vast consortium of benefactors finally coming together in an effort to kick someone else's ass for a change.

Now 47 days of doing nothing has got to be tedious, and of course boys will be boys. It wouldn't be long and the barbecue grills would show up. I think the beer was always there. The heat and the true mettle of some of the guys would eventually show up, making it tough on those dedicated to the cause. It wasn't long and UTU strike headquarters was begging for help. Some guys were too busy riding their motorcycles, ignoring the picket lines.

One day I received a call from "strike headquarters". The person on the other end of the line acted like I owed the UTU something. He said; "I should go out and picket because these guys were my buddies, and they needed support".

He was rather sarcastic. I told him that first of all - I'd been screwed by the UTU too many times and wasn't a big fan of that organization, and I'd already picketed and wasn't necessarily happy with either union. I didn't know it at the time, but I would vicariously save this same guy's life one day.

Five weeks into the strike, the BLE authorized its members to cross the UTU picket lines under the pretext of maintaining benefits. The company had announced that it would not pay health insurance premiums for employees that hadn't worked an entire calendar month. While other unions would absorb that cost, the rival BLE would not. That's another prime example of two entities working against one another. The company loved it. While the BLE was promoting its membership to become scabs the UTU membership was finding out for itself who the real brothers were. Witness the diminishing picket lines. By admonishing its membership to cross the picket line, the BLE showed its true colors. In an attempt to prove to the rank and file that they too were a union, what the BLE accomplished was to get a small portion of its membership branded as "scabs". Scab is a term that will stay with a person for the rest of his life. I remember hearing about an old yardmaster that allegedly worked during the switchman's strike of 1920. Every time the guy's name was mentioned, it was also stated "he scabbed in '20, you know". It was like a part of his name. Usually when a man scabs, it isn't for financial gain. Most scabs are basically "new men" and suffer from lack of exposure. They think a scab is a bi-product of a sore that will eventually go away. It never does, though.

Finally after 47 days and minimum negotiation, President Clinton intervened after the UTU announced its intention of picketing both the BN and C & NW commuter operations in Chicago. That was one door we were all glad to see closed. We could now get on with our lives

New jerseys were furnished by the company to the baseball team the following season. Each jersey had the same number on it. Ironically, it was the number 47, of course! In conclusion, our skeptical Canadian friends were surprised when the strike went 47 days. They didn't think that the U.S. powers that be, would tolerate a strike of that proportion.

The outcome would be that the company would be empowered to determine its crew size on any job, be it road or yard. As a trade-off, the UTU membership would get a new contract along with a raise. From a financial standpoint, for the rank and file - it wasn't worth it. However, from a moralistic viewpoint....albeit with scars, we won!

The flood of 1997 would exceed that of 1993 by almost three feet. It crested at 22.90 on the thirteenth of April. Snow melt and contributing waterways upstream of St. Paul caused the Mississippi River to overflow its banks, inundating

The flood of 1997 would exceed that of 1993 by almost three feet. It crested at 22.90 on the thirteenth of April. Snow melt and contributing waterways upstream of St. Paul caused the Mississippi River to overflow its banks, inundating both St. Paul Yard (CP) and Dayton's Bluff Yard (BNSF). Both mainlines were also under water. One track at Dayton's Bluff stayed open, for the most part. That was the recently elevated Bluff #1. Bluff #1 would, for a short time, be the only link between the Twin Cities and Chicago.

I was working the night Ford Hauler at the time and was told due to emergency conditions, to report for work at the Ford Plant instead of St. Paul Yard. While rail service was disrupted, traffic to and from Ford Motor Company would remain fairly constant. The Ford business was detoured over the Wisconsin Central. A Humboldt crew would take its Ford cars from Shoreham, across BNSF's University interlocking to the Midway Sub and then to the Minnesota Commercial at St. Anthony. Coming out the other end at Merriam Park and its junction with Soo's Third Short Line, the train would pull its hind end by Fordson Jct. until it was cleared. The head end could go no further than Chestnut St., due to high water. The distance between the home signals at Fordson and Chestnut was nine tenths of a mile which enabled most trains to fit comfortably. If any additional room was needed, the overflow cars would be cut off to clear Fordson. Once the hauler engine tied on to the hind end and pulled the train to clear Fordson, the Humboldt job would tack the extra cars back onto the opposite end of the train and presto, you had the usual day-to-day Ford Hauler. We operated like that for ten days.

Chapter 38

Lost Jobs

When a man or a woman goes to work in train or engine service, about all he or she has is seniority. A person is constantly evaluating their position on the board projecting the one day chance of holding a decent job. Moving up the seniority ladder didn't come without wondering about a senior employee's health, etc. You felt like a vulture thinking about it even discussing it with fellow rails, was awkward. The seniority system encouraged moribund conjecture.

Let's examine the plight of a Milwaukee Road employee in train or engine service around St. Paul. Let's say he hired out in 1972. This guy has already been through the mill what with bankruptcies, pay reductions and let's not forget the ulcers that stem from the "rumor" mill. There was always a tale spinning amongst the troops. And we have to remember that some of those "tales" came true.

Most if not all of the Milwaukee people were pulling for the Grand Trunk Western to assume ownership. The GTW pulled out early and that left the C&NW to vie with the Soo Line for ownership. The Milwaukee guys weren't exactly enamored with either one. The front runner was the C&NW, however, unexpectedly the judge ruled in favor of the Soo Line and the die was cast. 1985 comes along and now our '72 man has 13 years with the company and is almost in over his head. He just turned 30 and it's not too late to learn something else. After kicking his career around trying to justify a decision, he came to the conclusion that he simply liked railroading, had a lot of friends there and if it all worked the way it was supposed to, his career would be enhanced through perseverance. As we shall see - he wouldn't be the only one kicking his career around.

Our guy now works for an outfit temporarily or tentatively named Soo/Milwaukee. There will be dovetailing of seniority rosters, new places to learn and new faces to meet. The Milwaukee boys almost to a man wanted the Grand Trunk, but got the Soo Line.

Once the Soo Line had officially ingested the Milwaukee into its system, it found out that it was biting more than it could chew what with having to assume Milwaukee's debt, along with employee protection agreements. With two mainlines to maintain and pay taxes on, one would have to go. Was that the plan all along? No one is talking, but that is my guess.

The Soo found a buyer in the newly established Wisconsin Central effective October 11, 1987. The employees had an option - stay with the non-union neophyte or move over to the transplanted new Soo. Of course, that would entail re-location. Four hundred employees chose to remain with the new company, not wanting to move. Most of those guys were close to pension age, it was a logical choice. The guys that were caught in the middle were people that had 15-30 years invested in their seniority. If you happened to already have a rocky marriage, this would be the straw that broke the camel's back.

People would re-locate from former Soo Line and Milwaukee Road bastions. They came from Schiller Park, Fond du Lac, Stevens Point, Chippewa Falls, Rhinelander, Shawano, Gladstone (Escanaba), Green Bay, and Channing, Michigan Their future venues would be St. Paul (T.C.T.), Glenwood, Enderlin and Harvey, N.D. Many elected to work out of Dubuque, Mason City, and the Quad Cities, mostly Iowa terminals. Guys were in disarray. Families were uprooted. Hang on lads, Cavanaugh's not finished yet.

While all of that was going on, Soo Line was able to land a subsidy from the State of Wisconsin. With the money from the state, they could do exactly what they wanted, which was to single track the river. Talk about a windfall!

1988 was quite a year. Three subdivisions would be single tracked with CTC including the River. The bulk of the transplanted train and enginemen from Lake States made St. Paul their new home. There was an influx of about 50 men. It surprisingly didn't take long for the newcomers to get acclimated. Most of the Soo Liners would take road jobs if their seniority justified it. If our '72 Milwaukee man had any designs of working the River or the ID (interdivisional) pool in his immediate future, it no longer was feasible.

The belt still wasn't tight enough and Soo Line began looking at the H&D. They would put their heads together wih the Burlington Northern and re-route the lucrative Columbia coal business. The coal originated in Montana and would move east to the tune of three trains a week. BN and Soo negotiated a new agreement, while selling the Ortonville-Appleton segment to BN. Soo unloaded that portion of the H&D, adjusting its coal business with the BN to coincide with a more convenient juncture. The I.D. pool would benefit as always, but the guys that worked the H&D would have to start looking for work because they had just suffered another setback.

Effective 4-26-91 that portion from Tower E-14 (MP435) to Appleton (MP578.2) would be sold. The newly established Twin Cities and Western would purchase the final 143 miles of what was once known as the Hastings & Dakota. It would succumb to the machinations of corporate business.

Our employee now finds himself having to work nights two days a week. For the past few years our switchman has been able to hold the afternoon shift (3-11 etc.), as long as business stayed constant. He is beginning to feel the loss of jobs.

Before the Milwaukee Road came into the picture, the Soo Line had two jobs that operated over the Chicago & Northwestern. These jobs would service the Koch Refinery out in Rosemount. They were known as Transfer # 5 and Transfer #3. Transfer #5 would begin work at five AM, working five days per week. Transfer #3 would begin at seven PM with the same days off. Soo Line didn't want the business and it ceded the business to the CNW, soon to be the Union Pacific.

The Milwaukee had a job that also ran over the CNW. It would have trackage rights from East St. Paul to Junction Switch where it would access the Bayport Sub for the purpose of servicing the Anderson Window Co. It was too good a job and it too would be ceded to the ever expanding UP.

Considering the influx of Lake States switch and train personnel, about 30, and then factor in the refugees off the H&D, plus the three jobs given to the UP, our now beleaguered friend is steadily losing ground. That makes it about 50 people looking for a place to work, when you total it up. Most if not all would have more seniority than our anguishing friend.

The wheeling and dealing wasn't' quite over yet. The now CP had put up for sale the Chicago-Kansas City line along with its corn lines in Iowa and southern Minnesota. A new company evolved from this entitled: I&M Rail Link. Effective 2-3-97, the once transplanted Lake States would be given another option either stay with the new company and hopefully remain in place or follow the parent company and re-locate, again!

What the IMRL would mean to the men at St. Paul would be the loss of trains 222 and 223, two trains originating and terminating at St. Paul yard on a daily basis. These trains handled traffic from Kansas City and points in between. St. Paul yard crews would still do the switching. Looking at it from a manpower standpoint - about four engineers and about eight trainman would be affected.

Two guys, both from Fond du Lac would be affected by it in different ways.

One guy elected to go to Mason City the other to Dubuque as a result of Lake States. When the railroad was sold, the guy that went to Mason City elected to move his family to St. Paul. The other fellow opted not to move his family, however brought his seniority to St. Paul. He was able to work a regular job with Saturdays and Sundays off. On Friday evening he would make the 250 mile drive back to Dubuque. There wouldn't be enough time or paper to describe each individual situation. Some guys along with their families persevered and did well, while others lost their families, homes, and lifestyles, not to mention their health.

And lastly, let us not forget the ever presence of crew down-sizing which always loomed large in the career of the rank and file railroader.

This chapter is not intended to berate the rail companies but is meant to be factual with an overview of the plight of an employee out of the operating department or departments at this time in the corporate scheme of things.

Chapter 39

~~~~◞

Crew Comfort or Lack Thereof

Locomotives weren't always designed with crew comfort in mind. Take the ubiquitous GP9's, of which some railroads had hundreds on their rosters. These units came delivered with "toad stool" seats. You could adjust the height of the seat, but little else. The seat itself was horizontal and the backrest was vertical. Some guys would spend 16 hours daily, six days a week sitting on them. Judging by their posture, I don't think those seats did them any good.

From time to time I would experience back pain and would seek the aid of a chiropractor to get an adjustment. After describing my work requirements, these guys always concluded our conversation with "your job isn't doing your back any good". The x-rays didn't lie either.

Air brake systems on the engines weren't exactly user friendly either. The 6BL brake system on the geeps was designed to exhaust into the center of the cab. While the exhaust of the 6BL was obnoxious, it wasn't nearly as bad as the newer 26L brake system that came out on the GP40 and SD40"s. Ordinary service reductions off the trainline would make you wish you were wearing ear muffs.

Radios were another source of audio irritation. Each crew was issued one radio per locomotive consist. The major radio component weighed about 40 pounds and was ungainly to handle especially when changing ends. They would get bumped against the stanchions that supported the railings. Because of that they took a beating. The squelch on a bad radio was almost unbearable. At times in order to avoid hearing the scratching squelch guys would turn their radios down and forget about them. That could lead to a dangerous state of affairs. Eventually all units were equipped with radios and because of that the radios were spared much wear and tear. A bad radio was definitely hard on the hearing. Radios were abused and were not maintained by optimum standards.

I joined the army at the end of August 1962. We had no radios on the IC Chicago Division at that time. I came back to the railroad in October of 1965. By then all of the jobs, yardmasters, towerman, and trainmasters had radios. It was enough to make you wonder how they operated in the pre-radio era. In fact, I remember an old timer complaining because his handset wasn't functioning properly. One of the other guys assailed him with "you worked around here 40 years without radios and now you're lost without one"!

The railroad was a loud, noisy and violent place to work. One of the other less than pleasant sounds was the screech of the retarders as they pinched a boxcar rolling off the hump.

Another interesting sound that we would encounter while operating a geep, would be heard within the cab when going from throttle #2 to throttle #3. At throttle #3 there came this incessant vibration from under the locomotive. For some reason the RPM's of the prime mover while it turned the main generator at around 250 RPM's didn't seem to be comfortable while doing so. Of course, you could easily eliminate that by going to throttle #4. By doing that, all the wonderful sounds that emanated from a geep would return to normal. I loved listening to a brace of geeps marching uphill with a heavy drag. That was a good sound.

The first time I sat in front of the control console of a SD70Ace, my first thought as I leaned back into the plush engineers chair was "this is too comfortable, it's a death trap"! And then I noticed the console itself, replete with little toggle switches here and there. I asked myself "What was wrong with the original setup"? I knew that the new BN units were equipped with this "newfangled" outfit and so it only stood to reason that we would also have to have it. Keeping up with the Joneses, you know.

It wasn't too long after that that I caught a trip in the ID Pool (interdivisional). On the return trip we had a new engine with the "cute" controls. The CTC was out between River Jct. and Hastings, and I would get a crash course on the use of those new controls. We would have to stop at each control point and hand line the switches. We did that eight times before we finally arrived at Hastings. I was thankful that it was a short train.

I worked an awful lot of nights during my railroad career. For the most part I worked for two different railroads, meaning that I had to start over once. Because of this and during this, my greatest fear was falling asleep. I wasn't getting any younger.

When I first went firing, the staccato roar of those 567C's would lull me to sleep. The switch engines weren't much better. I had a very difficult time staying awake. This occurred at a time when firemen were laughed at because everyone thought that we came to work simply to sleep. Everyone, jokingly, had a "hayboard" stashed around somewhere.

I wanted to be an engineer and the only way to do that was to fire one of those "self-firing" diesels. Unlike a lot of people involved in railroading, this was going to be my life. I was serious about it and yet I couldn't stay awake. At the time, I didn't realize that eventually I would get used to it.

There is much talk between rail unions and management about a more practical approach to sleep management. Better scheduling is often mentioned. Freight trains ran when they ran, they held little sway in the scheme of things. Every now and then we hear about a train that simply doesn't stop when it is supposed to. That usually happens in the wee hours of the morning. I am amazed that more accidents don't occur due to sleep deprivation.

I don't have a degree in the study of somnolent behavior however, I can speak from experience. As long as humans are humans and as long as trains run at all different times of the day - there will be the occasional sleep related accident. I've never had an accident due to lack of sleep and believe me there were times when I came to work so tired, I had difficulty driving myself to work. My greatest fear on the railroad was falling asleep and never waking up, or being the victim of another train whose crew was fast asleep.

Humans simply cannot sleep for the sake of getting ready for work. The average guy might have a houseful of toddlers, the telephone or even a noisy neighbor or his dog or maybe the family dog. It would be nice if we were all equipped with "ON" and "OFF" switches. However, it doesn't work that way.

Any crew with experience in pool service would usually work together. They would determine who was tired and who wasn't. The pool crews on CP had only a conductor and engineer, both on the head end and almost all of the conductors would run the engine and do a good job. If a guy needed to close his eyes for 20 minutes or so, he would communicate with his crew member because it wouldn't do for both of them to be in the arms of Morpheus. This occurred for years, long before the railroads sanctioned organized rest periods on the job.

One railroad had the audacity to suggest running its road trains with only the engineer. It is really ludicrous that a company would want to run a 50-60 MPH freight train with only one man in the cab. Of course they would have alertors all over the place. The poor guy would be "wired up" to the extent that he might not be able to get up. Railroads today should accept the fact that with two men in the cab, they have arrived at the optimum level. Two men can now perform the job that was once done by five and do it most efficiently. Any thought of going to one man is incongruous and surely hedges on greed.

Once the companies put the crew issues to rest, they can lay off the head choppers or efficiency experts. That's money saved. Now take the money saved and totally focus on the infrastructure of the railroad. Make it a good place to be for all concerned. Make it a competitive place to work.

Chapter 40

～

From an Employee's Standpoint

I have spent the greater part of my life working for a railroad. It is truly in my blood. At one time that blood was pretty thick. I've seen a lot of changes some good and some bad. My heart was always for the railroad itself, not labor, not management. The railroad was my life. I wanted it to be a utopian place where the company made money, we made money and it was a good place to be. Throughout my career, up until a few years ago, I always felt that, no matter what the companies and the unions haggled over, once they got it together, it would get better. It hasn't. Railroad employees are what you might call "middle men". Scapegoats, if you will. We are victims of mismanagement and a union structure that simply collects money.

The railroads historically have been a haven for thieves. It is an industry that provides a good basic playground for embezzlement. Most of these guys aren't in the limelight, they're very quiet and methodical, and usually disappear into oblivion. Like Al Capone once said, "Gimme one good lawyer for a bunch of machine guns." Our industry should be monitored by a more efficient federal agency. Let's face it, if the railroads didn't make money, they wouldn't be here today.

Let's go back forty years or so and trace railroads to date. Most railroads went into bankruptcy during the depression. What company didn't? They came out of it, and thrived when the economy was good, didn't when it was bad. So went America.

With the fifties came the diesels. The diesels were easier to operate, fuel and definitely to maintain. They were able to cut maintenance forces initially by around 60 percent. The next big stumbling block would be the fireman. The diesels fired pretty well without a fireman, so the fireman had to go. It took ten years for that to happen, and it did. The railroads began training programs for engineers taking the place of the age old "osmosis" stratagem. Are we making money yet? Don't know, do we. Let's let that sit for a while and then we'll go after the third man. That's pretty much done. Why not go after new employees? Now the companies are close to probably around 50 percent of employees they are paying a 75 percent rate not to mention whatever else they don't get. Eventually they get 100 percent after five years. At present most crews are down to two men.

The Milwaukee Road was a great railroad. Somebody ruined it for personal gain. At least that's my opinion. What isn't opinion, but fact, is that the Soo Line once ran a tight ship. How else could they get away with painting their locomotives and cabooses white? They came together and suddenly the white went to hell. So did the orange and black. This wasn't carefully planned. We're all victims or pawns manifested by court decisions and this is what we ended up with. Let's face it the entire situation has been nothing but a chaotic controversy. We merged, we moved and then we moved again. If it didn't at least inconvenience you, it may possibly have ruined your life. No problem. We're a corporate giant now.

Soo Line elected to use "Pig's Eye" as their Twin Cities hub. Let's sell Shoreham and make some bucks! As I said before, there wasn't a whole lot of research involved in the merger, and so the powers that be elected to sell Shoreham. Shoreham was no longer a viable switching yard when they finished with it. While they were pulling up tracks with happy thoughts of more money for the new Soo coffers the DNR said, "No, you can't sell this. It stinks. It is polluted."

Soo Line bought Milwaukee for its double track main line to Chicago, but what happened? Can they still compete with the BN on single track? Ask a big time Soo Line official if he feels that we can compete with the BN. If he says yes with a straight face, it would be understandable.

On a more local note, while the Soo Line officials were trying to find the Milwaukee officials for the key to the washroom, we were out making friends or enemies on the physical property. The Milwaukee guys were into "wish the Grand Trunk would have gotten us", and we were into "wish we hadn't had to move". It caused considerable internal strife.

Suddenly, we were exposed to a different way of thinking. It's now a "you don't think for yourselves you do what we tell you to do" stratagem. You tried to be conscientious, so here you are in a new environment, trying to do something and they tell you to mind your own business. We began to see mismanagement as close as you'll ever see it. A curious employee is or will be a good employee. Don't discourage him when he wants to know about his job.

A few years back, a Canadian vice president by the name of Rice was quoted as being a proponent of talking with the crews, getting feedback, and generally helping to boost morale. He expressly mentioned the "night brothers". Those are the guys in the trenches with little or no respite from the doldrums of the night shift, he alluded. Not all management types are blasé toward labor. Here was a man that was trying to make a difference.

Let's talk about the typical employee, say a guy with 20 years. With 20 years going, he's been through the gamut. He starts out working for a company in good faith. If the company didn't need him, why did they hire him? This starts off on the extra board with probably Monday and Tuesday off and no days off if he's on the road. There were no cellphones or beepers back then. Wherever he worked, while the rest of the world was socializing on Saturday night, he was at work. Ever have someone with a "normal" job ask you if you and your wife can come to a party and all you can say is "maybe". Then the guy wants to know what you mean by "maybe". Of course, we all know what transpires then. A guy works five or six years to where he might be able to work a regular job with a day or two off, or at least have some control over his life from time to time and suddenly the bottom falls out. Three man jobs go to two men and the fireman goes wherever he can. Whatever was built up is out the window. Back to the extra board and start over. This kind of situation, from day one, has never been a good place for a family man. Never being able to tell someone that you don't know where you're going to be from day to day preys on those around you. It puts pressure on you. Everything related to the life style that you don't have, puts pressure on you. You've lost a good portion of all you have strived for in the last five, six years or more.

We have often said that corporate management is out of touch with the troops, the guys who actually oversee the physical operation and the people who operate it. In Vietnam, all the generals were interested in was "body counts". We sort of have that too. Our executive offices don't seem to know the difference between tangible and intangible assets. The intangibles are assets that cannot be measured on paper. Those that came up through the ranks forget, and the college educated ones who never left the office, never knew. When I first came to St. Paul, there was a definite openness of hostility towards employees from the local management level. The leadership was in a word, immature. There was no encouragement to do a good job. The company wasn't concerned about working together. Employees were given a urinalysis test at the drop of a hat, never mind the cost. It was sort of like a kid with a new toy. We had a three way hate relationship going: Milwaukee guys versus Soo Line guys versus management. The unions played an important role in this pandemonium also. You would think that railroad unions, at least by the time Soo and Milwaukee came together, would have been old hands at implementing mergers, etc. The answers to every question should have been readily available. Agreements that applied on one former property didn't apply on the other and so on. Agreements were often entirely circumvented for lack of an answer. Since coming to St. Paul, I have seen quite a few new people come in, victims of the Wisconsin Central sellout with a smattering of transfers from other points. Wouldn't it have been great if the company (with the help of the unions) would have had a packet containing information as to the operation at St. Paul, maps to the various yards and profile maps of the hills we encounter, not to mention the entire division? That would have been constructive. All of that energy was spent screaming at people instead. It would have been nice to have had a few more student trips down those hills, too! That goes back to one of those intangibles, experience. Management, both corporate and local, show little regard for that priceless factor.

I wish that I had kept a log from the day I arrived at St. Paul. You would not have believed the screw-ups. I'm talking big bucks type screw-ups. Most of it was attributed to lack of communication. Also, several new innovations were being put into effect, consolidations which led to an over worked, over stressed people trying to keep these "streamlined" departments going. Throw in whatever is currently going down on the overall picture, such as the prospect of having to move, maybe get laid off, and it makes for a demoralized employee. It doesn't do much for efficiency either. Let's take a prime example, the "Crew Management Center", one of the consolidation "biggies". If you are in train or engine service, you probably talk to these people once or twice or ten times a day. You are irritated before you even pick up the phone. A good deal of your personal life is spent trying to get through to these people because they are overworked. You're not alone; they're depressed, too.

We have seen the work force drastically reduced over the years. The work force has given way to consolidation, computers and abandonment. One of the things that I have noticed about management's zeal for technology is that they will not let some new innovation, stabilize i.e. let's shoot for a better way, but let it be done gradually so that the new system can be learned and be functional. This allows the other departments to adjust also. Before the new system is basically familiar within their respective areas, a new one is already in the works and the learning process starts over, nothing stabilizes until the company itself comes down to realizing that it takes people to run a railroad—yes, and a profitable one. We are and have been in a transitional period, but if you stay in transition, that's all you are—between gears. Soo Line has its train crew force pretty much the way they want it by hook or by crook. There isn't much to cut there. I can't see where you can cut, anywhere, unless you bring in robots if you haven't already. Every time there is a contract negotiation, the company comes in with "we have too much dead weight", not enough productivity. We won't get into what was then, they were right in a lot of ways. Let's deal with today. If they can't make money today, with the productivity they are getting, then we are either "scapegoats of mismanagement" or victims of greed.

Another factor to contend with were the unions. Most of us feel that they are a necessary evil. Throughout my 42 year career, the unions were and are membership conscious to the extent of a closed shop (UTU). I don't feel that closed shops are constitutional but, yet, I don't feel that a guy should go for a free ride. I realize that it is expensive to operate a union as large as ours. It is even more expensive when nothing gets done. Maybe the unions should be kept honest. The latest anecdote, the catchall answer from Cleveland goes something like this… "We can't do anything with the current regime in power". Why can't we? Unions have rested on their laurels long enough. An alternative must be found. Let's face it, unions are a business. They provide big paying jobs for people. Union means just that - unity. In unity there is strength. Enginemen were divided to the point that they wouldn't talk to one another. Who benefitted? The railroads. Instead of coming together and working for a common cause, they did nothing but fight. With friends like that, highly paid friends, providing a dual service we got a lot less than we could have. We had our enemies, too. Don't misunderstand me, I'm not anti UTU or BLE, I am just providing an example of what went down. Unions are looking forward to hard times. Get out there and earn your money or start selling insurance on a full time basis.

Granted the guy that hired out 20 years ago probably did so at the least opportune time. Railroad employees today are between a rock and a hard place. We're definitely in the middle and must seek alternatives. If you hired out twenty years ago and were part of a merger etc., you probably have seen it all. The railroad is greatly reducing its expenditures, and is close, if not there, to being where it wants to be. We're getting back to "body counts". I'm convinced that if our company cannot afford a pay raise at this juncture, somebody's doing some powerful lying.

I would like to briefly go over some other facets, most being in the "foolish spending" department. Let's go with drug abuse. I feel that the railroads in general are realizing that we aren't the addicts the public was led to believe. These drug tests are proving that. These drug tests are also costing tons of money. Can't the companies and the unions collectively go to the powers that be and kill this thing?

Ford Motor Company and 3M volunteered to show Soo Line how it wants their traffic to be moved. It was sort of "let us volunteer or else" program. It kind of makes you think…gee, we've been in this business for a hundred years and a tape company is showing us how to operate.

You can't say changes have to be made because changes have been made. Management can't blame the labor force anymore. This company got big overnight and any changes should be made in the higher echelons. Labor is not out of control…could it be management? As I said before, Soo Line has never tried to stabilize. There has always been some new "scheme" to contend with. CP bought the Soo and hopefully brings a positive note. Hopefully we can now get down to business and forget about past executives that were trying to make a name for themselves.

Employees have often echoed that Soo is trying to copy the BN. Forget about copying the BN—we can't. We made that decision when we single tracked. St. Paul employees have an opportunity to observe BN trains as they pass the yard. For a while I noticed that BN was using "fuel tenders" (rolling fuel reservoirs between locos). Wouldn't you know it, but we went and made four of them at Shoreham. Had to have 'em. About the time we put them on the road, they vanished from BN, don't know why, neither does Soo. If BN no longer uses theirs, what are we doing with ours? I always see two or three of them at the roundhouse. What happened? Did we do our homework or was it simply a case of "me-too-ism".

I would like to cover the buyouts that occurred and the company's lack of recognition for experience. The "buyout" was a good deal if you were ready to retire. It was even better if you took the money and they let you work for a year or so. What happened there? How do you buy a guy out and then profess that you need him? How does that work? Let's look into an incident that happened on the Soo Line shortly after it single tracked its River Division. An inexperienced man gets called to be the engineer on a train that goes to Portage. He wants, and rightfully so, a pilot. The pilot had made a few trips to Portage and always when the river was double tracked but wasn't familiar with the "new river". He had no business accepting the call as he had less seniority than the engineer. He knew nothing of the track and signal changes that were made. As it turned out, the engineer had to put the train in emergency to get stopped at a signal on the east end of the newly located "Duke" siding. If this pilot didn't have brains enough to know where he was, why didn't the caller have some control, something that tells crew management the man has no business either running a train or being a pilot. His lack of common sense could have gotten four or five guys killed. Albeit the call board should have had more information as to his work background, the man was void of ethics, thus jeopardizing an already un-thought of and unstable "pilot policy". We're talking big league death here. We're talking big league everything. Why wasn't more thought given to this aspect of "employee training"? We have people that are supposed to have a say so to that effect. This is another argument toward overloading a company agency. Cut three crew callers to make one, then buy off ten engineers and put two new ones out on a strange railroad because you want a body to run a train. Unfortunately we can't write the rule book to cover violation of the "corporate manslaughter rule" etc.

One of the really big problems you've got on the railroad is when you've got an official that is trying to be noticed. These guys get pretty ruthless. They know their own field and in their zeal, they forget about the repercussions that come down through the channels that are affected by them. On the corporate level, when a new regime comes in, a railroad has to endure the changes made there also. When a new man takes over a department, changes are made, some good, some bad. Changes are made because the man has to justify his new position. He has to be noticed.

In the last two years or so, Soo has hired or re-hired several men as switchmen-brakemen. They have implemented a training program, and, of course, is inadequate because of the "rush" factor these men aren't given enough training. Local management is plagued by these guys. It's not their fault, but then what more could you ask from a corporate management whose point of view suggests that anyone could just walk in and do our job. Of course, some are better than others. In the almost three years that I worked the midnight top end, I am proud to say none of these guys suffered an injury of any kind, not a scratch, I might add.

In fairness to management on the CP I have been told that local managers are "brow-beaten" by our Canadian owners. The most common complaint is that the Canucks don't see the interchange picture clearly". "They don't have interchange problems in Canada because there is no interchange".

The aforesaid is simply an honest opinion based on the truth and not intended to be rancorous.

Chapter 41

~

The End of the Line

With the onset of the new decade, the 21st Century held promise and ultimately happiness. Initially the year 2001 would bring both bad and good news. The bad news meant that my moderate growth mutual find continued to fail and if I was going to buy that pick-up truck, I'd better get it while the gettin' was good. The new, shiny, money green truck would be the good news. We called it the "Big Unit".

The entire time I worked at St. Paul, the company would continuously stress good safety habits or lack thereof. It got to the point where it became obnoxious. They acted like the rank and file enjoyed pain and relished injury. We were told that "any time you have the slightest discomfort or suspicion that something is not right because of a job related accident, do not hesitate to report it to your superiors".

In June of 2001 I was lucky enough to meet my future wife. I waited a long time for her and it was worth every minute.

On the 21st of December 2001, railroaders would receive a wonderful Christmas present from President Bush when he signed the "Railroad Retirement and Survivors Improvement Act of 2001". The enactment of this new bill would truly bring joy to the households of many an American railroader. Among the highlights provided in the act was that an individual having thirty years service could retire with full benefits when he or she turned 60 years of age. It wouldn't be long and I would be 60 and I fully intended to take advantage of this federally mandated godsend. Another part of the new revision that would affect our lives was that now I only needed to be married one year in order for my new wife to be eligible for a R.R.T. pension. I must have been like a knight in shining armor to my future wife. If we hadn't met, she would have had to work until she was

66. With the R.R.T. revision she would only have to work until she became 60. Factor in the one year requirement of having to be married and we wouldn't miss by much. We were married on the third of June 2002, and she was eligible for benefits on September 12th of 2003, her 60th birthday.

It wasn't very long after that, I went to see a neurologist. He in turn, would send me for a MRI (magnetic resonance imaging) and a CAT scan. The MRI revealed progressive cervical degeneration, diffuse cervical degenerative disc disease and bulging discs at four locations in the spine. A CAT scan of the lumbar spine revealed a herniated disc on the left and two bulging discs. For this, I was deemed incapable of performing my occupation as an engineer. In the doctors own words "it is my opinion that this patient's cervical and lumbosacral back injuries are causally related to his railroad occupation". I was out of service.

At this time, we applied to the Railroad Retirement Board for an occupational disability. At the end of April I received a letter from the office of the Chief Medical Officer admonishing me to keep Health Services apprised as to my progress, and to provide that office with copies of any medical decisions made by my doctor.

Another letter comes at the end of May. Again it comes from the Chief Medical Officer through one of his subalterns with the title Disability Case Manager. The letter stated that the Chief Medical Officer has reviewed my records, and has determined that I was fit to return to work, but first I must submit to a return to work physical and a drug screening. My question was, if I am fit to return to work as determined by the good doctor, why do I have to take a physical? How does the doctor know that I am fit for work, he hasn't seen me? Is there a doctor? Now I am getting phone calls from CP on a weekly basis.

The sawdust was still on the dance floor when another letter came signed by someone with a fancier title. Apparently our incommunicado doctor had washed his hands of the affair and they moved a more annoying person in to do their bidding. They would give me until June 19th (my birthday) to capitulate or else. I did not. For this omission I was invited to attend an investigation on July 10th. During that time our invisible Chief Medical Officer extends a letter, this time with his own signature on it. He says that I am good to go, but yet he hasn't examined me.

Let's talk about the physical and the drug screening. This process would be performed by nurse practitioners or physicians assistants. The drug screen was a joke and had nothing to do with my health. What they wanted was that drug screen. The other thing that pissed me off was the fact that I lived 60 miles from that clinic which meant a drive of 120 miles round trip. I was in a dilemma after being badgered, bludgeoned, and beaten by this company for 20 years. I was in no mood to cooperate with them. They took a well- intentioned, decent, and conscientious employee and turned him into a monster. I was still in Superior when I finally realized that this company wasn't my friend.

Just at the time that I was ready to succumb to their demands….a letter arrived with "Railroad Retirement Board" up in the corner of the envelope. It seemed to have a few papers in it, could this be what I'm waiting for? It was! I'm a free man! Forty-two years is now enough. The next day I received a letter from CP telling me that because of my failure to submit to their desires, I am assessed with a five day suspension. Okay. A few days later I opened a letter from that nice lady from health services. She not only writes but she calls me on the phone, too! Where was she when I was in the army? I have yet to inform the company that I was awarded a disability.

Another investigation was held, for which I attended. That was when I told them that I was awarded a disability and wasn't sure why I was there because I didn't work there! Once again they thwarted me. I would not receive the satisfaction of a disability through the sanctions of CP Rail. I should have been used to it. One trainmaster explained it to me this way: "you can't quit unless we authorize it". So now this guy tells me I can't quit, but yet I'm guaranteed a disability pension no matter whose idea it is. Are those management types that naive or do they think we're the ones that lack cerebral abilities.

Another letter comes from a lady I deem "Director of Bodily Fluids". She was a real hound dog for that most coveted "golden nectar". It seemed like they had a regular department dedicated to the extraction of urine. Once the random drug testing got into full swing, guys were more than judicious because of the consequences of a positive drug test (in this case positive means: not good).

At this time I am reminded of this one fellow that was selected and tested positive. Everyone was surprised, even the company couldn't believe it. After a careful interview with the guy, it was revealed that a fair amount of bread encrusted with poppy seeds was ingested by this man. Poppy seeds contain trace amounts of opium. From opium comes morphine, heroin, and codeine. One teaspoon of poppy seeds is enough to make the drug-o-meter needle change direction. I began sprinkling poppy seeds on my pizza.

September comes along and they still don't get it. I received another invite to go to an investigation. I attended the event only to reiterate that I no longer worked there. On the 8th of October 2002, I was formally fired, drummed out of the corps if you will. It was a piss poor way to go out, but it also was a piss poor company to work for.

In the course of reading this book, you will have noted a certain amount of negativity. As may also be noted, the railroad would always throw the first punch drawing first blood tends to alienate an employee, when it happens frequently.

In closing this book I want it known that it was always my intention that the union and the company would one day come together to work for a better railroad which would translate to better employees which would again translate to happier employees.

As I look back over those 42 years, I can say with great satisfaction, that I did my job well and was better than most. I had a meaningful sense of accomplishment. As I sit here pondering my future, I wonder if maybe I should write a book?

One early spring morning I was called at LaCrosse for a train whose designation I cannot remember. It had rained off and on all morning, but the sun shown from the east and had the promise of a bright, sunny day. For power we had two nearly new SD60's and the maximum train of 120 cars. The train was close to being a mile and a half long. Once we rounded the wye at River Junction, we had clear signals all the way. We would encounter patches of rain here and there however the sun kept coming undaunted by the scattered clouds.

Our train ran well and at track speed, fifty miles per hour. Somewhere between Read's Landing and Lake City, along Lake Pepin, I happened to look back at the train snaking its way around the many curves the Mississippi River offered. The rain had made the cars glisten as the sun arose beaming across the lake. The power was now leaning into a curve and as I looked back I could see the train coming around two more curves. The sight of that gave me a majestic, grandiose aura, a strong sense of power and of importance. My thoughts that morning what with the diversity of life and its struggles concluded with: "you know what? I've got the best damn job in the world"!